IMAGES
of Rail

NEVADA NORTHERN RAILWAY

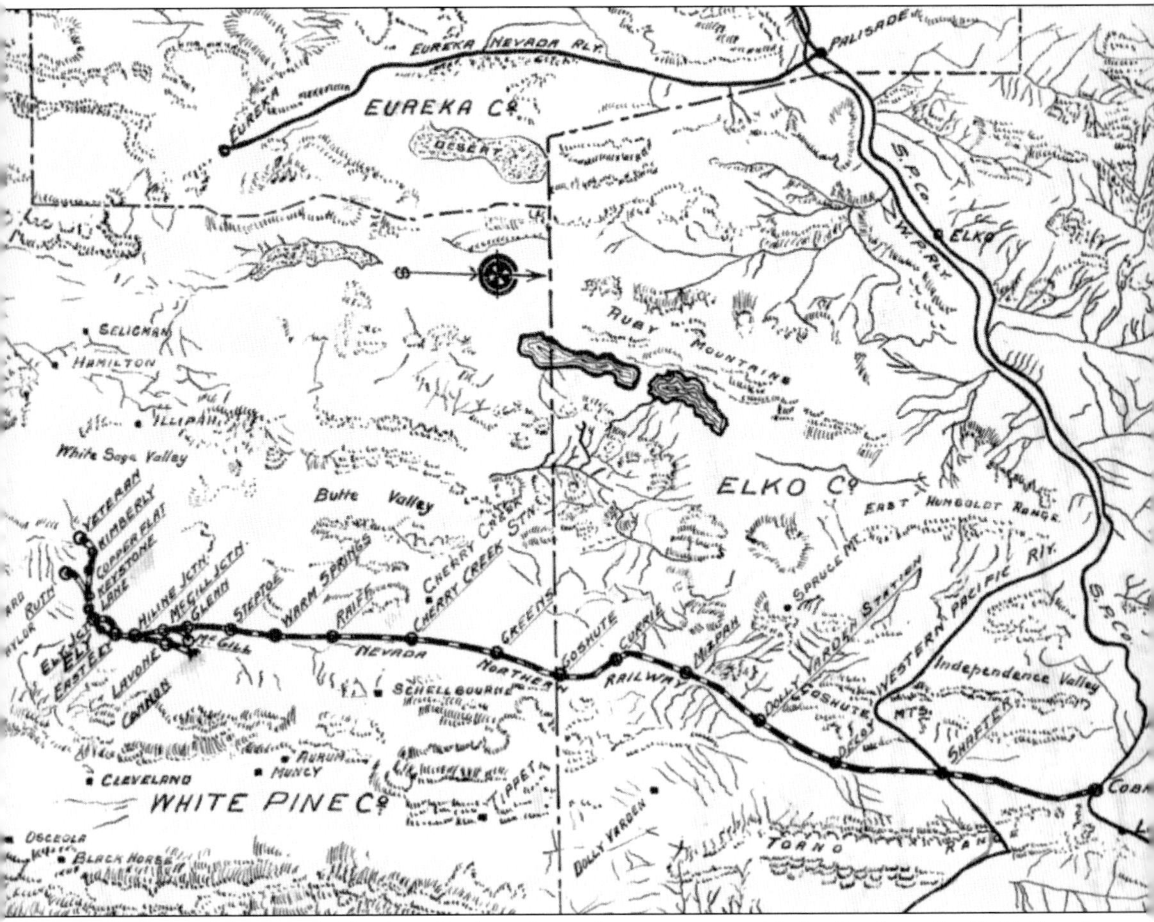

This map of the Nevada Northern Railway shows the connection with the Southern Pacific Railroad at Cobre, Nevada, and the Western Pacific connection at Shafter. The end of the line was Veteran. The map is unusual because north is to the right. (Nevada Northern Railway Museum.)

On the Cover: It is July 9, 1938. Locomotive 40 is in front of the East Ely Depot preparing for departure to Cobre. In three years, passenger service will end, seemingly, for good. But in 1987, a renaissance would occur. And locomotive 40 would once again pick up passengers at the East Ely Depot. (Stephen G. Swanson collection.)

IMAGES
of Rail

Nevada Northern Railway

Mark S. Bassett and J. Joan Bassett

ARCADIA
PUBLISHING

ISBN 978-0-7385-7475-2

Published by Arcadia Publishing
Charleston, South Carolina

Printed in the United States of America

Library of Congress Control Number: 2010939057

For all general information, please contact Arcadia Publishing:
Telephone 843-853-2070
Fax 843-853-0044
E-mail sales@arcadiapublishing.com
For customer service and orders:
Toll-Free 1-888-313-2665

Visit us on the Internet at www.arcadiapublishing.com

To Mark Requa, whose vision created the railroad, and to the people who resurrected the railroad and continue that vision by keeping it running today

Contents

ACKNOWLEDGMENTS

Joan and I may be the authors of this book, but our work is based on the efforts of others. Our goal is to tell the story of the Nevada Northern Railway. This would have been impossible without the outstanding contributions of Keith Albrandt and Steve Swanson. They have spent countless hours researching and documenting all aspects of the railroad—from the Guggenheim family's financial manipulations to documenting the locomotives and equipment. To Keith and Steve—thanks!

Several other individuals went above and beyond in helping with this book. Ted Benson graciously shared his photographs, which were taken toward the end of operations. Steve Crise shared not only his photographs but also the photographs of the late Donald Duke. Paul Newitt allowed the use of his grandfather's photographs, which are priceless in documenting the early days of the railroad, long before digital cameras made it a snap. Collector Robert Novich welcomed Joan and me to take over his dining room table, allowing us to scan his remarkable collection.

A side benefit of this project was the amassing of photographs for the project. Most of these photographs have never been published before. To adhere to the strict word count for this book, photographic credit is given at the end of the captions with one word, either a name or initials. Photographs in the book appear courtesy of the following individuals and organizations who generously granted access to their collections: Steven and Nolan Bechtold collection (Bechtold); Ted Benson collection (Benson); Gordon E. Chappell collection (Chappell); Steve Crise collection (Crise); Donald Duke-Golden West Books collection (Duke); East Ely Railroad Depot Museum (EERDM); Jolene Gardner collection (Gardner); Joel Jensen collection (Jensen); Library of Congress (LC); J. Brent MacGregor collection (MacGregor); Nevada Historical Society (NHS); Philip E. Newitt collection (Newitt); Novich family collection (Novich); Sundance Publishing collection (Sundance); Stephen G. Swanson collection (Swanson); Robert Timko collection (Timko); Utah State Historical Society (USHS); White Pine County Historical Society (WPCHS); and White Pine Public Museum (WPPM). Photographs with no credits are from the Nevada Northern Railway Museum.

Additional thanks go to Arcadia Publishing for giving historians the opportunity to publish books that capture the stories of America.

INTRODUCTION

The Nevada Northern Railway was the vision of one man—Mark Requa, a mining engineer and railroader. His travels to White Pine County made him aware of the low-grade copper deposits and the profitable opportunity that awaited there. The recent inventions of the electric light and the telephone were being commercialized. Every building in America would need to be wired twice: once for electricity and again for the telephone. The demand for copper would be colossal.

When he was owner of the narrow-gauge Eureka & Palisade Railroad (E&P), Requa's first idea was to extend the rail 75 miles to the copper deposits. He faced two obstacles. First, the E&P would have to be standard gauged. Secondly, the route would cross four mountain ranges. These obstacles killed the idea.

But there was still all of that copper ore. D.C. Jackling proved that ore containing as little as three percent copper could be smelted profitability. But to get at that copper, a mountain of copper ore would have to be moved. A mine, mill, smelter, and railroad would need to be constructed if copper deposits were to be developed.

Requa had a vision, and he was in a hurry. He optioned copper claims in October 1902. On February 15, 1903, he organized the White Pine Copper Company to develop the copper claims. An experimental mill proved that the low-grade ore could be smelted profitably. He also undertook a geological survey that confirmed the extent of the copper ore body.

As Requa was developing his claims, others were also doing exploration work. On November 17, 1904, Requa merged his companies with the neighboring claims to form the Nevada Consolidated Copper Company. Requa had proven that it was economically feasible to mine the copper, but millions of dollars in capital was required if the project was to be successful.

The Guggenheim family had been exploring the district since 1904. A New York banking firm brought the Guggenheims and Requa together. Capital was raised, and on June 1, 1905, the Nevada Northern Railway Company (NNRy) was incorporated. On August 29, 1905, a contract was signed with the Utah Construction Company to construct the 150-mile railroad.

Construction commenced on September 11, 1905. Requa was confident and optimistic; he predicted that the railroad would reach Ely by January 1, 1906. Unfortunately, the winter was the severest of the past 20 years, and by January 1, 1906, work had come to halt. The ground was frozen, the snow was deep, and railroads were being built in southern Nevada where it was warm. Crews and laborers abandoned the NNRy and headed south.

As work ground to a halt, Requa had another problem—the Guggenheims. They wanted control of the copper district. By March 1906, the Guggenheims out-maneuvered Requa and established partial control over his Nevada Consolidated Copper Company and the Nevada Northern Railway.

At about the same time, the weather improved, and construction resumed. Requa now predicted that the railroad would reach Ely on June 1. But when the San Francisco earthquake struck, many of the railroad workers, originally from San Francisco, dropped their tools and headed home.

Labor shortages plagued the railroad, and progress continued slowly. By late May, the rails reached 63 miles to Currie's Ranch. The first passenger train on May 22 carried Requa and his associates. They continued on to Ely via Requa's new Thomas automobile. Regular train service between Cobre and Currie started on June 2.

By July 16, 1906, tracks reached Cherry Creek, and Railroad Day was celebrated. At the same time, the Guggenheims were tightening their grip on the district and the railroad. On July 24, Requa was again out-maneuvered and lost complete control of the Nevada Consolidated Copper Company and the railroad to the Guggenheims. Yet, he stayed on the as vice president of the Nevada Northern.

A new problem now confronted the railroad. In 1905, the commissioners of White Pine County granted the railroad a right-of-way through the business district. As track crews neared Ely, the business owners on Aultman Street decided that having trains running through the business district was not a good idea. They convinced the county commissioners to move the railroad right-of-way one block south. This met with opposition from the property owners along Clark Street, but the business owners carried the day. With track crews entering Ely, the right-of-way was moved south.

On October 2, 1906, the headline read, "Rah, Rah, Rah Requa! Railroad's Here on Time." Described were the Railroad Day festivities that took place on September 29 and 30. Overlooked were the previous promises of the arrival of the railroad. As it was, the railroad barely made it to Ely for the Railroad Day celebration. Requa drove the ceremonial last spike, made out of Ruth copper. On October 1, passenger service started between Ely and Cobre, and freight service started on October 12.

Despite the celebrations, there were bitter controversies just below the surface. Mark Requa resigned on November 2, 1906. The Guggenheims were in firm control of the district and the railroad. Two issues upset Ely residents. First was the realization that the ore trains would be running through the heart of the community every 30 minutes or less. This was unacceptable. The copper company agreed and built a bypass north of the community, completed by December 1907. Secondly, when the railroad arrived, it started a new community called Ely City, just east of the existing city of Ely. Here is where the yards, shops, freight barn, offices, and the depot would be built. The residents of Ely objected and petitioned the new Railroad Commission of Nevada. They insisted that a depot be built in downtown Ely and that the railroad change the name of Ely City. After lawsuits and counter-lawsuits, a depot was built in Ely, and by 1908 the name of the Ely City Depot was changed to East Ely.

The copper spike ceremony marked the completion of the railroad to Ely, but the work was not done. The railroad continued toward the mines 10 miles away. Rails reached Lane City in the middle of July, and another Railroad Day celebration was held. The Star Pointer Mine was reached August 16. It has been reported that the 10-mile extension to the copper mines cost as much as the building of the railroad from Cobre and took almost as long.

Also during 1907, the rail yards at Ely City (East Ely) were expanded to include a concrete brick engine house and machine shop complex, additional tracks, a track scale, and water standpipes for watering the engines. The railroad was preparing for the start of ore service.

East of town, the nine-mile Hiline branch was constructed to service the new mill at McGill. Used exclusively by the ore trains, Hiline was completed on March 15, 1908. The signature structure on the branch was the 1,720-foot-long, double-track trestle that was 109 feet tall, reported to be the tallest double-track trestle in the world. In McGill, construction was proceeding on the smelter and mill.

On April 12, 1908, operations at the mill commenced with the arrival of the first ore train, witnessed by a large crowd. In less than five years, copper mines were developed, a railroad constructed, and a mill and a smelter built. Towns sprung up where there once had been only sagebrush.

Steam railroading was king. The railroad served as a steel conveyer belt, delivering ore to the mill. At the copper pits, small, steam-powered dinky locomotives hustled dump cars to the immense steam shovels that were removing waste rock. Other dinkies spotted ore cars for loading. The track spiraled down into the pit. As the pits became larger, track was moved when the digging areas changed. Almost 20 miles of track was laid in the pits. Work continued around the clock every day of the year.

Under the auspices of the Nevada Consolidated Copper Company (NCCCo), the ore trains were made up at Copper Flat. The equipment was lettered NCCCo. From the mines to East Ely, the track dropped 632 feet in only nine miles. The steepest part of the grade was three percent—this was mountain railroading. As ore trains departed Copper Flat, small, 4-wheel bobber cabooses waited on the caboose track. As the ore train went by, the brakes were released on the caboose, and it started rolling, thereby chasing the ore train down the hill and coupling to the train on the fly.

All ore trains stopped at East Ely where they were inspected by car men who checked for hot boxes and turned down the retainers. Retainers were not needed for the uphill stretch from East Ely to the mill. There the cars were unloaded, sorted, and turned back to the mine to begin the cycle again. The operation was gigantic. In May 1909, 100,000 tons of ore were taken to McGill, and an equal amount of waste rock was removed.

Under the banner of the Nevada Northern Railway, all of the freight needed for the mine, mill, smelter, and the community came by rail. In addition to the freight, the railroad also provided passenger service.

Each day, 32 passenger trains departed East Ely. White Pine County boomed, and laborers were needed. The copper company recruited people from around the world. Traveling from either coast, immigrants arrived in White Pine County by rail to start a new life.

The transcontinental passenger trains departed Ely at 6:40 a.m. and arrived at Cobre at 10:50 a.m.—140 miles were traveled in four hours and 10 minutes. The trip back from Cobre started at 11:20 a.m. and arrived back in Ely at 6:25 p.m. At Cobre, only 30 minutes were allotted to turn the train and water the locomotive. Timetable speed was 33 miles per hour, and the conductor was very proud of making it on time; arrival times were reported in the newspaper. From 1907 until 1920, daily Pullman service was also offered.

The railroad moved people. It offered shift trains, school trains, ping-pong trains, party trains, church trains, and rabbit-hunting trains. Workers were transported on shift trains. Since the county high school was a block away from the Ely Depot, school trains carried students from both Ruth and McGill. In the age before the automobile, the railroad offered ping-pong trains between East Ely and Ely. Since Ely was the established town, most of the amenities in the county were in Ely. People needing to go shopping would hop on the train.

On Saturday night, the railroad provided a party train. "By arrangement between businessmen of Ely and the Nevada Northern, an extra train will operate every Saturday night." Then on Sunday morning, the railroad offered a church train to bring the people back to Ely to attend church.

During the next decade the demand for copper seemed insatiable. The start of World War I in 1914 caused copper prices to soar along with demand. But the copper boom stopped with the ending of the war on November 11, 1918. By the beginning of 1919, layoffs struck the communities, and the bad news continued. The mines operated at about half-capacity through 1920. By 1921, operations were suspended. All workers were laid off, except for a lucky 250 employees who made improvements and repairs to the plant.

In mid-April 1922, the demand for copper began to increase. After a year of being closed, three shifts were again working, and the trains resumed. Then disaster struck. On July 9, 1922, a fire broke out at the mill. Strong winds fanned the flames until the massive mill complex was completely engulfed. About the only thing saved were the concrete foundations—the mill was a total loss.

It was feared that this was the end of the copper dream. A detailed telegram was sent to D.C. Jackling, president of the company, explaining that the mill burned. The next morning, a two-word reply was received: "Rebuild it."

Within 45 days after the fire, a temporary mill was in operation. Continuous operations were resumed 69 days after the fire. The rebuilt mill reached a full capacity of processing 9,500 tons of ore a day just 523 days after the disastrous fire. For the next 69 years, ore trains continued to deliver ore to the mill. The rebuilt mill could handle more ore more efficiently, creating greater profits for the company.

The introduction of the automobile was hurting the passenger trains. In September 1931, the ping-pong trains ended. Shift trains ended June 30, 1938, and service from Ely to Cobre ended July 31, 1941. But the order allowing the railroad to stop passenger service included a condition that the railroad needed to keep the passenger equipment and locomotive in case it was needed in the future. And in 1984, it would again be needed.

Back in 1906, the Guggenheims developed a copper property in Alaska called Kennecott. Through financial manipulations on June 12, 1933, Kennecott acquired all assets of Nevada Consolidated Copper Company. With a nod toward local history, the name was changed: the word *company* was dropped and replaced with the word *corporation*. The new name lasted only 10 years, as the Nevada Consolidated Copper Corporation would soon be absorbed by Kennecott. On January 1, 1943, it became the Nevada Mines Division of the Kennecott Copper Corporation (KCC).

Other changes were coming. On October 20, 1948, locomotive 101, a RS-2, diesel-electric locomotive, proved it could haul more ore at less cost than a steam locomotive. On February 17, 1950, steam locomotive operations ended in the pit. Within eight years, pit rail operations would end because of cost and unstable pit walls. The last train in the pit operated April 23, 1958. Trucks had now replaced the trains.

The 1970s were a period of low copper prices and new environmental regulations that severely and adversely affected Kennecott. On April 25, 1978, T.J. Lani, a 36-year veteran engineer, used locomotives 101 and 109 to haul the last ore train to the mill, ending 70 years of ore train operations.

Smelting continued at McGill, fueled by ore from Utah, Arizona, and other operations in Nevada. But by the 1980s, higher costs associated with wages and environmental compliance combined with the lower grade of ore available signaled the end of Kennecott operations in White Pine County. The end came on June 15, 1983. All workers, except for 65 employees, were laid off. The permanent closure of the McGill Smelter also brought about the end of the railroad. The Nevada Northern Railway was built to serve the mines and the smelter. Now with both of them gone, the railroad had no purpose. The last revenue freight left East Ely on June 20, 1983. It delivered seven cars to Cobre and returned the next day—just engine and caboose.

That should have been the end of the railroad. But farsighted individuals at Kennecott and in the community realized that there was an opportunity to preserve the railroad, completely intact, as a museum for future generations.

This is a magical book. If you enjoy the images and wonder what it was like to be part of the Nevada Northern Railway during the day, well, you don't have to wonder. Put the book down, and make the trek to East Ely. Today, original, century-old steam locomotives still pull passenger trains and, on special occasions, freight and ore trains too. Here, you can still witness and participate in, firsthand, what it took to move a mountain of copper.

This is only made possible because of the dedication of the staff, volunteers, and members of the museum, whose tireless efforts and financial contributions have allowed the Nevada Northern Railway to highball into its second century of operations. Join us on a photographic tour through time as we explore the Nevada Northern Railway—All aboard!

One

The Railroad Comes to Town

For the past century, the Nevada Northern Railway has served as an economic generator for White Pine County. It served as a steam-powered Internet, connecting the county with the rest of the country. It made the copper mine possible, supplied the towns and mines with everything they needed, and when it appeared that copper mining was ending and the railroad was no longer needed, it transitioned into a working historic railroad museum.

The Nevada Northern Railway was built to service the copper boom in White Pine County. It was the vision of Mark Requa. Construction started September 11, 1905 at Cobre, Nevada, 140 miles north of Ely. It would be a little more than a year before the railroad arrived in Ely.

The arrival of the railroad changed everything. It connected White Pine County to the national transportation system. A few hundred people had lived in what was to become Ely since the late 1860s. In 1904, 307 people lived in Ely. The coming of the railroad transformed the small community. By 1910, the population in the county had jumped to 7,441. According to the *White Pine News*, "The growth was so rapid that the old timers are made dizzy by the kaleidoscopic changes." No longer isolated, the communities of White Pine County grew and thrived because of the railroad.

The building of the railroad was delayed by the worst winter in memory (1905–1906), the San Francisco earthquake, and the scarcity of labor and capital. But Requa persevered. September 29, 1906 was the celebration of the arrival of the railroad to Ely. Requa drove home a spike made of Ruth copper. In celebration of Railroad Day, the community threw the biggest party that White Pine County has ever seen, before or since.

It was a bittersweet celebration for Requa. He had been out-maneuvered by the Guggenheims and lost control of his dream—the railroad. By November 1906, Requa had left White Pine County and the Nevada Northern Railway.

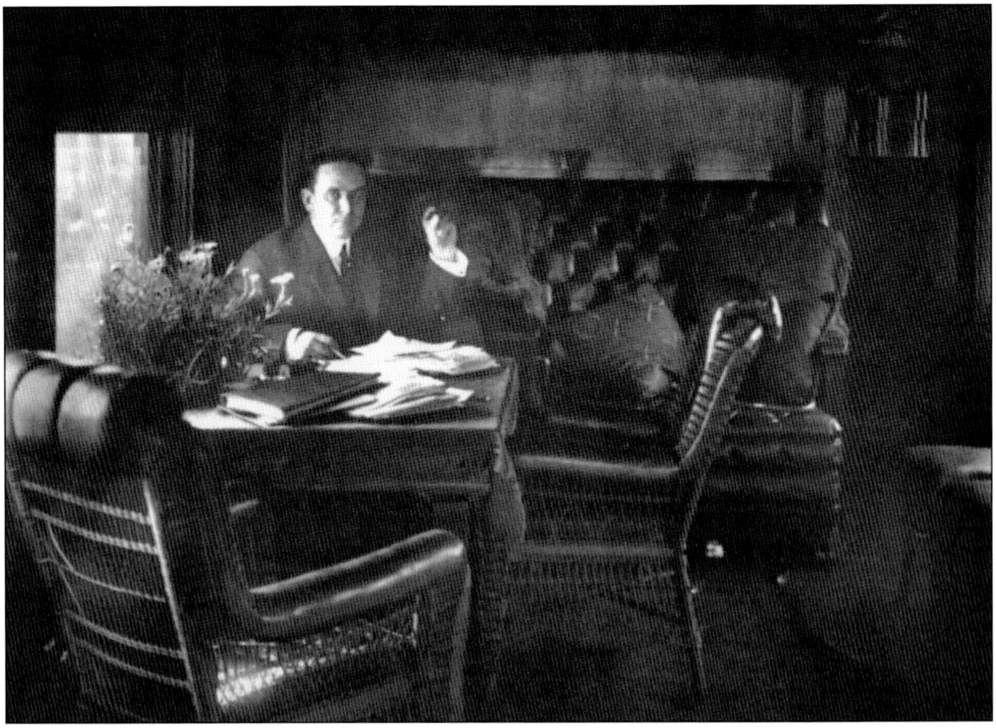

Daniel C. Jackling is seated in his private railroad car, the *Cyprus*. While in Utah, he developed the revolutionary technique of using steam-shovel-loaded railroad cars to move the low-grade copper ore to the smelter, thereby making the extraction of low-grade copper profitable. Jackling eventually became president of the Nevada Consolidated Copper Company, which later morphed into Kennecott Copper Company.

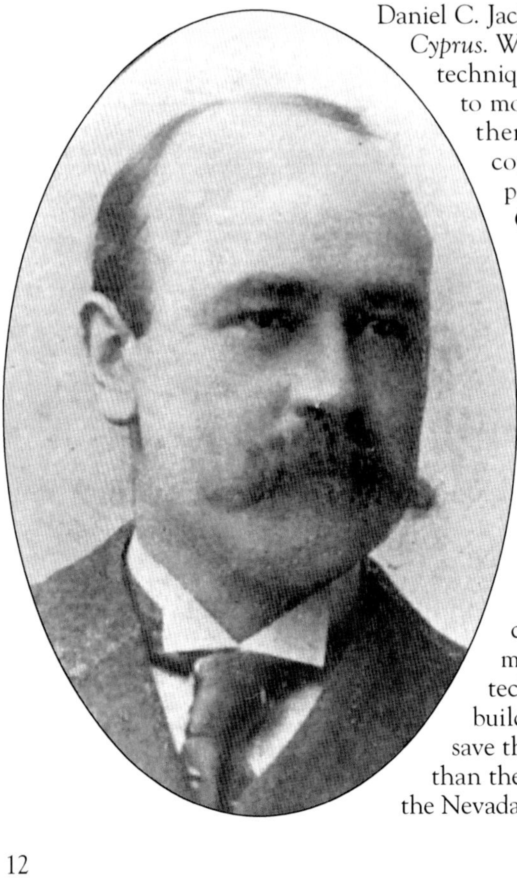

Given that he had a railroad with no traffic (the E&P), Mark Requa's big challenge was creating some business for the rail. With his mining background, he concluded that Jackling's technique would work in Nevada. He envisioned building a copper mine, a mill, and a smelter to save the E&P. Unfortunately, the project was bigger than the E&P could handle, so he created a new rail, the Nevada Northern Railway. (WPCHS.)

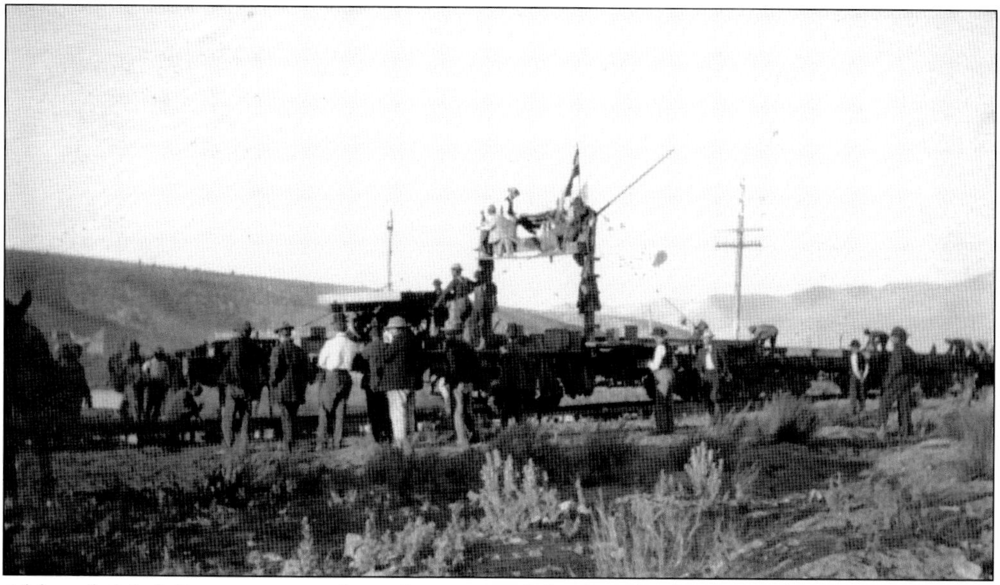

Although Mark Requa constantly underestimated the length of time needed to construct the Nevada Northern Railway, he did use the latest techniques. Here, a crew is laying track just outside of Ely, with plenty of trackside supervisors to watch.

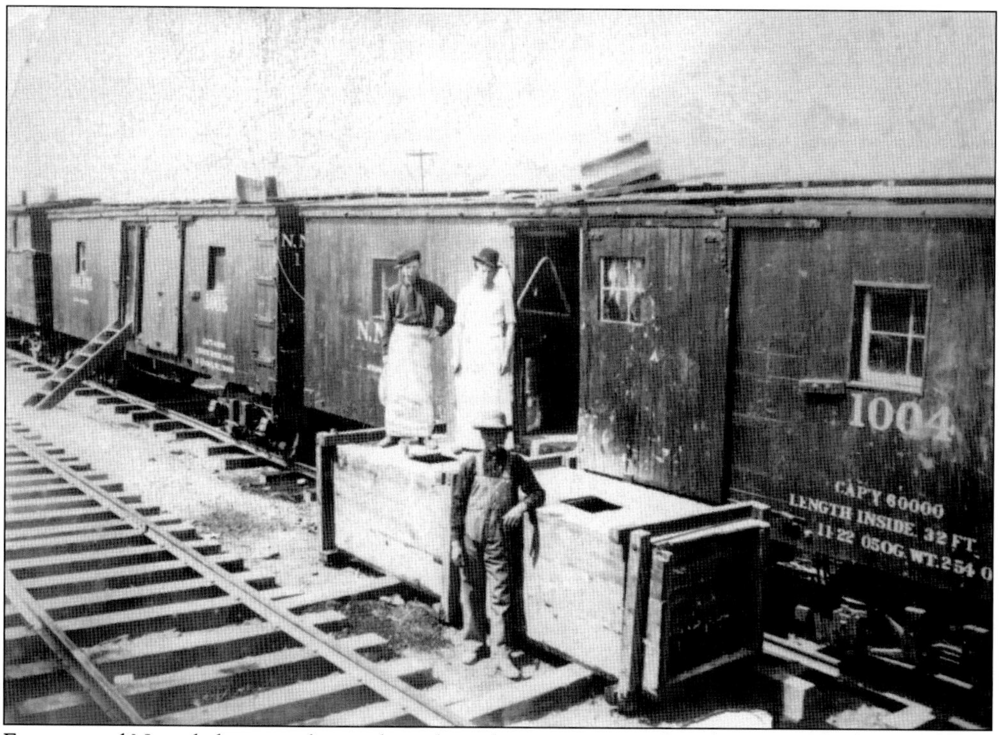

East-central Nevada has not changed much in the past century. Residents outside the cities need to be self-sufficient. The photograph shows the work train parked on a siding. Standing next to the open boxcar are the cooks, and hanging from the boxcar is a metal triangle that would be used to call the workers to meals.

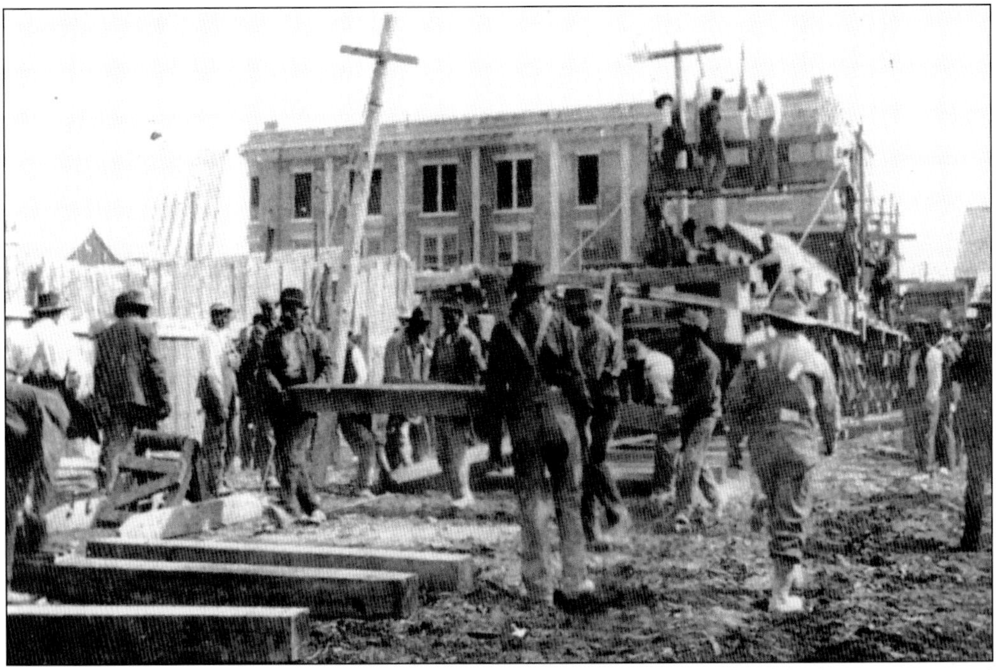

Originally, the track was to be built on Aultman Street, one block north of the location pictured (to the left of the fence). Business owners on Aultman Street came to the realization that having a railroad in front of their shops might harm their business. At the last minute, they petitioned the change that moved the railroad to Clark Street.

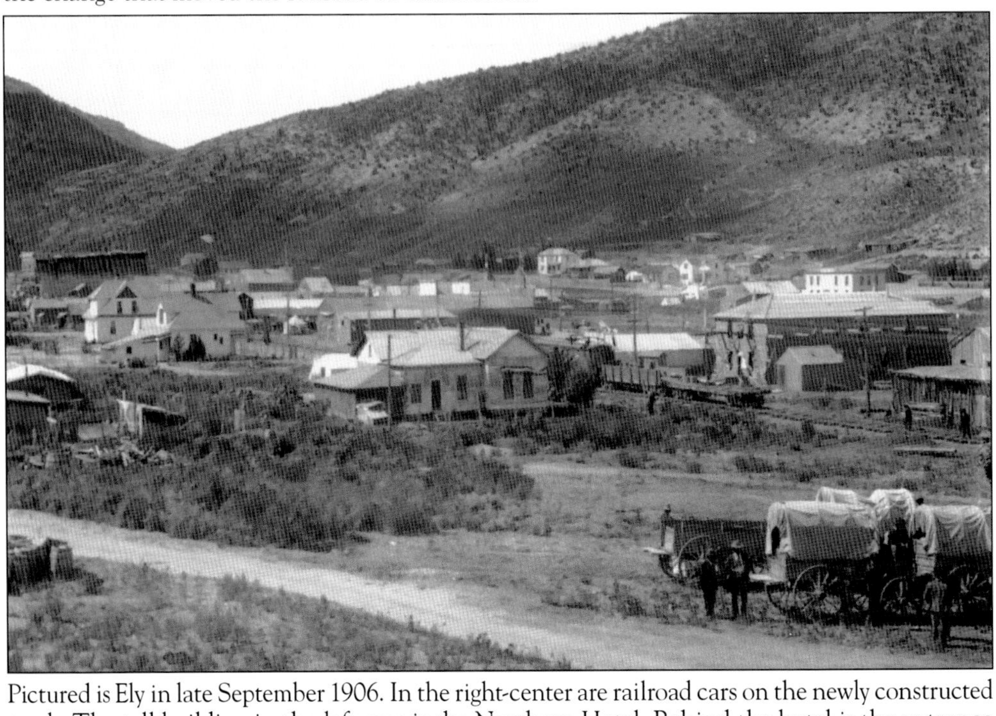

Pictured is Ely in late September 1906. In the right-center are railroad cars on the newly constructed track. The tall building in the left rear is the Northern Hotel. Behind the hotel is the entrance to Robinson Canyon. The copper mines are 10 miles farther west up the canyon. (USHS.)

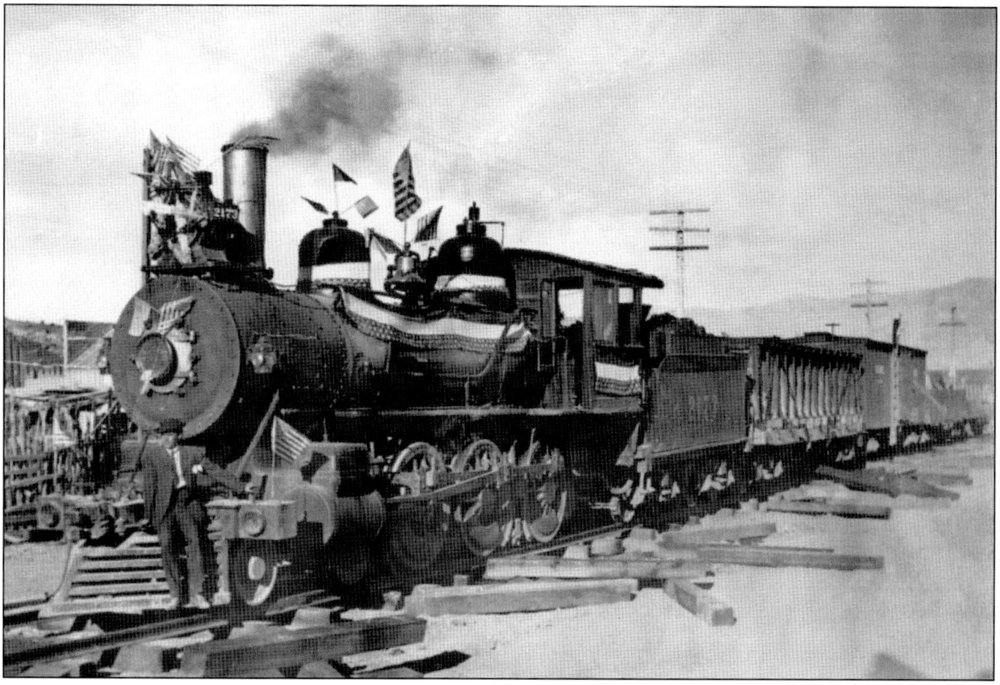

This photograph is often referred to as the first train picture, but it is not the official first train. It is actually a work train arriving in Ely just before the Railroad Day celebration. The train is lead by a Southern Pacific (SP) locomotive. In its early days, the Nevada Northern (NN) leased and purchased locomotives from the SP. (WPCHS.)

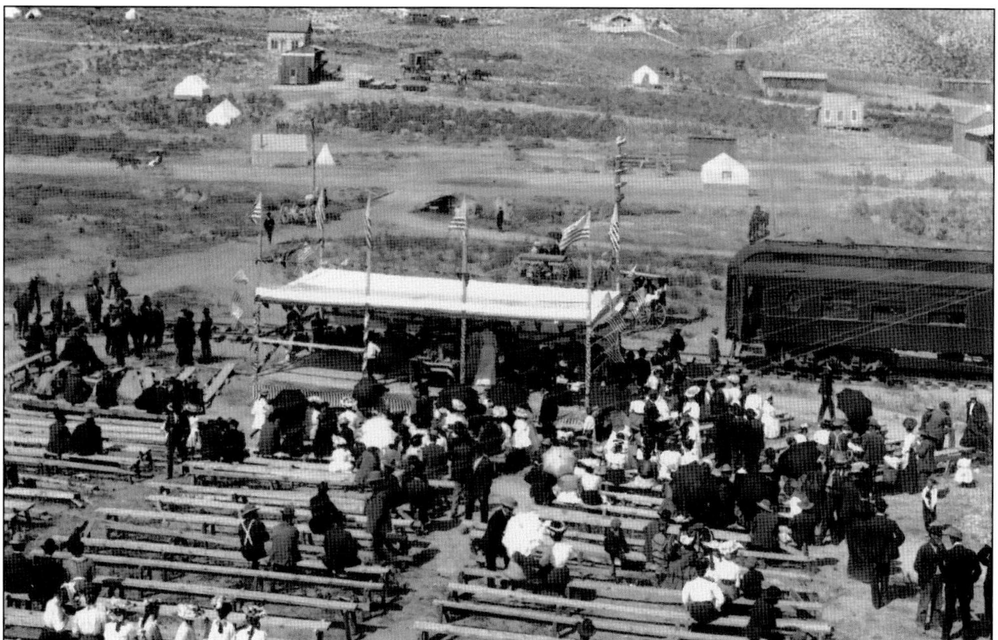

An enormous celebration was planned to welcome the railroad to Ely. Committees were formed, and duties were assigned. The highlight of Railroad Day would be the speeches and a community barbecue. This is the speaker's platform with benches set up for the public. (USHS.)

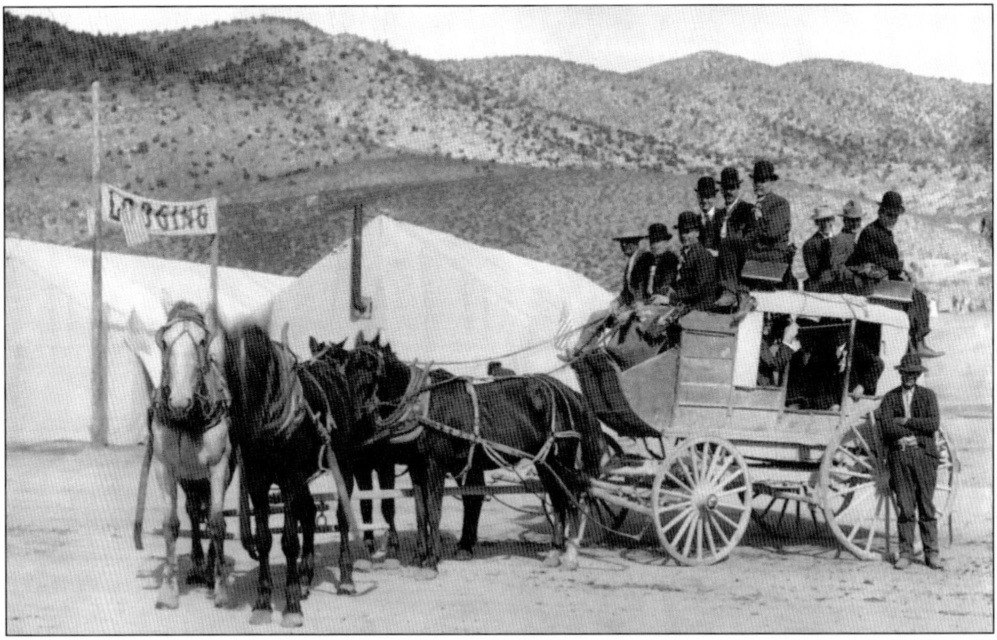

Railroad Day weekend was September 29–30, 1906. Special trains arrived in Ely on the new Nevada Northern Railway. The 500 residents of Ely hosted celebrants, who converged on the region to welcome the railroad, almost seven-times their number. All of these people needed a place to stay. A tent city was set up to accommodate the celebrants. In addition to lodging, transportation was needed to move the visitors around the community. In 2006, at the centennial celebration of the railroad, the town should have followed the historical precedent and set up tents for lodging once again. Visitors that weekend filled the town and all of its motel rooms; tents were needed. (Both, USHS.)

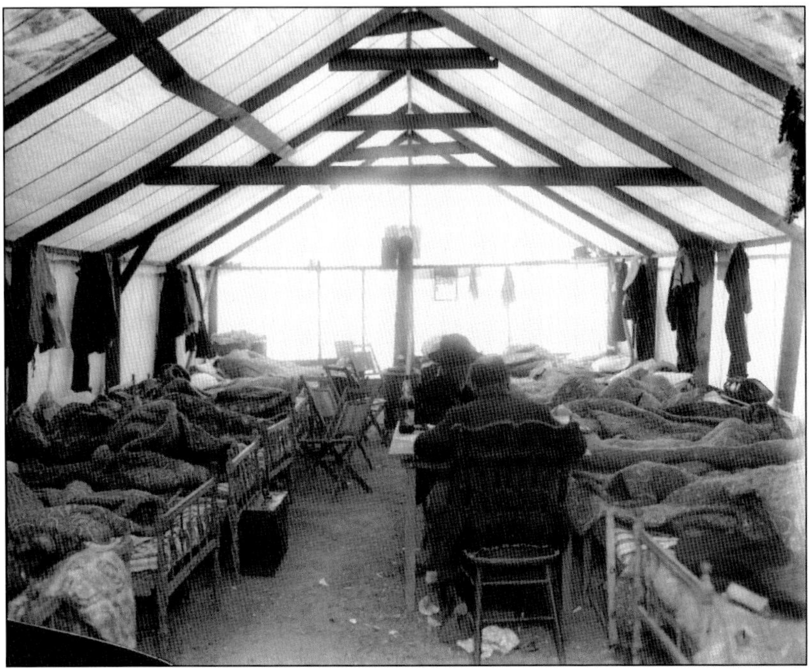

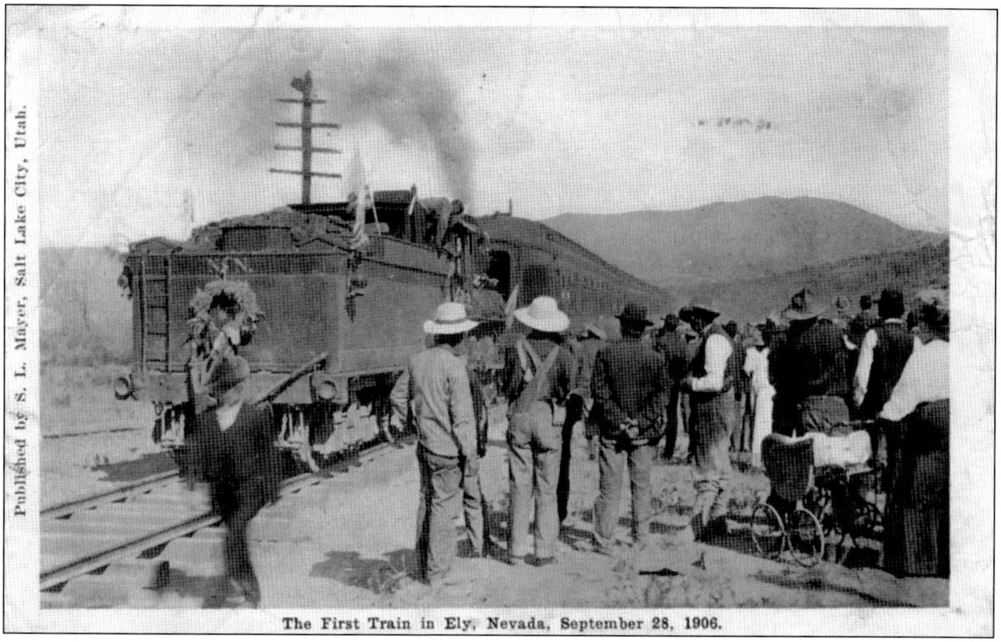

Special trains whisked hundreds of visitors to the festivities in Ely. The first train was from Salt Lake City and included five luxury Pullman sleepers, three tourist sleepers, and a private car transporting Mark Requa, members of the railroad's management, and their guests. The second train originated in Ogden, Utah, and awaited a contingent of cars bearing political dignitaries traveling from Carson City to Cobre via the Southern Pacific Railroad. The SP train was delayed by repeated problems with the steam locomotive, which caused it to be hours late. If the caption on the picture above is correct, this is the train from Salt Lake City, the first passenger train to arrive in Ely for the celebrations. (Above, Novich; below, USHS.)

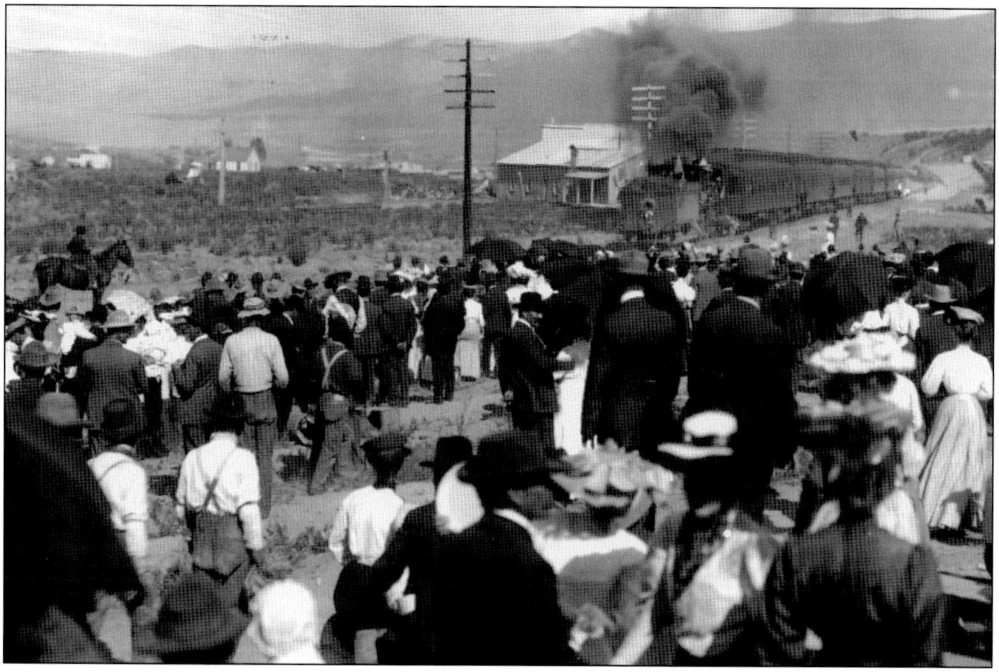

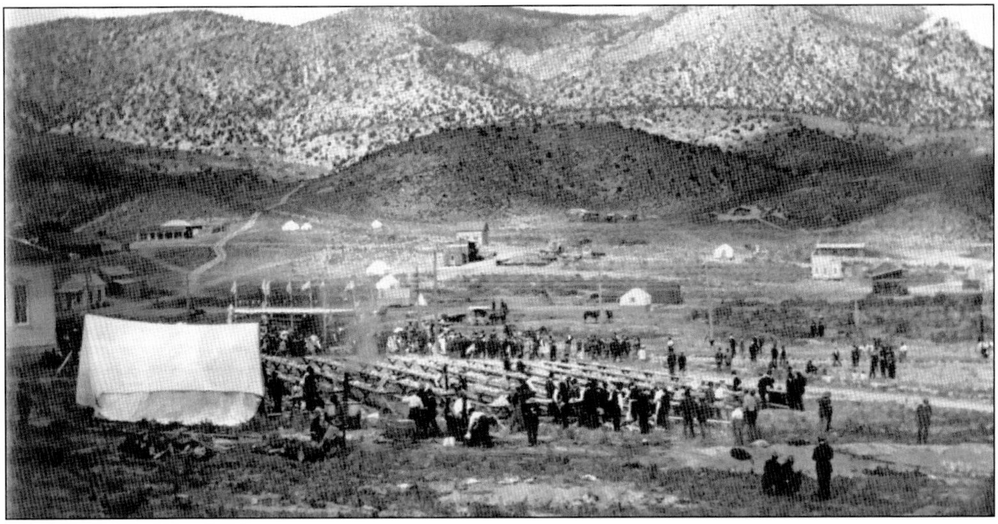

Shown are the preparations for the Railroad Day Celebration. The building on the left is the White Pine County courthouse, in front of which the celebration took place. Today, the building is used for county offices. The tent is a cook tent, and above the cook tent is the speaker stand.

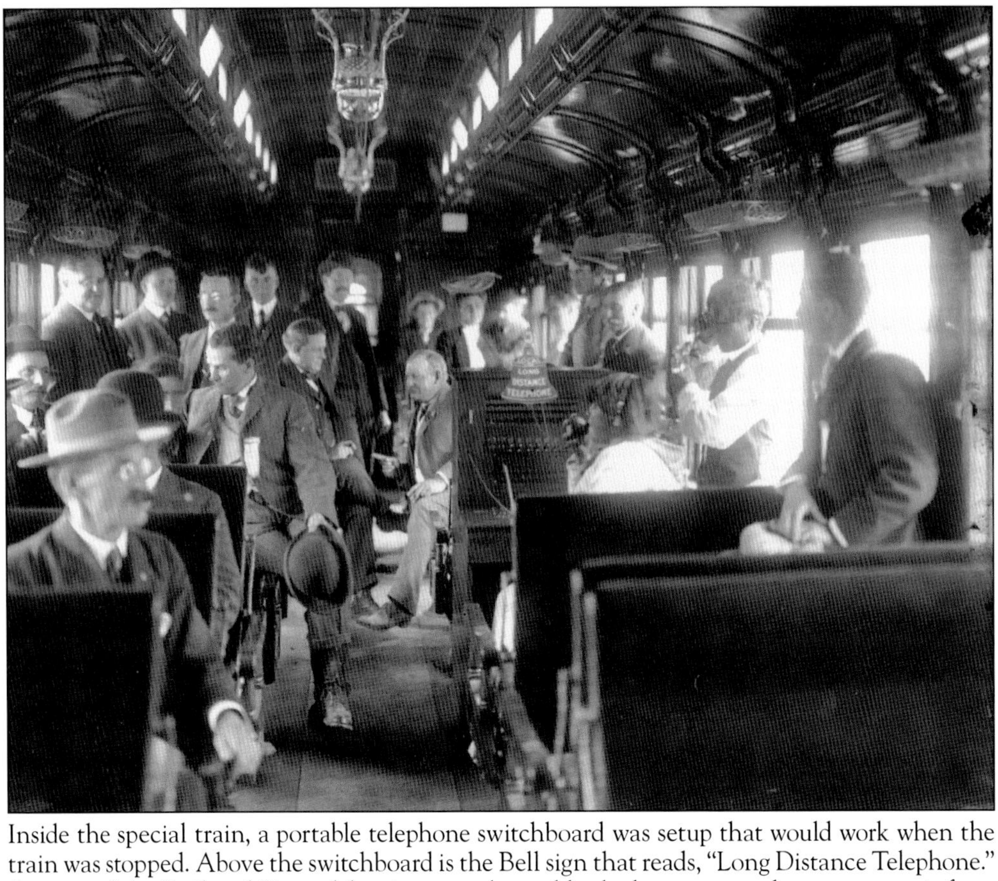

Inside the special train, a portable telephone switchboard was setup that would work when the train was stopped. Above the switchboard is the Bell sign that reads, "Long Distance Telephone." As part of the Railroad Day celebration, people could telephone across the country to inform their friends and family about the railroad coming to Ely. (USHS.)

"Rah, Rah, Rah Requa!" read the headline. On September 29, 1906, at 3:00 p.m., Mark Requa, the builder of the railroad, drove home the ceremonial last spike made of Ruth copper. It was a bittersweet moment. By November 1906, Requa was forced into retirement from the railroad. Today, the mineral wealth of the mines has exceeded the wealth of the famous Comstock Lode. All of this was made possible by Mark Requa's vision.

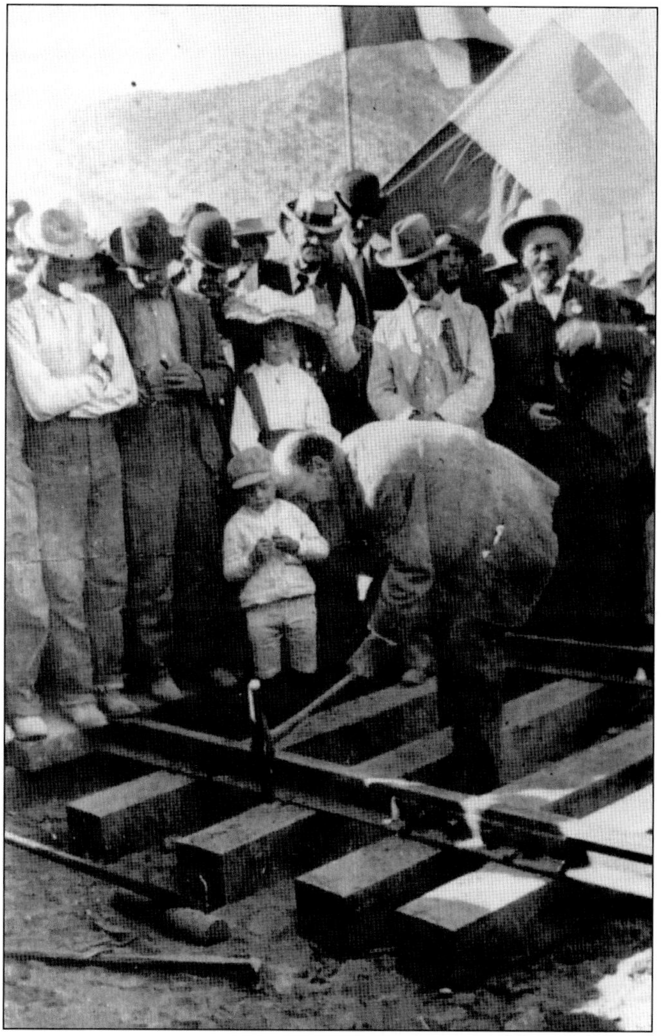

The railroad required space for shops and a yard. A new community called Ely City was to be built to the east of Ely. Here, grading crews are laying out the streets. But things did not go as planned. First, the community objected and did not move. Secondly, the mill and smelter site was moved to McGill. (USHS.)

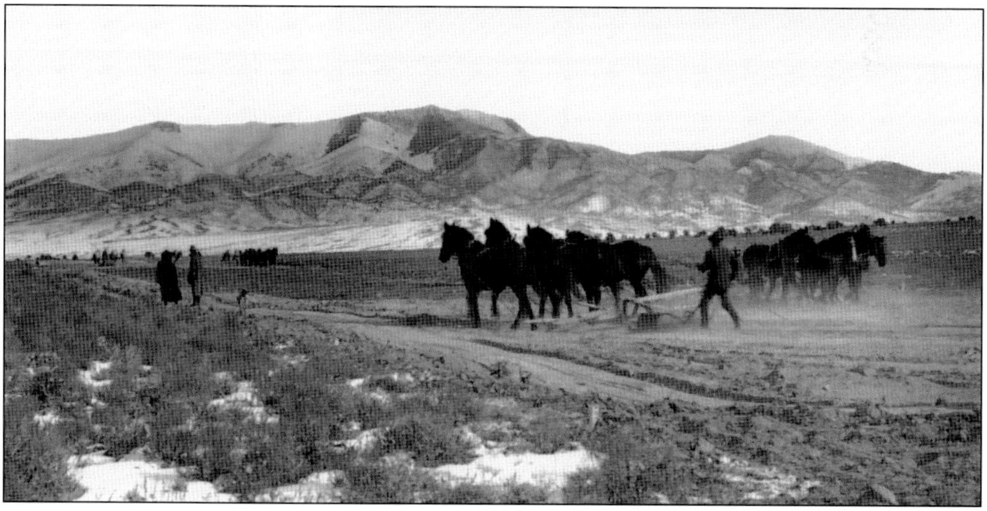

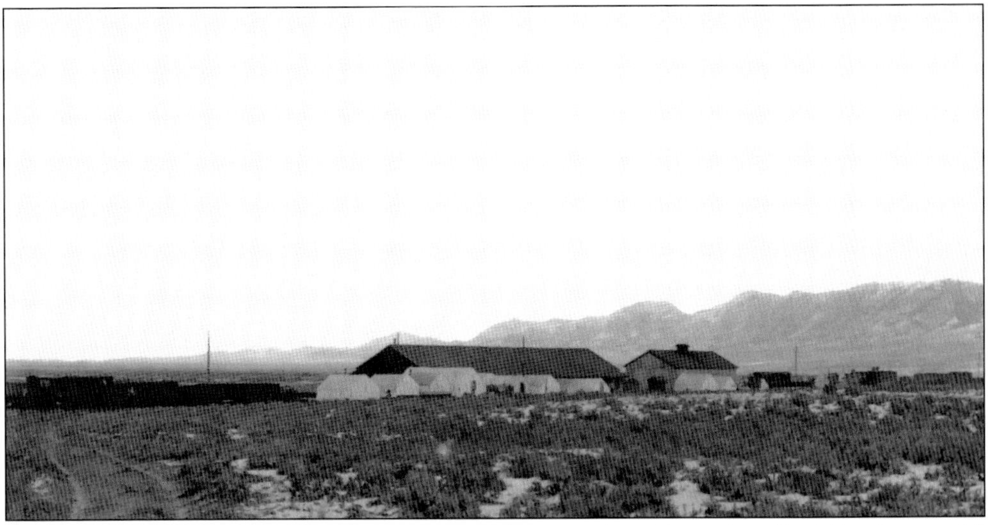

Construction of the railroad yard is evident in this view from December 1906. Freight cars fill the yard. The long building behind the tents is the freight house. It served as the first depot. The first engine house is on the right. Mark Requa planned to build the mill and smelter on this site to the north of the railroad yard, but the Guggenheims moved the site to McGill. (USHS.)

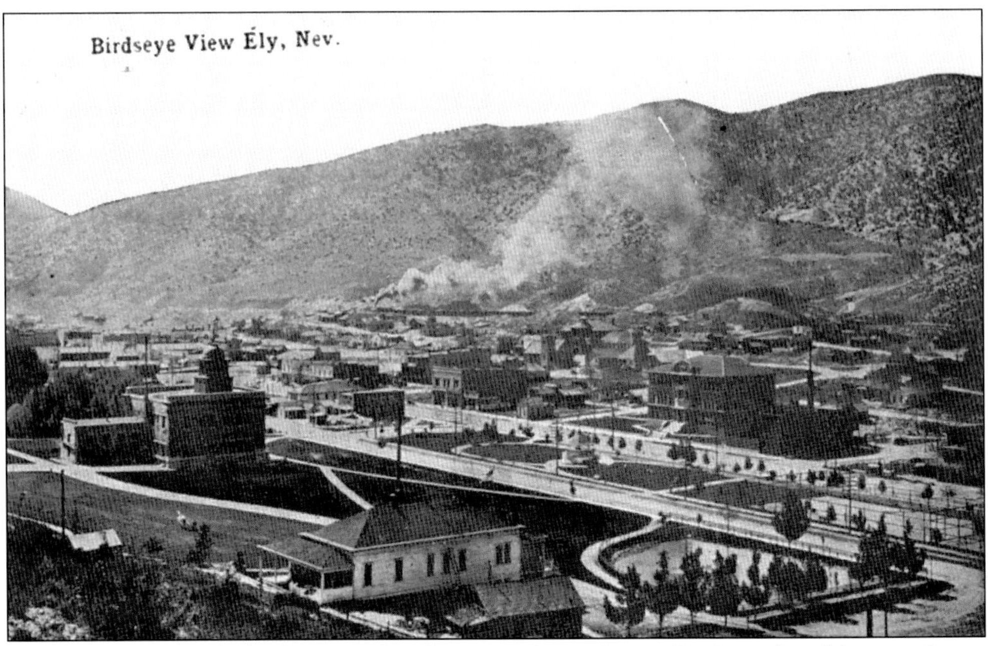

The white building in the foreground is the original courthouse. To the right of the courthouse is the duck pond facing Clark Street, left of the new courthouse. Barely visible in Clark Street is the original track through town. The plume of smoke in the center is an ore train heading to the mine on the bypass track. (Novich.)

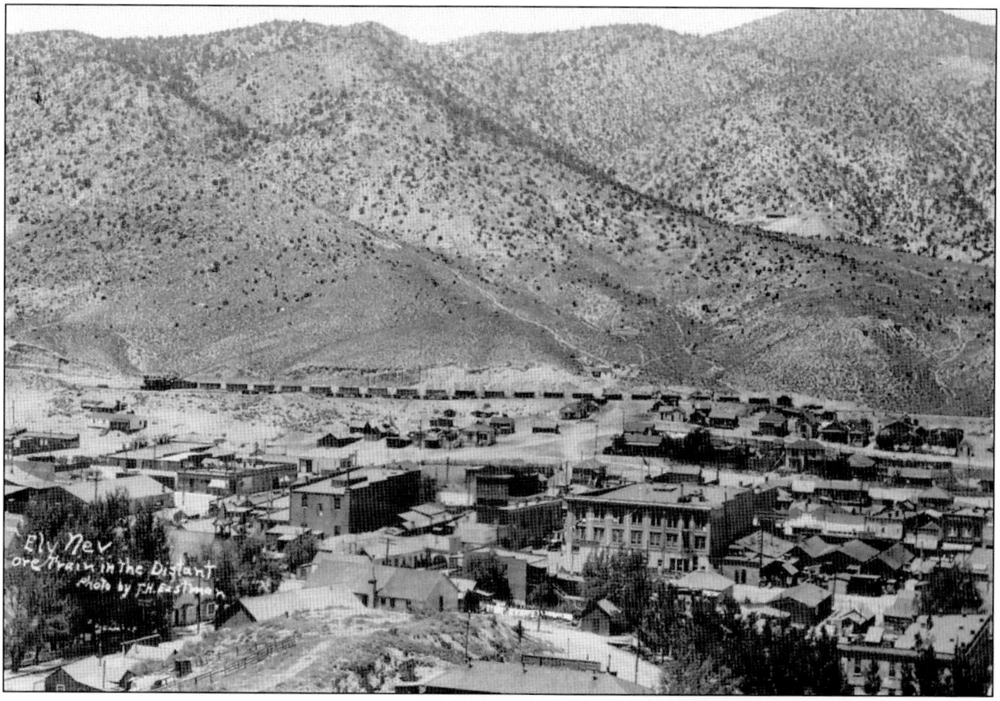

An ore train on the bypass track is visible in the background. The large, three-story building in the right-center is the Northern Hotel. The original plan was for the ore trains and freight trains to go through downtown Ely. The community objected, and the bypass track moved those trains to the north and above the community. (Novich.)

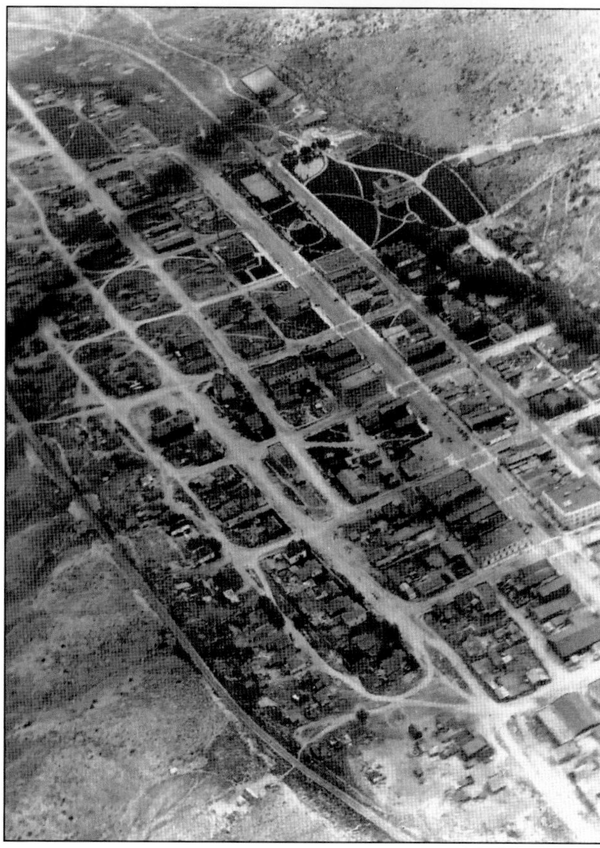

In a rare aerial photograph of Ely, the domed building in the top right is the new courthouse on Clark Street with the railroad track in front. To the left of the courthouse is the duck pond. The building next to the pond is the Ely Depot. On the left bottom is the bypass track. The community was squeezed between the bypass track and the mainline track. (Novich.)

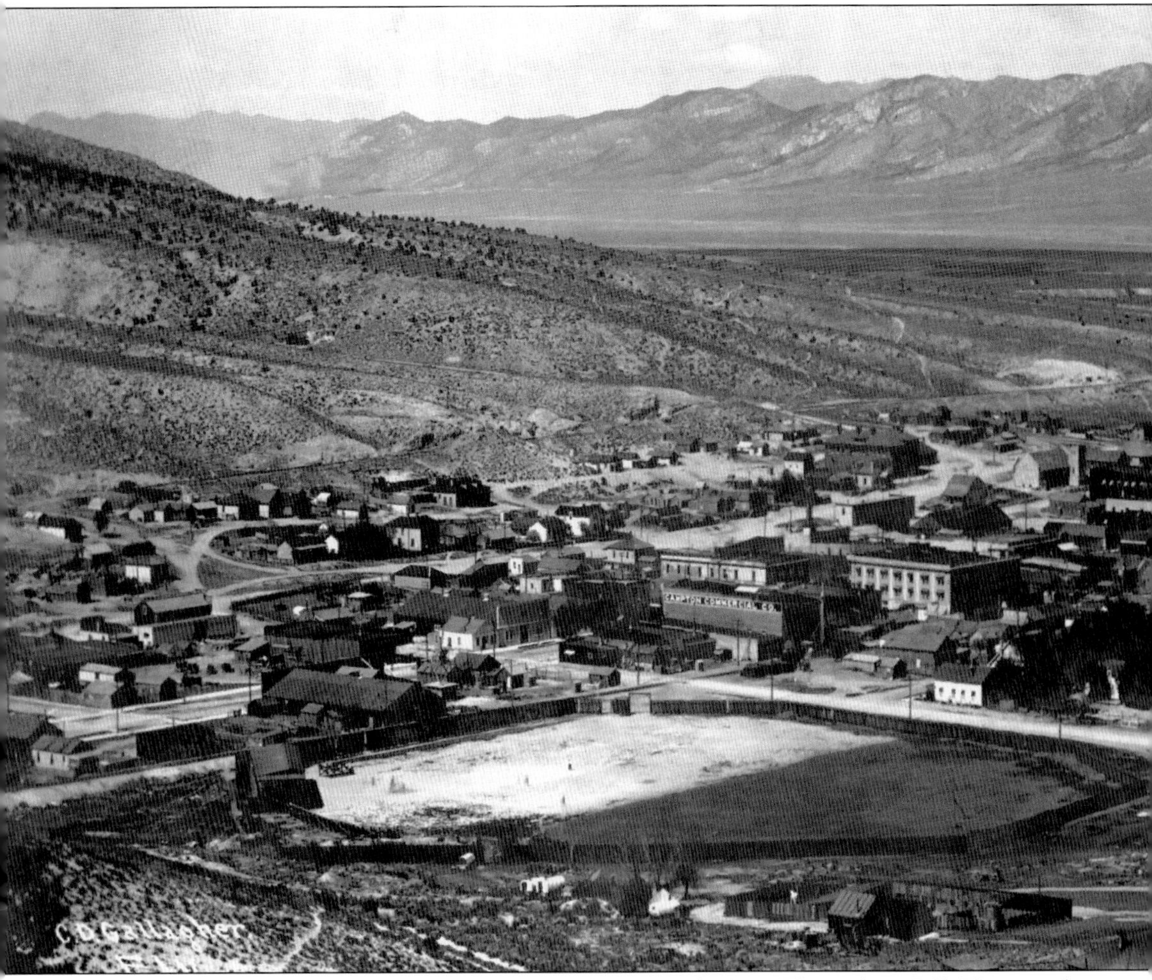

This 1910 photograph shows the relationships between Ely, East Ely, and McGill. Ely is in the foreground, East Ely is to the upper right, and McGill is barely visible in the upper left. This photograph can be compared to the earlier image of the same area on page 18. In four years, Ely had boomed. The domed building in the right-center is the new courthouse where the copper

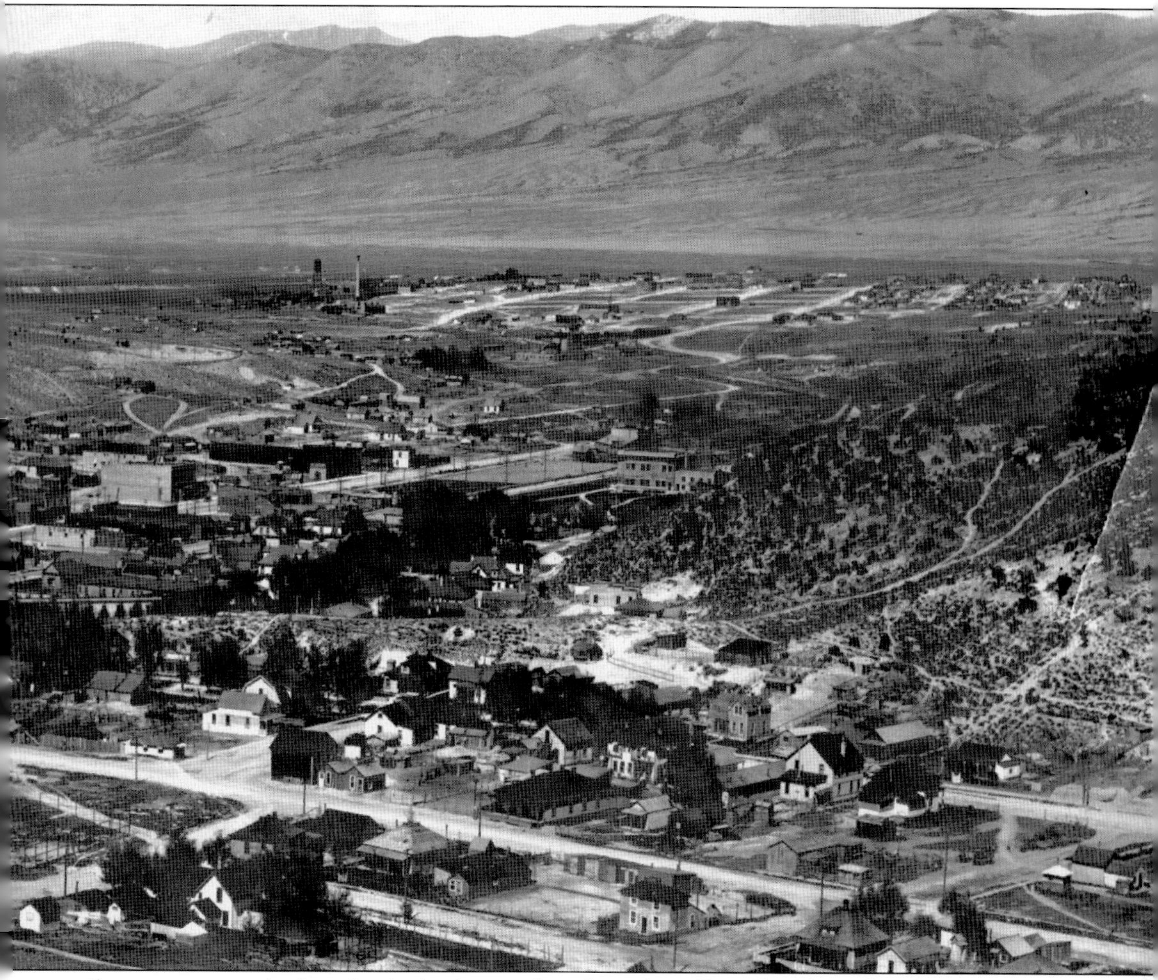

spike ceremony took place. In the background to the right is East Ely. The railroad's water tower is also visible, and to the left of it is the fill required for the new ore bypass track built around Ely. Also visible are the broad streets that the grading crews built in 1906. It is evident that Ely is not dying as the railroad, perhaps, hoped it would; rather, East Ely is struggling to build itself up.

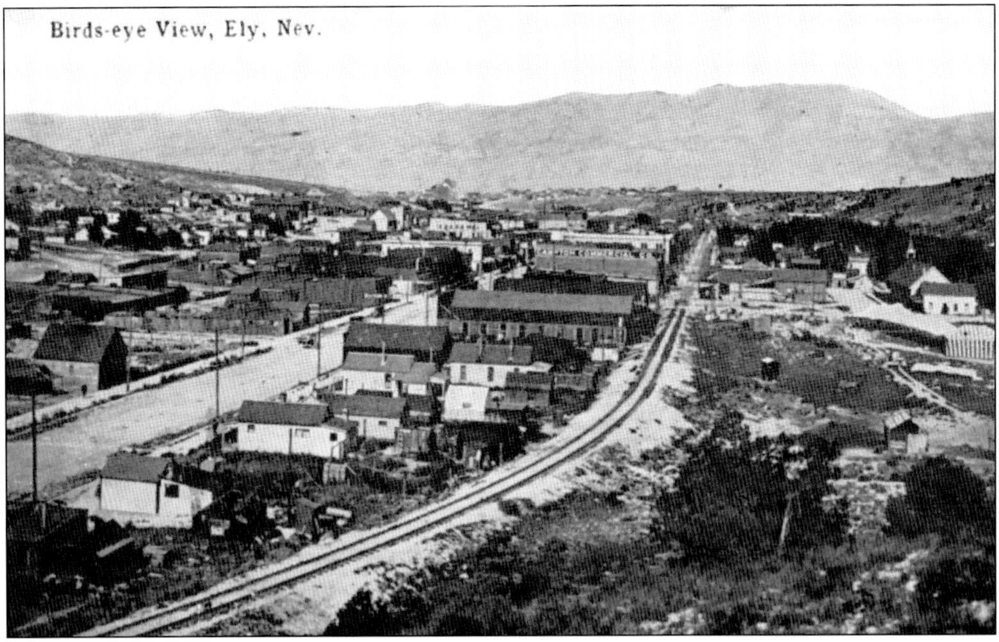

This is the mainline track through Ely. Its proximity to the heart of town demonstrates why the community demanded the ore line bypass track be built. The street to the left is Aultman Avenue, which was the proposed original route of the railroad through town. Businesses on Aultman forced the track on to Clark Street, which was only a partial solution. (Novich.)

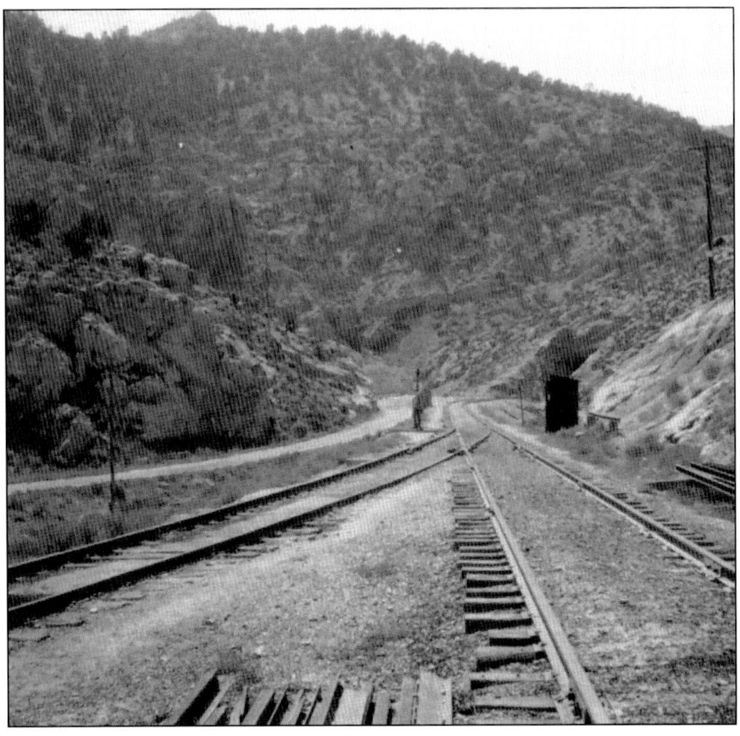

The mainline track (left) and the ore bypass track (right) came together at Ely Junction to the west of town and just before tunnel No. 1. Passenger trains and the occasional freight train used the mainline. All ore trains used the bypass. To the right of the switch is a switchman's booth with a telephone. (Newitt.)

Two

Copper Mining Moves a Mountain

White Pine County copper ore is a very low-grade ore, containing only about three percent copper; 2,000 pounds of ore produces about 60 pounds of copper. To profitably produce the copper, tens of millions of tons of ore needed to be mined annually. To get to the copper ore, overburden or waste rock, needed to be stripped off of the copper ore and dumped out of the way.

It was very labor intensive. The copper was mined by massive steam shovels, the ore and overburden was dumped directly into the railroad cars, and the copper was dug from benches. As the pits became larger, the track would spiral down into the pit. Small steam locomotives called dinkies would run around the pit, delivering and removing the railroad cars.

As the pits spiraled into the earth, track was constantly being moved and built. The original steam shovels were mounted on railcars. As they dug, new track needed to be built for the steam shovels to reach the ore. When the bottom of the pit was reached, the shovels started digging a new upward spiral headed to the top of the pit. At the top of the pit, another spiral heading back down was started.

Approximately 19 miles of track was in the pit. It was constantly being moved as the pit was dug deeper and wider. At Copper Flat, the ore cars were grouped into trains for the trip to the mill.

Mining went on constantly. It was an industrial symphony on a colossal scale. Blasting was done to break up the rock. Track was relentlessly moved. Steam shovels were dumping rock into the cars. The dinkies delivered empty cars and removed full ones. The steam shovels and churn drills needed coal and water, which had to be delivered in between the ore cars. Day in and day out, around the clock, the pits were in operation. Steam whistles blew, cars clanged, and smoke and dust filled the air.

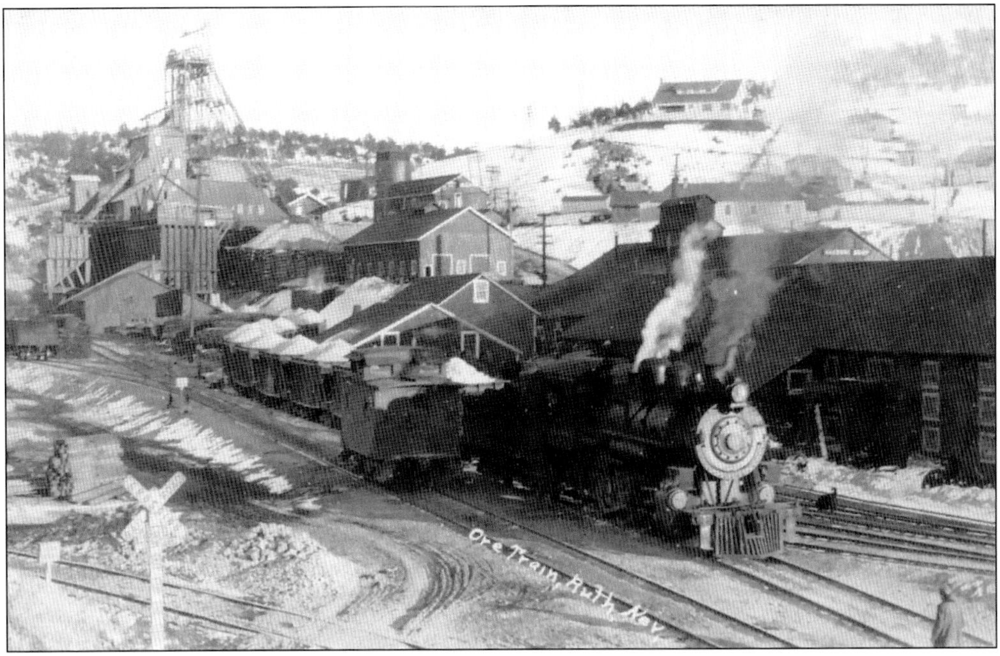

These photographs show Ruth around 1918. Above, ore cars are being loaded from the mine in the background. Next to the locomotive is one of the little four-wheel bobber cabooses. Once the ore cars were loaded, the caboose was coupled on to the train for the trip to McGill. Notice the railroad crossing sign. The lettering going down the post warns, "LOOK OUT FOR THE CARS," referring to railroad cars, not automobiles. Below is a view north from the mine. Originally, an underground mine, it eventually became an open-pit mine. In the lower right are timbers used underground to stabilize the shafts. (Novich.)

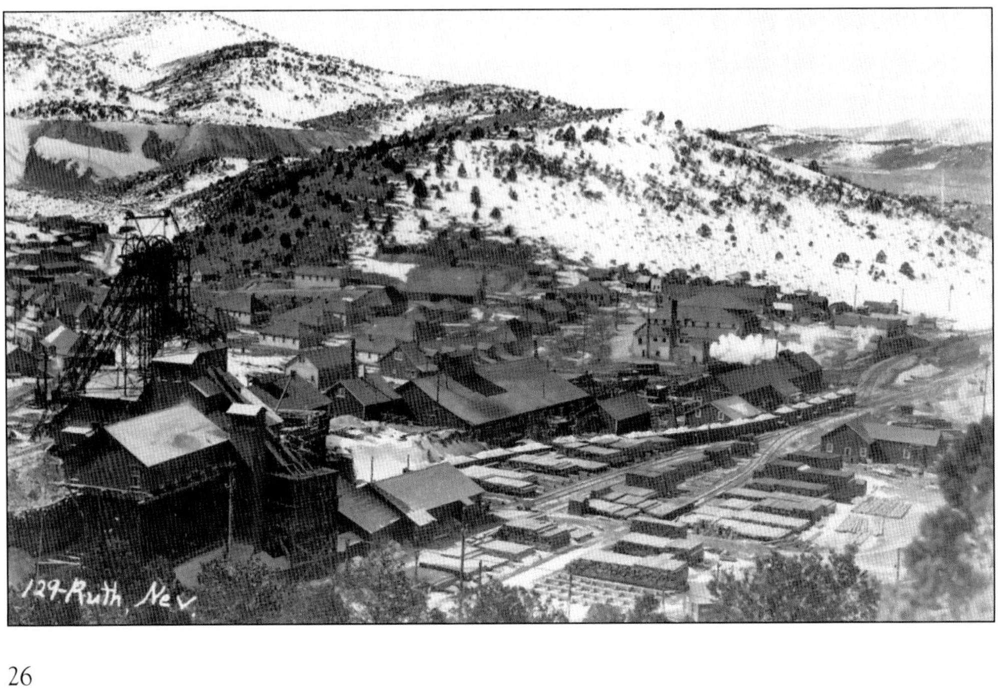

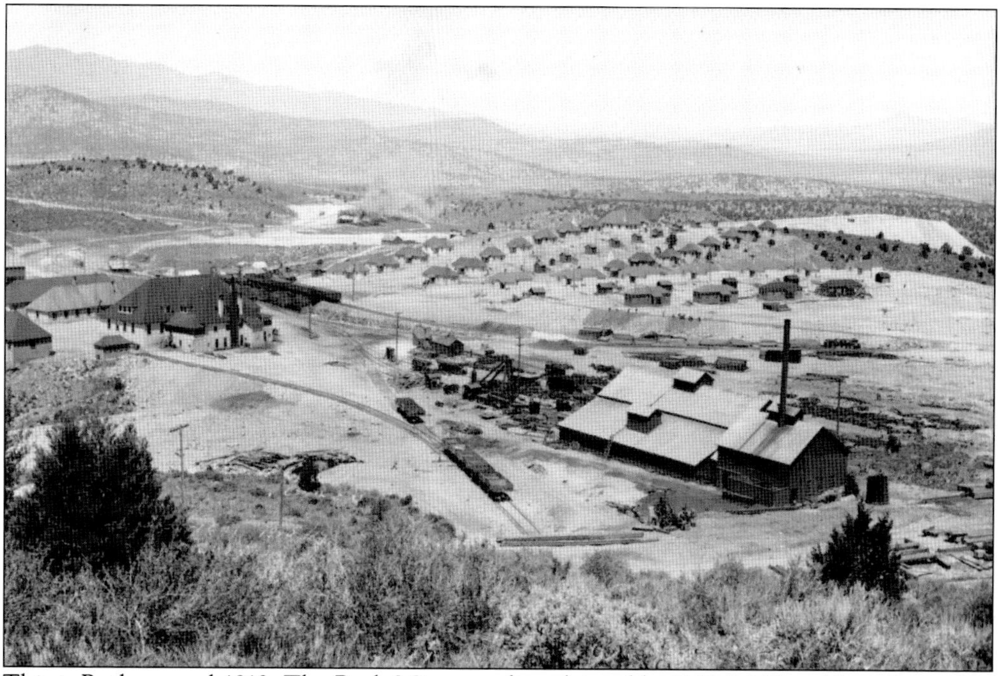

This is Ruth around 1912. The Ruth Mine was first claimed by D.C. McDonald on September 22, 1899. He named the mine for his daughter, Ruth. McDonald sold the claim to E.F. Gray and D.P. Bartley for $3,600 on October 8, 1900. Mark Requa optioned the Bartley and Gray claims in October 1902. (NHS.)

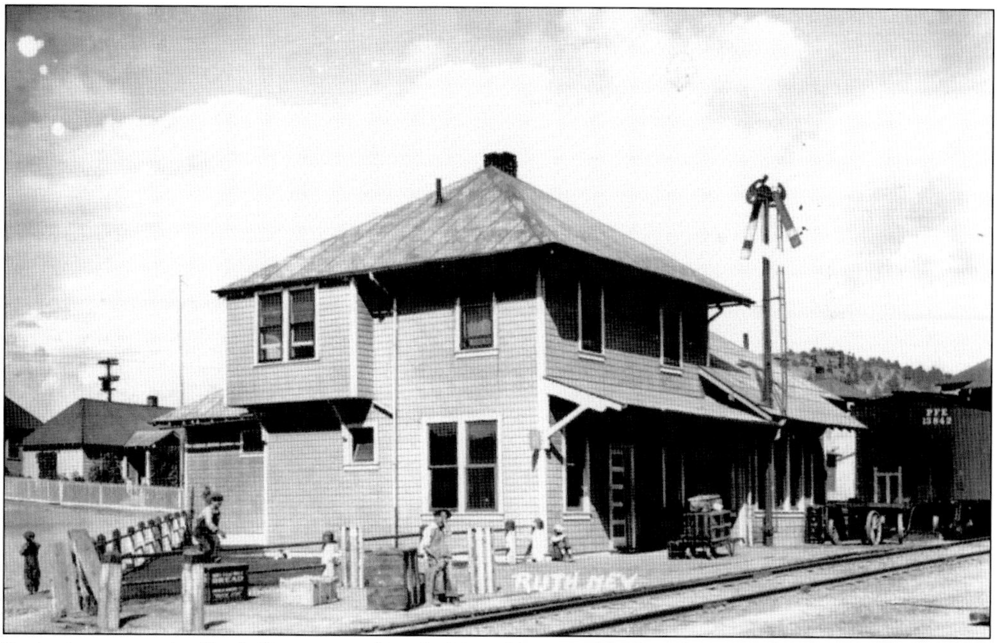

Parked next to the Ruth Depot is a Pacific Fruit Express (PFE) refrigerated car. PFE refrigerated cars delivered fresh fruit and vegetables throughout the country. The child on the left is jumping over a Butternut breadbox. All of this will disappear when the pit is expanded in the 1950s. (WPCHS.)

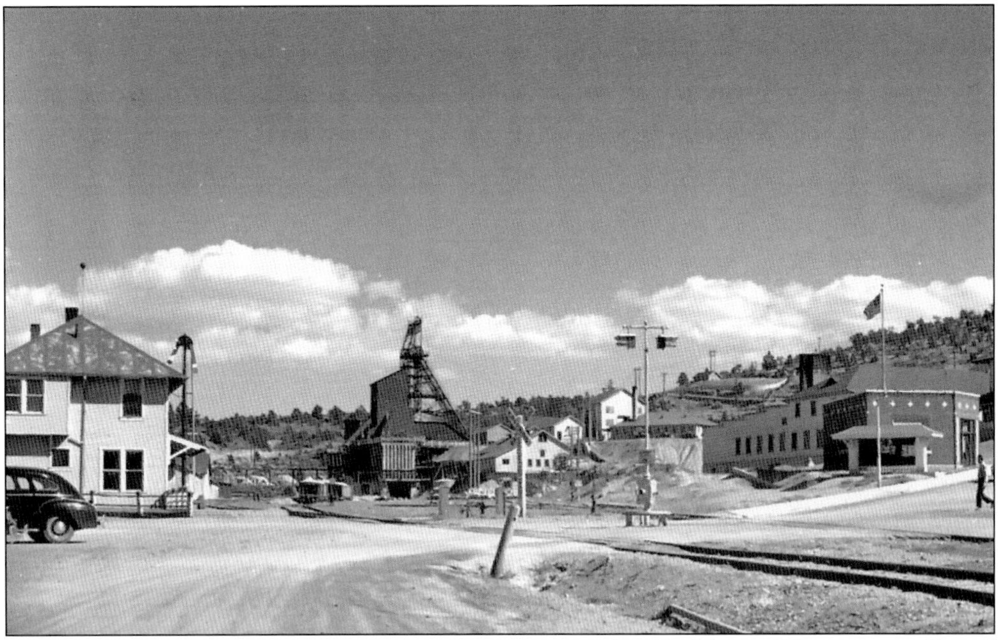

This photograph shows Ruth in the 1940s. Within a decade, all of this will be gone, swallowed up by the Liberty pit. The town will be moved. The building on the left is the Ruth Depot with the train order board in front. The railroad crosswalks have been updated, and the lettering now reads, "LOOK OUT FOR TRAINS." (Novich.)

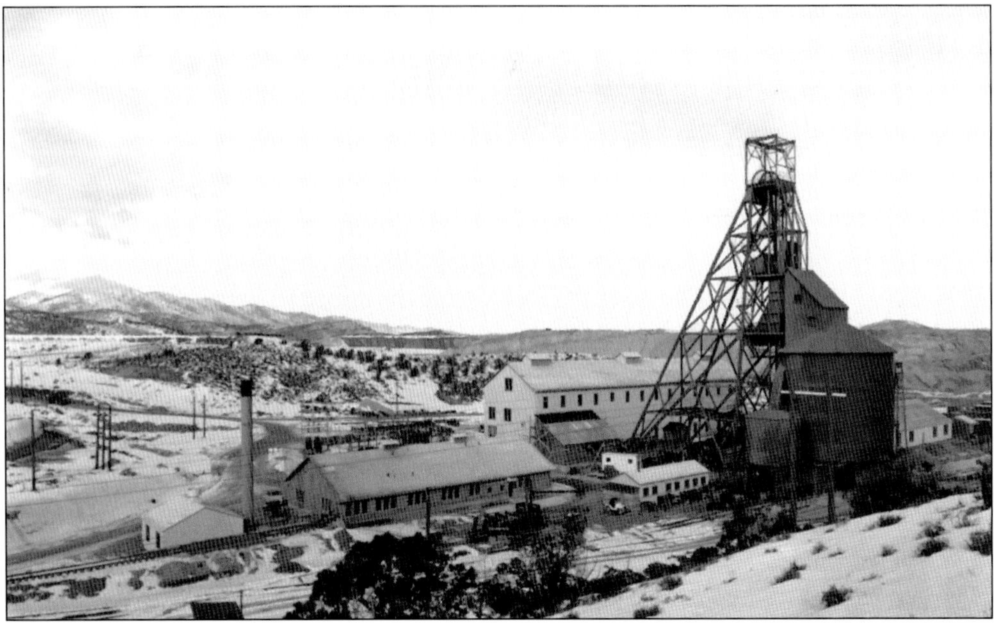

Between Old Ruth and New Ruth was the Deep Ruth Shaft. The shaft provided access to the deep ore body located there. Mining ended in 1965. The headframe and buildings were removed in 2009. By 2010, overburden was being dumped there, and the location is slowly disappearing under the waste rock.

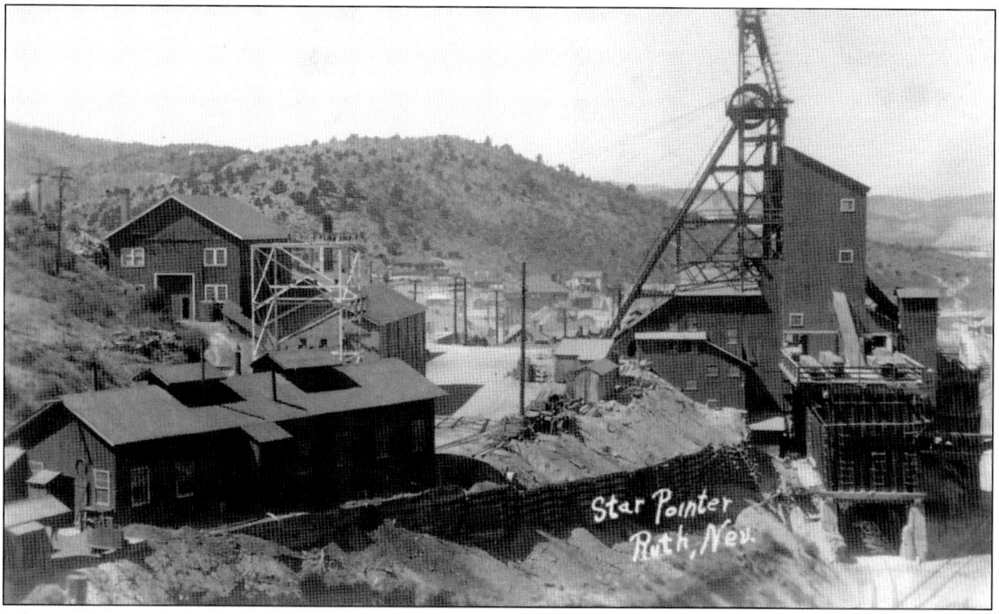

The underground Star Pointer Mine was located near Ruth. It too was served by the Nevada Northern Railway, which hauled the copper ore to McGill. Today, the Star Pointer no longer exists, and its location is part of one of the pits. (Novich.)

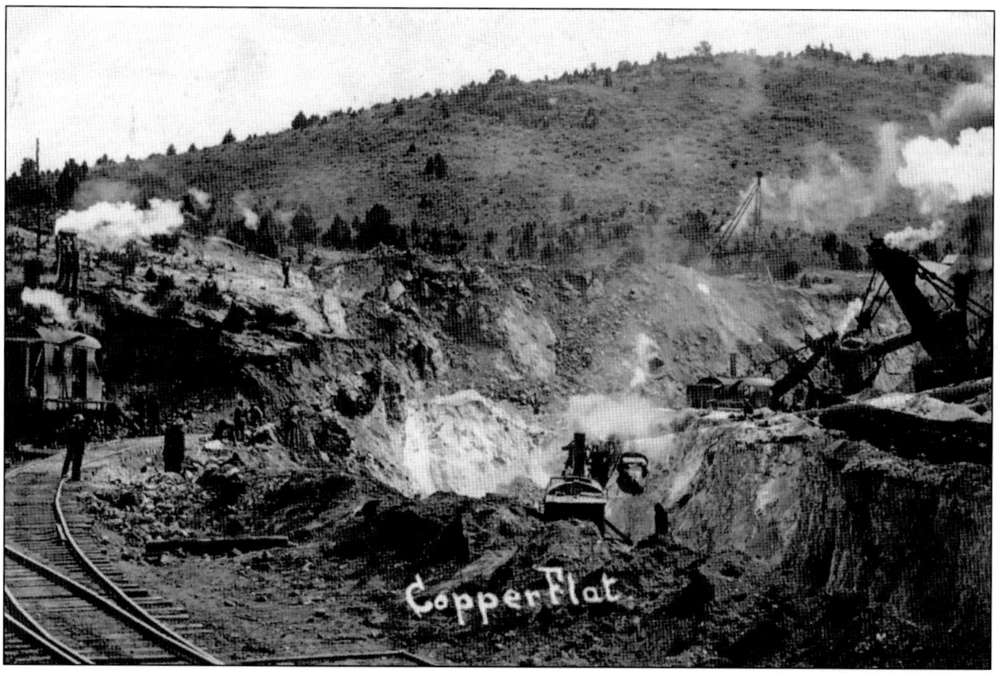

Though the picture is labeled Copper Flat, this is most likely the beginning of the Eureka pit around 1908. There are four steam shovels and a churn drill working in the pit. Before any ore can be removed, the overburden will be removed. In 1916, the Eureka pit merged with the Liberty pit. (Novich.)

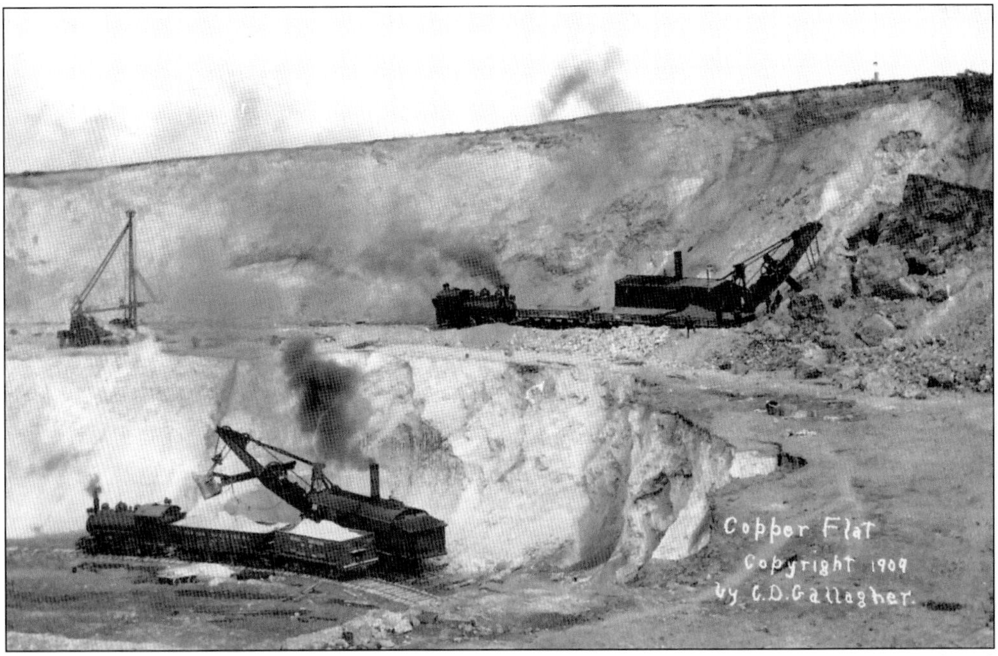

By 1909, the Eureka pit (renamed Copper Flat pit) is considerably larger. The upper steam shovel is removing overburden that will go to dumps. The lower shovel is loading ore. Pit trains were small, usually two to five cars. The locomotives were called dinkies. Both trains will spiral out of the pit to deliver their cars and bring back empties. (Novich.)

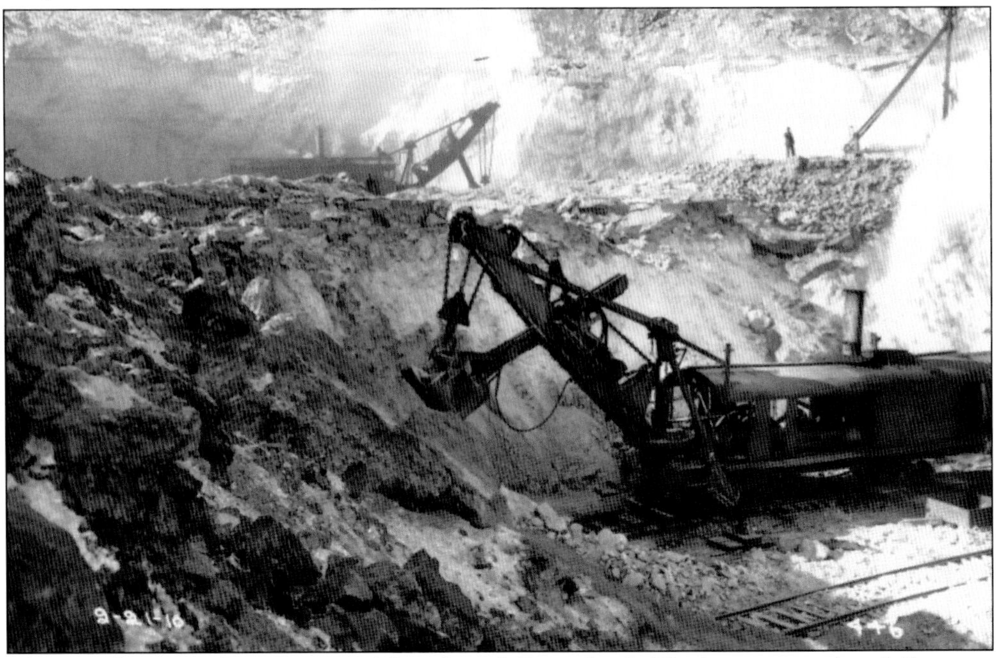

This view from 1910 shows two steam shovels on different levels. The lower steam shovel illustrates the major drawback of this equipment—they were mounted on railroad trucks. A small piece of track is visible in front of the shovel. As the shovel removes the ore, track will be extended in front of the shovel and on the adjoining track.

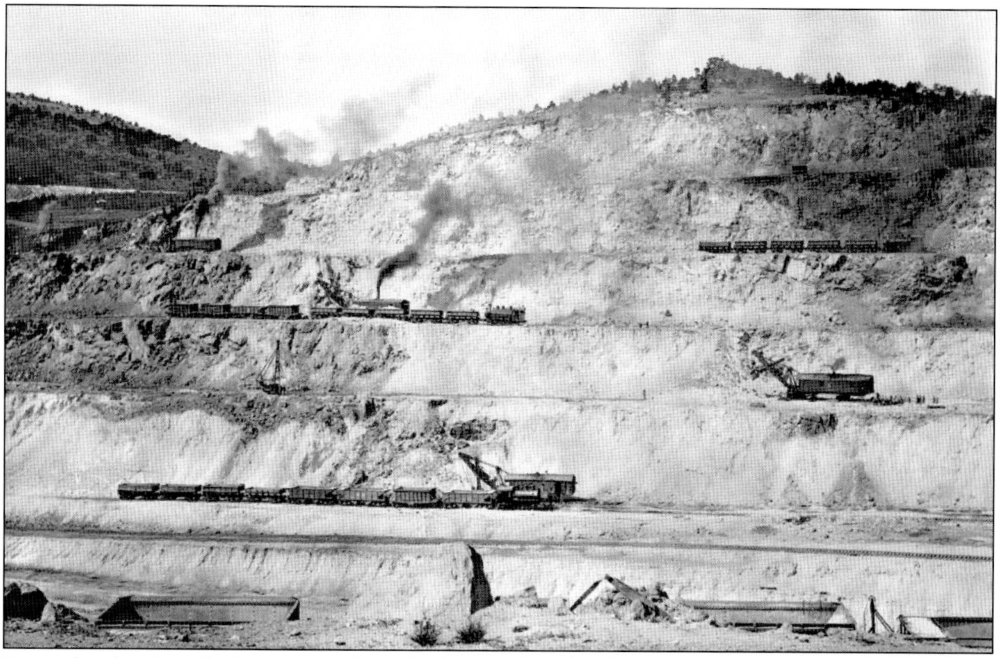

Seven levels of track, four steam shovels, four dinkies hauling trains, and two drills are visible. Overburden and ore are being removed. Empty cars are being brought back. And at shift changes, a shift train will run through the pit delivering workers. As the pit is widened and deepened, track will be laid and moved. (NHS.)

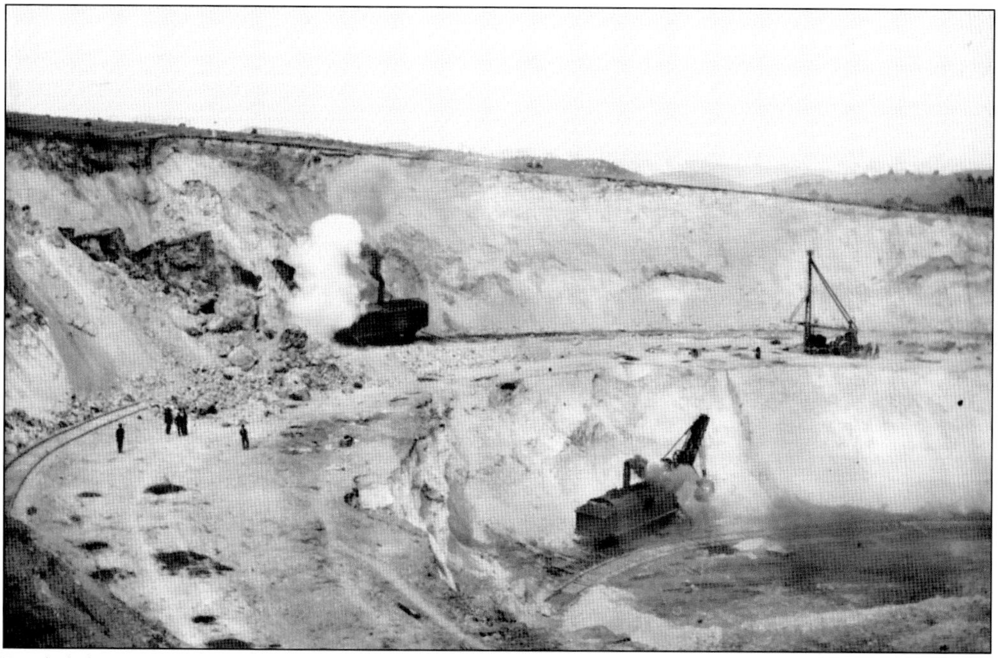

Rockslides were one of the hazards of working in the pit. It appears that a slide had just happened and has blocked the track to the lower part of the pit. The upper steam shovel is removing the blockage. Until it is removed, everything below the blockage will come to a standstill until supplies and workers are again able to pass. (NHS.)

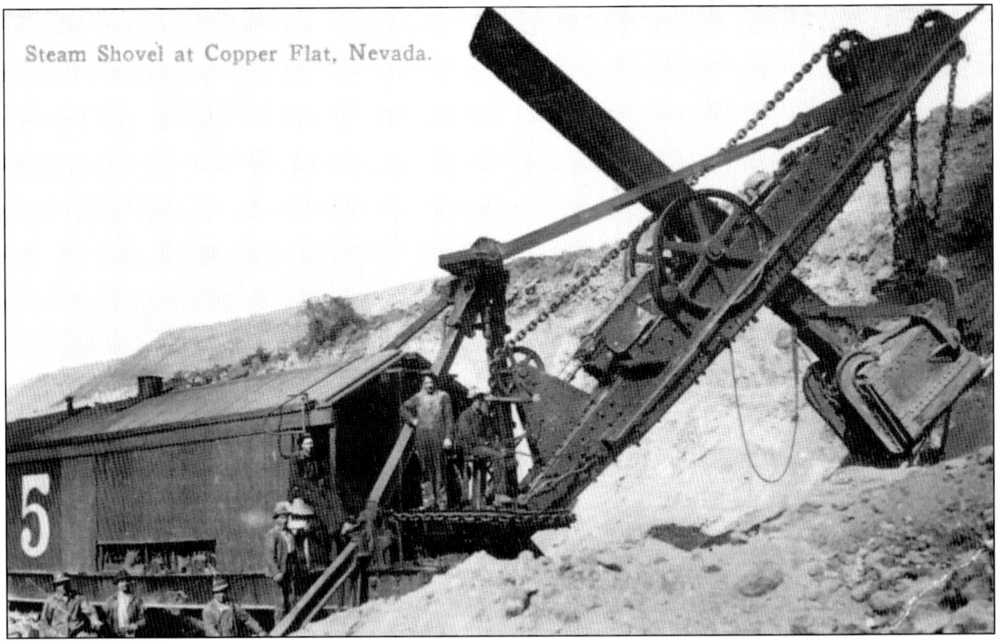

The steam shovels were coal-fired behemoths requiring a three-man crew that included an engineer, a fireman, and a ground man. These were similar to ones being used on the Panama Canal, and some of the operators had worked there. When digging, the operator simultaneously raises and extends the dipper stick to fill the bucket with material. (Novich.)

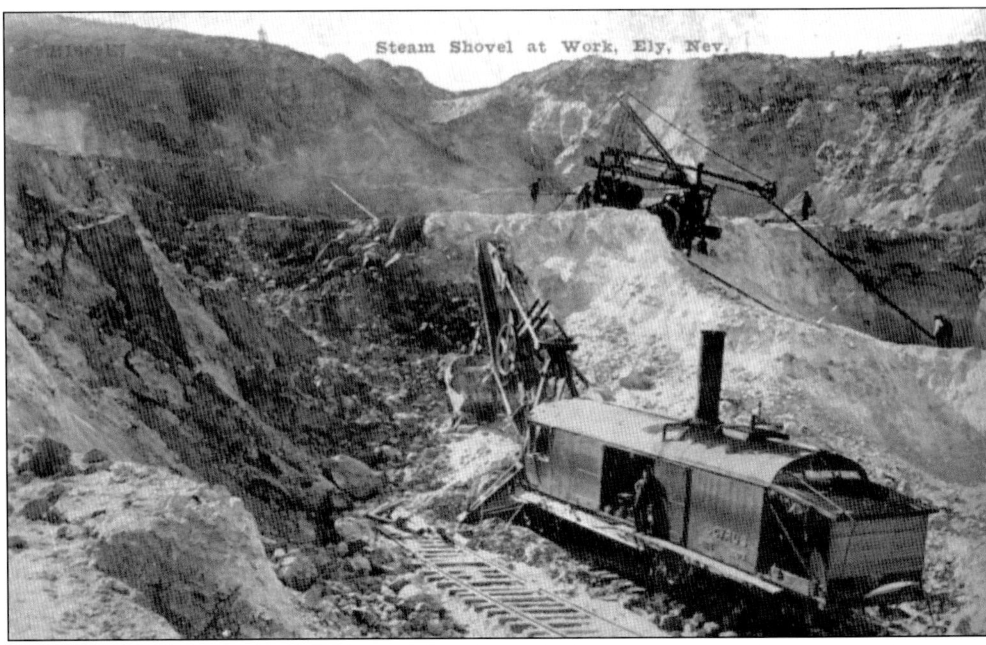

This is a Bucyrus steam shovel. The stack is above the boiler, which produces steam for a steam engine. Just like a steam locomotive, the steam shovel needed the coal and water delivered by the dinkies. Above the steam shovel is a steam-powered churn drill that was used to drill holes for blasting and for core samples to determine the ore body. (Novich.)

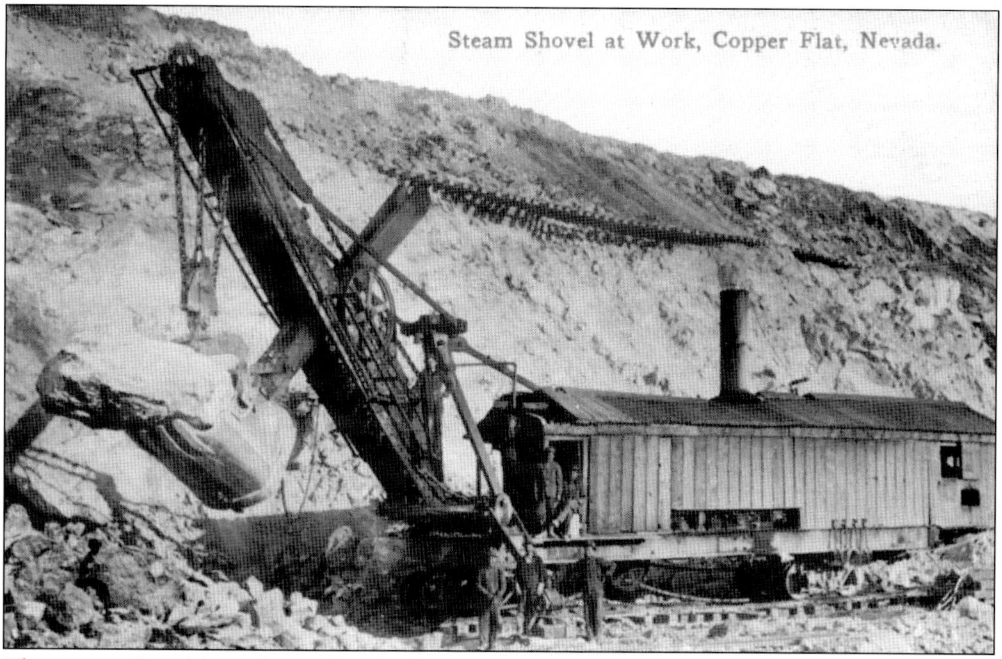

This steam shovel has a large chunk of copper ore in its bucket and is on railroad track. This shovel is self-propelled, but not all were. The drive chain is visible underneath the unit. Above the shovel, the sidewall has collapsed, leaving the track hanging in the air. (Novich.)

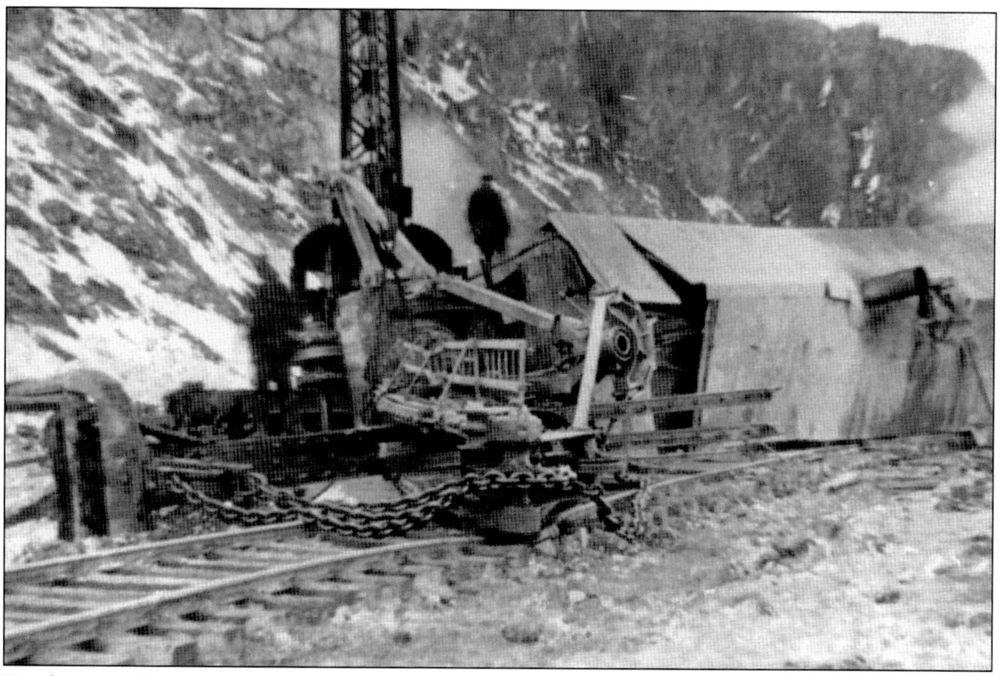

Working in the pit on the steam shovels was a hazardous job. The steam shovels needed to be leveled and blocked to keep them upright, a delicate balance. Soft ground, large boulders, or just plain bad luck, could put the steam shovel on its side, as evident in this photograph. (EERDM.)

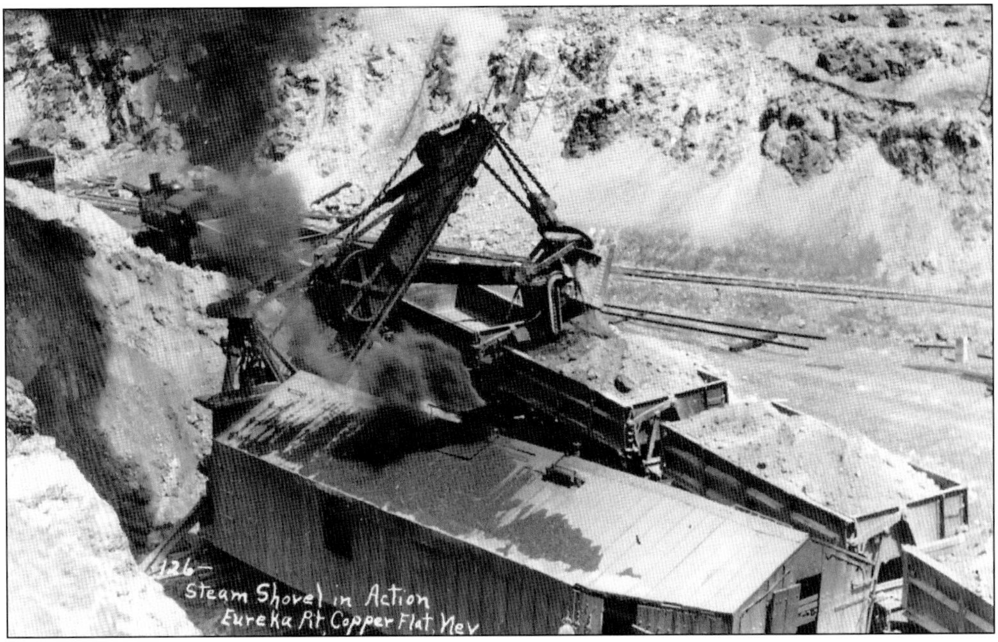

A bird's-eye view of a steam shovel at work reveals the cinders on the roof. It just filled a car, and the dinky will move another one into position. Across from the ore train, a new section of track is being laid. Smoke, steam, cinders, and dust made the mine a dirty place to work. (Novich.)

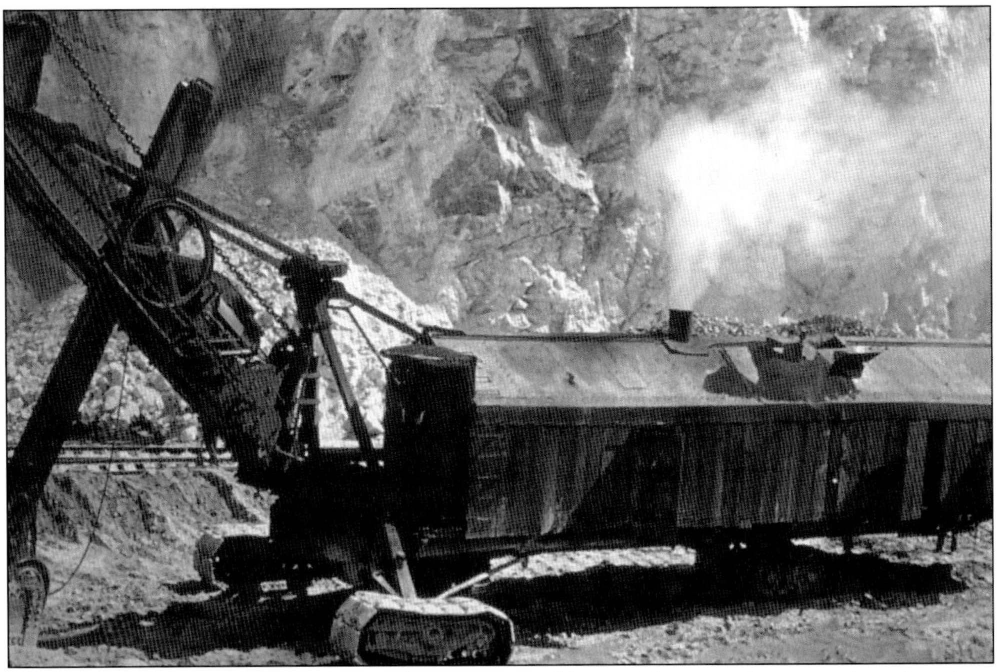
Using railroad track to support steam shovels was inefficient. To move the steam shovel workers needed to build track. And the need for track was constant because the shovel was always digging. This is an early example of putting crawler treads under a steam shovel. To move, the operator would use the dipper to drag the unit forward or push it back.

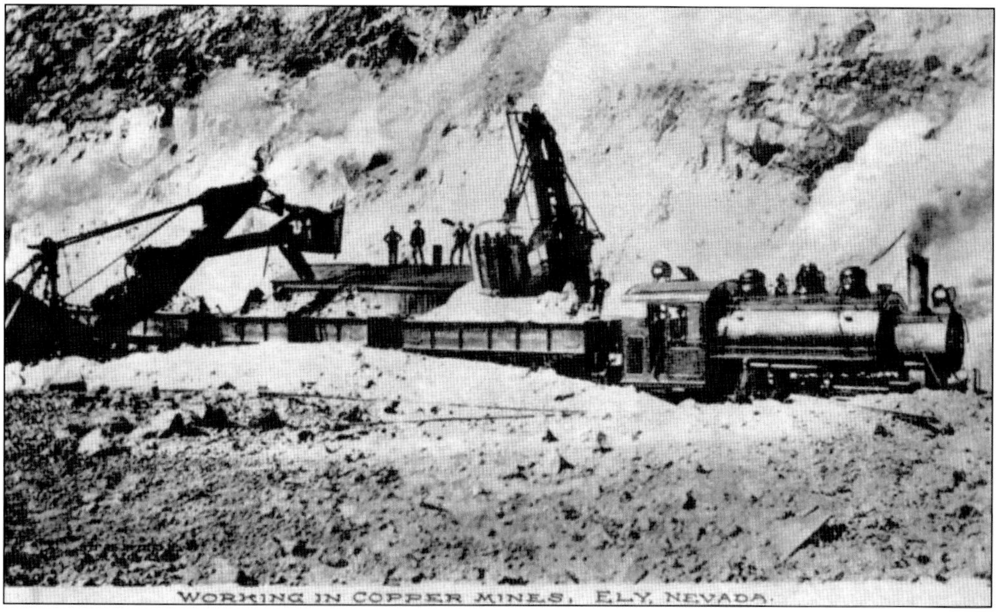

The copper mine fed the McGill mill and smelter, which had colossal appetites for ore. By the end of 1909, McGill could process over a million tons of ore a year. Annually, 20,000 carloads of oar were needed. The railroad served as a 49-mile-long conveyer belt to keep McGill satiated with ore. (Novich.)

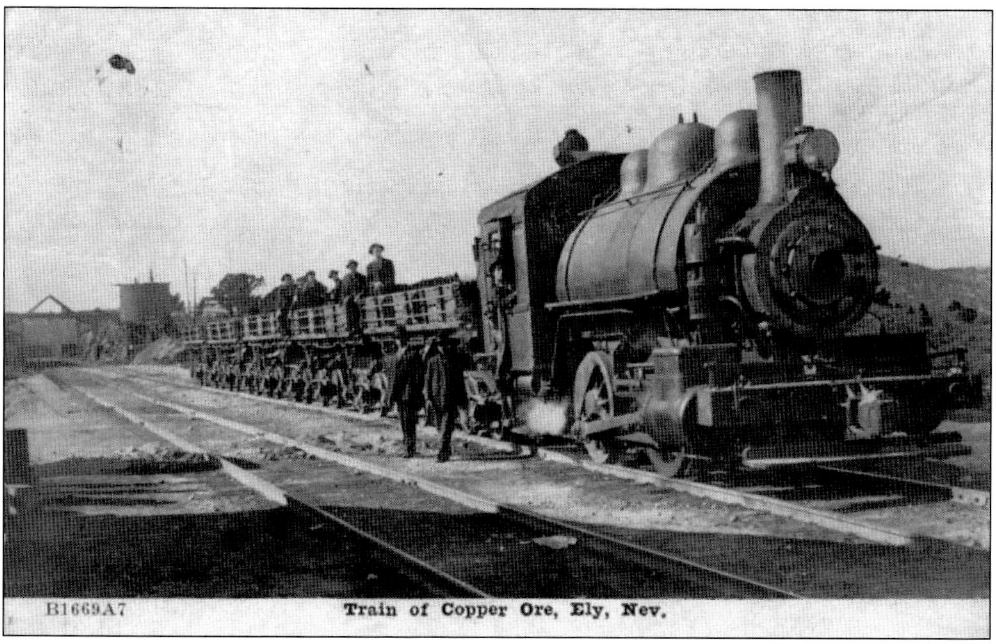

This is a pit ore train. The small locomotive pulling it was called a dinky, in this case an 0-4-0, which means the locomotive has four driving wheels and no other wheels. The advantage to this arrangement was that all of the locomotive's weight was distributed on the driving wheels, making these locomotives powerful for their size and weight. (Novich.)

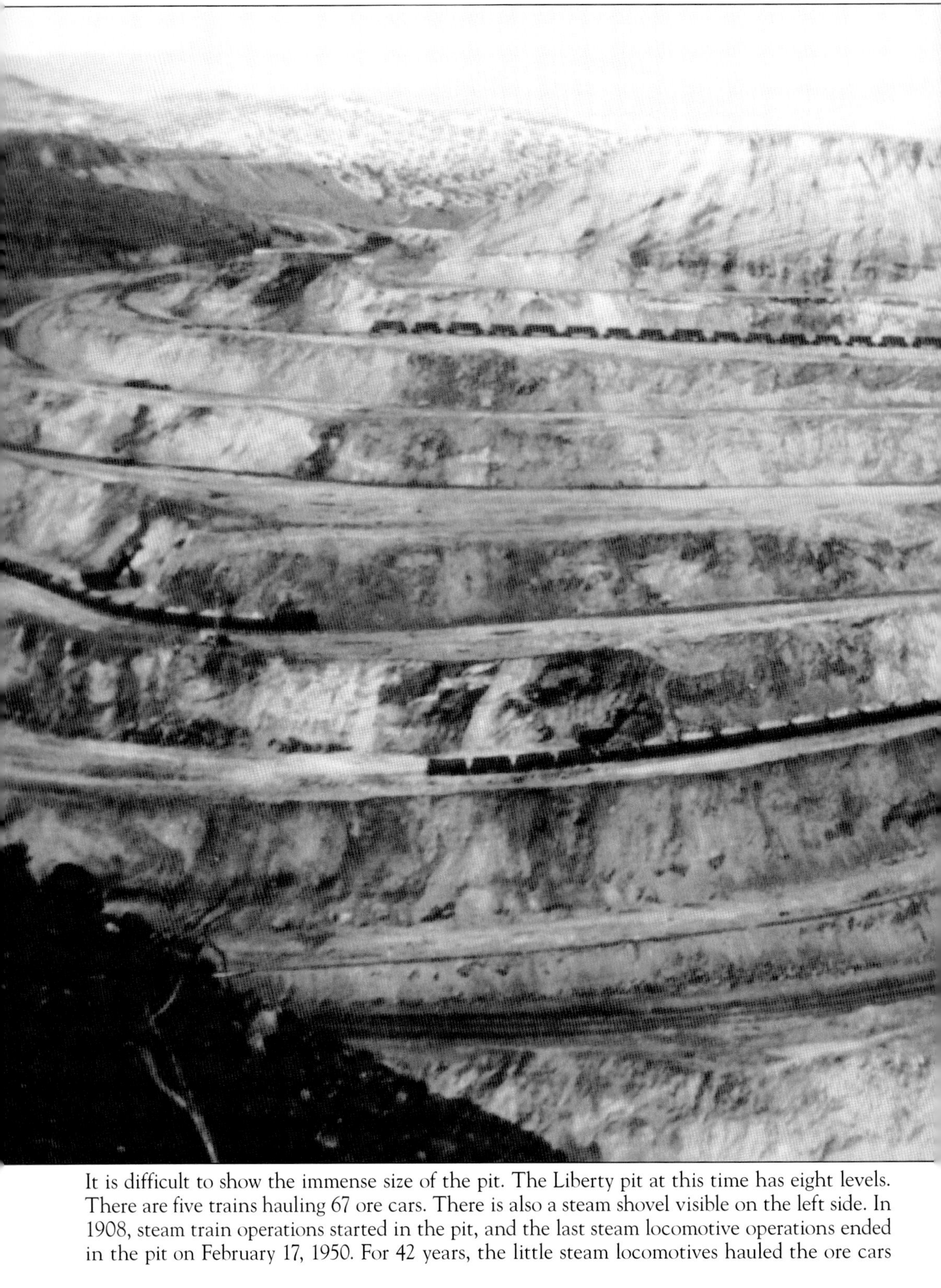

It is difficult to show the immense size of the pit. The Liberty pit at this time has eight levels. There are five trains hauling 67 ore cars. There is also a steam shovel visible on the left side. In 1908, steam train operations started in the pit, and the last steam locomotive operations ended in the pit on February 17, 1950. For 42 years, the little steam locomotives hauled the ore cars

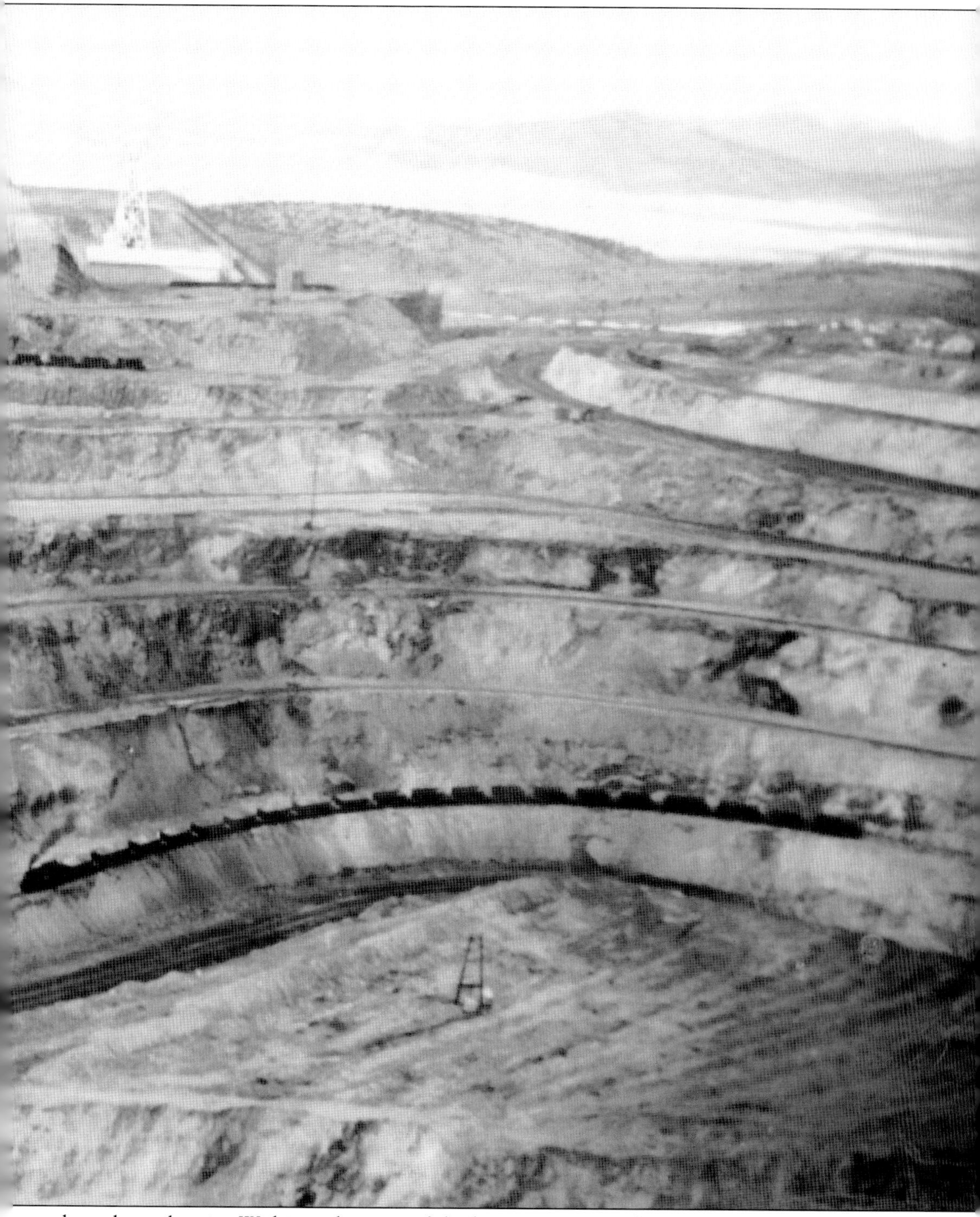

throughout the pits. Within eight years of the last steam-powered operations in the pit, all pit rail operations would end. Unstable pit walls and the already high cost of operations made it economically unfeasible. The last train in the pit operated on April 23, 1958.

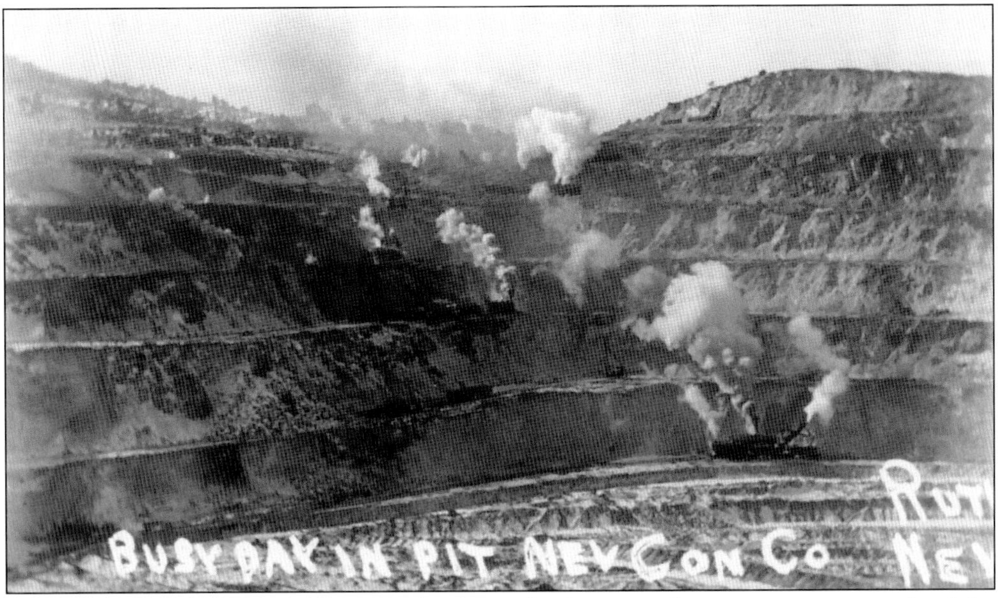

A photograph taken on a cold winter day shows the location of equipment on one side of the pit. There are 18 plumes of smoke visible, and the amount of equipment in the pit could easily be three times that. Because the pit is so large, only a small section could be photographed at any one time. (Newitt.)

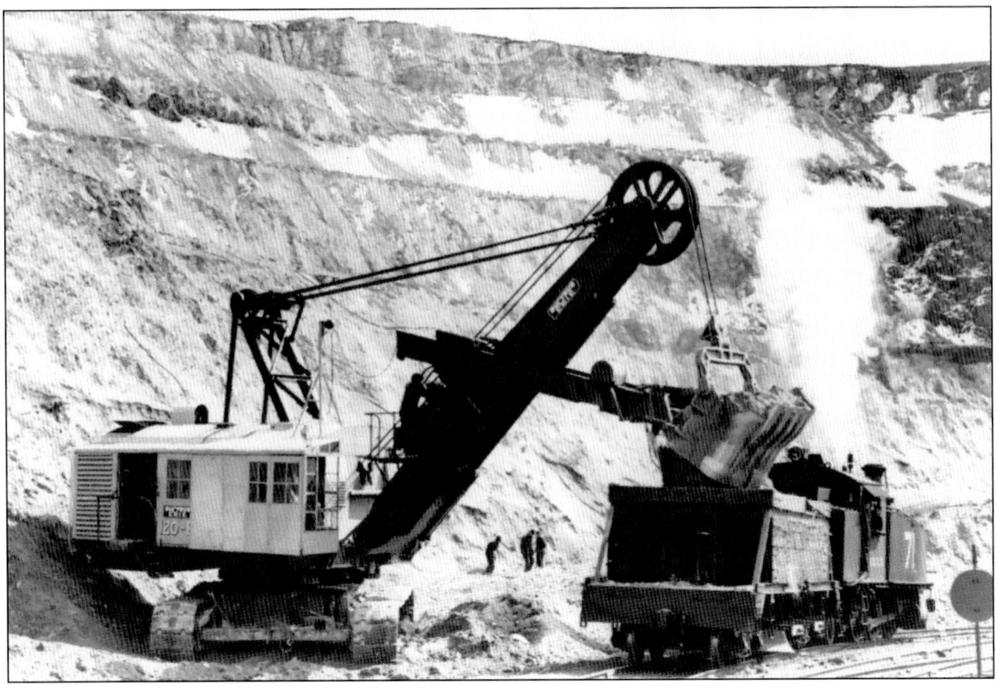

Rail operations did not change much in the 42 years that the steam locomotive hauled the cars, but the copper mine was constantly improving the shovels. The ballast car shown is part of the Nevada Northern Railway Museum's collection. Beneath the car is a steel plow. The contents could be dumped from doors at the bottom of the car and spread along the track.

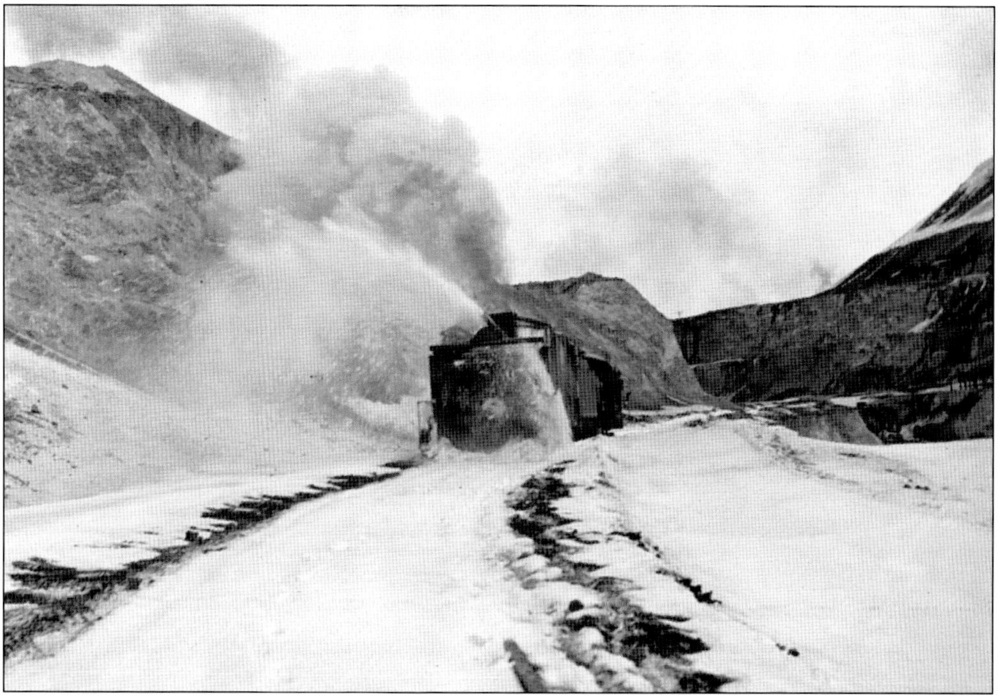

Nothing was allowed to stop the flow of ore to the smelter. This photograph was taken around the winter of 1910, and the railroad's steam-powered, rotary snowplow is being pushed through the Ruth pit to clear the tracks of snow. Because the snowplow was not self-propelled, steam locomotives were needed to push it. (NHS.)

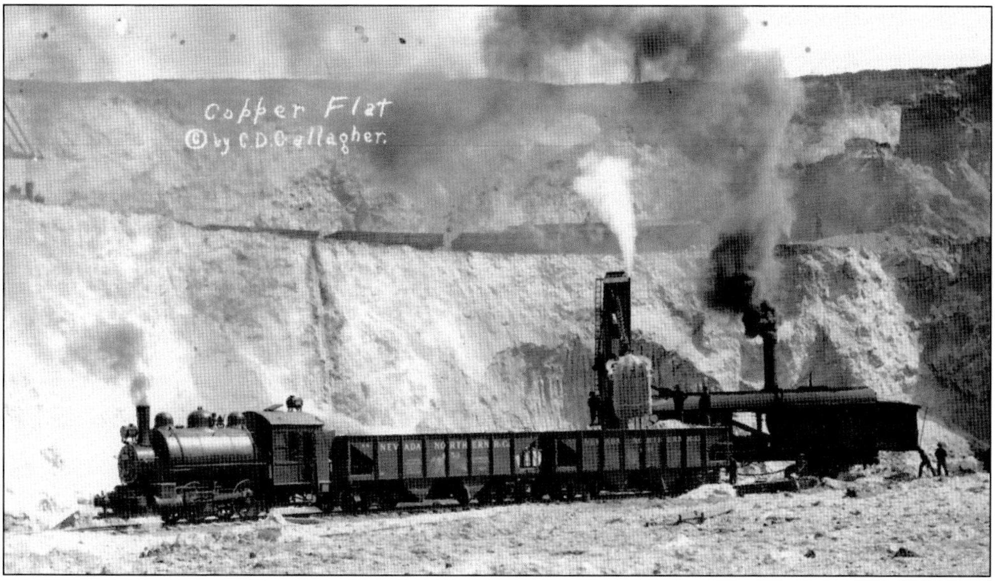

One of the small dinkies with two ore cars is being loaded. The sides of the ore cars boldly proclaim, "NEVADA NORTHERN Ry. Co." Originally, all equipment was lettered by Nevada Northern Railway. In 1920, pit operations were split from the Nevada Northern Railway. The equipment would be transferred to the Nevada Consolidated Copper Company, which eventually would become Kennecott. (Novich.)

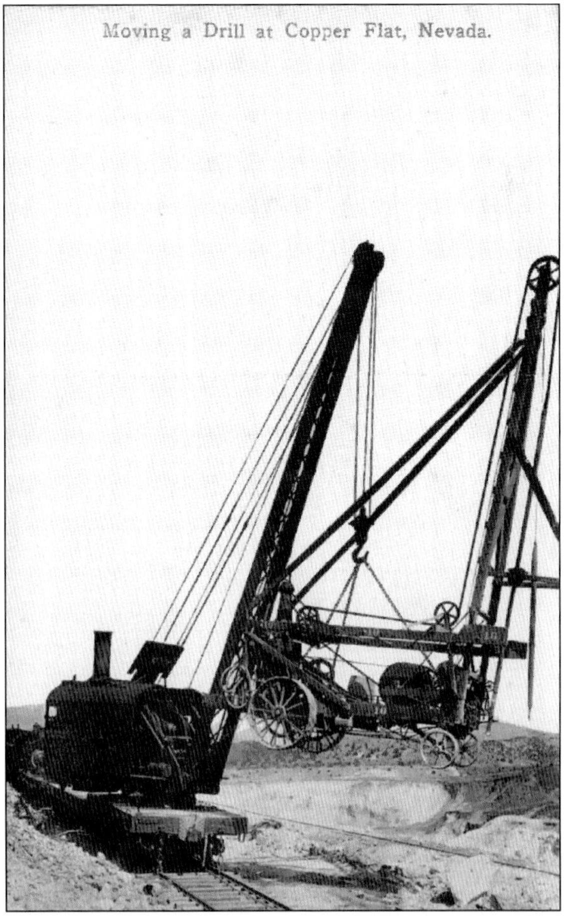

Moving one of the Keystone drills required some heavy lifting. The drill was first rigged with a sling for hoisting by a steam-powered derrick. Since the derrick was not self-propelled, it had to be pushed by a steam locomotive. This entire top-heavy ensemble with its high center of gravity was pushed over a hastily constructed pit track to its new location. (Novich.)

Throughout the pits, steam-powered drills manufactured by the Keystone Manufacturing Company were used to drill blast holes and sample the ore body. A series of holes would be drilled along one of the benches in the pit. Blast teams would then fill the holes with explosives. (Novich.)

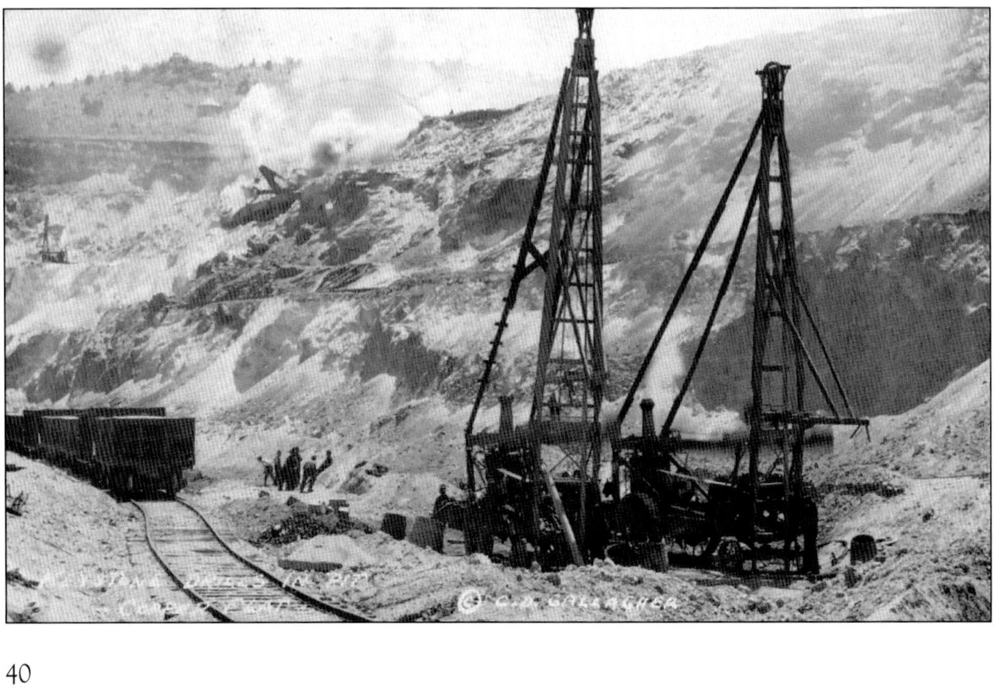

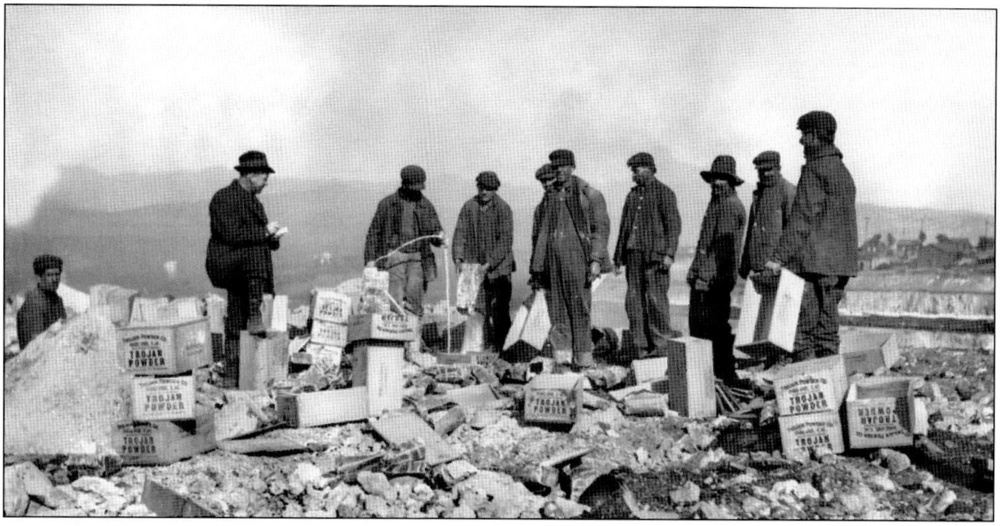

Instead of dynamite, which contained nitroglycerine, the blast holes were packed with Trojan Powder, which was a dry, nitrostarch-based powder that was mixed with various oxygen carriers and other combustible materials. It is obvious that the mine purchased Trojan Powder by the boxcar load. Notice the homes in the background. (NHS.)

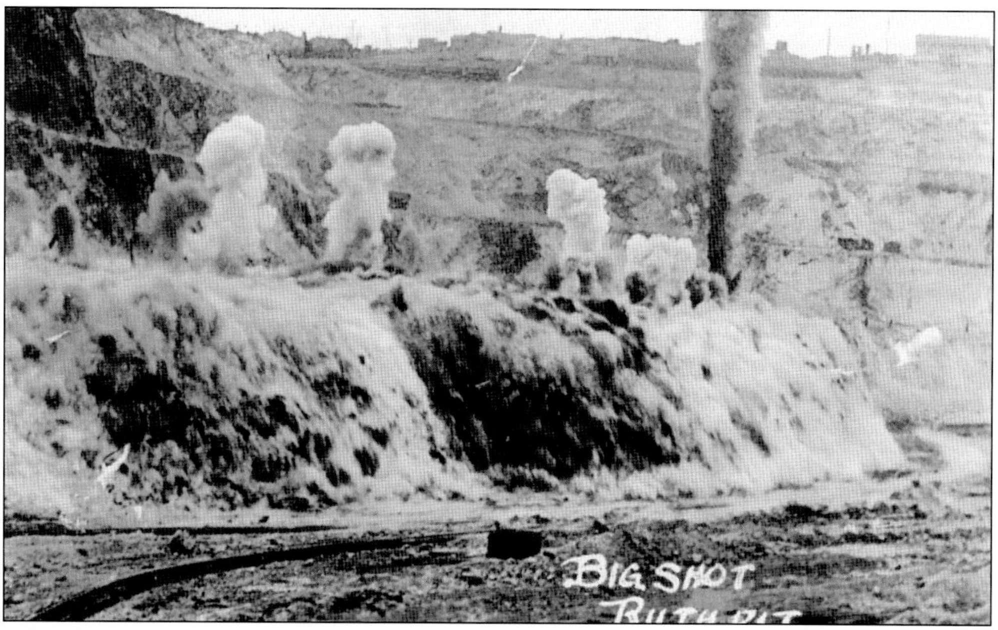

After the holes were packed and people and equipment moved to a safe zone—*Bam*! The ground shook, dust flew, and more earth needed to be moved. Just barely visible at the top of the photograph are homes and buildings lining the rim of the pit. (Novich.)

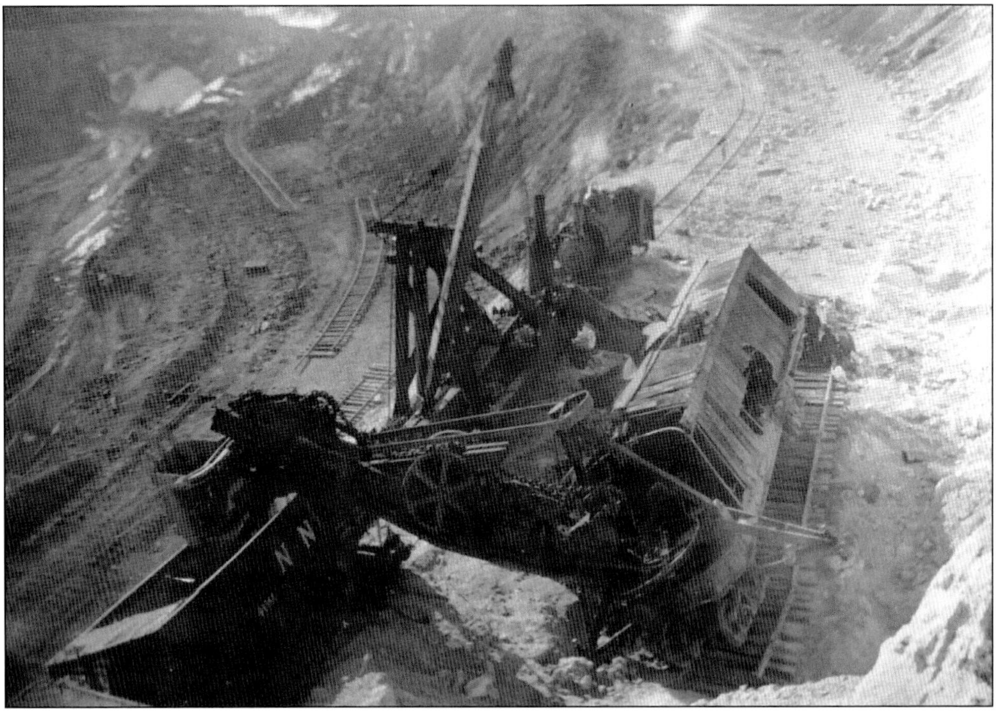

The dipper bucket was supported by outriggers on both sides. Here, the outrigger closest the ore car was undermined by soft ground, causing the steam shovel to tip over. The dipper caught on the ore car, and this prevented the steam shovel from completely overturning. A steam-powered derrick is attempting to lift the steam shovel. Notice the short pieces of track in the background. (WPPM.)

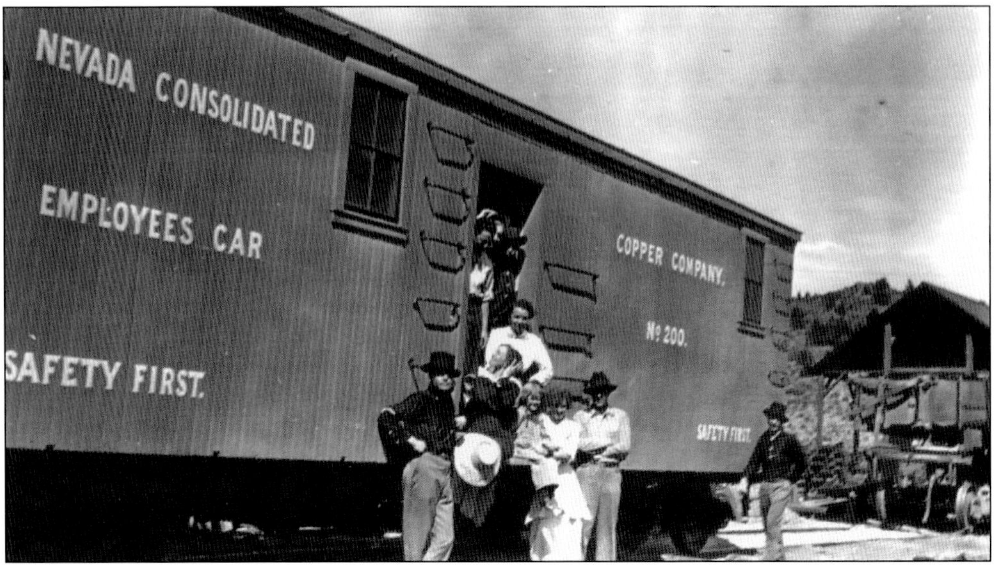

Because the pits were so enormous, crew change cars were provided by the mining company at shift changes. Workers would gather, and the cars would convey the crews around the pit, dropping off and picking up workers at job sites. The cars were converted boxcars that were pushed by one of the ubiquitous dinkies. (Newitt.)

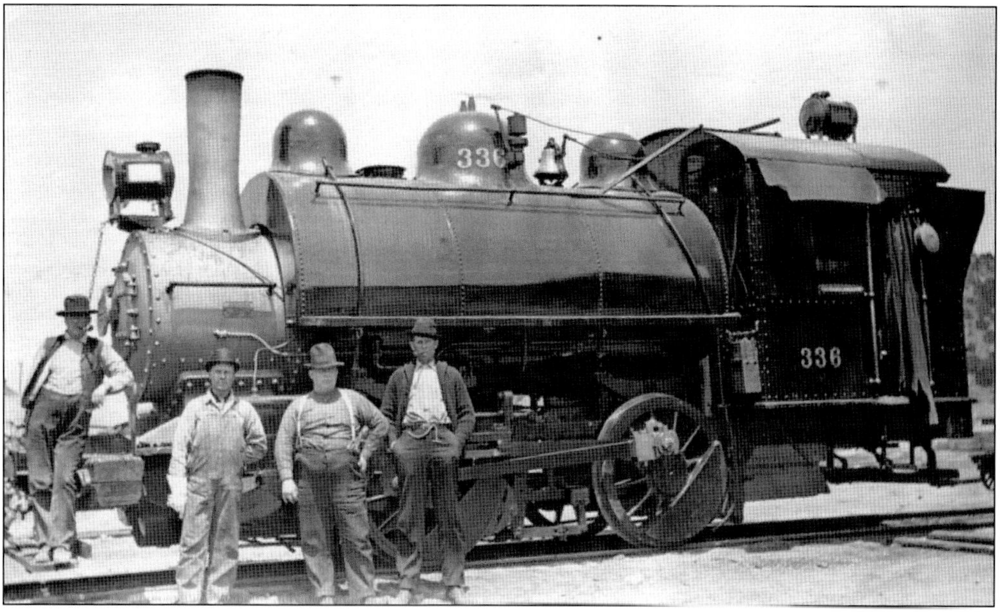

Shown is a close-up of locomotive 336, one of the dinkies purchased for use in the pit. The locomotive was built by the American Locomotive Company, weighed 42.5 tons, and the wheel arrangement was 0-4-0, meaning it had no pilot wheels, four driving wheels, and no trailing wheels. These locomotives carried their water in a tank on top of the boiler.

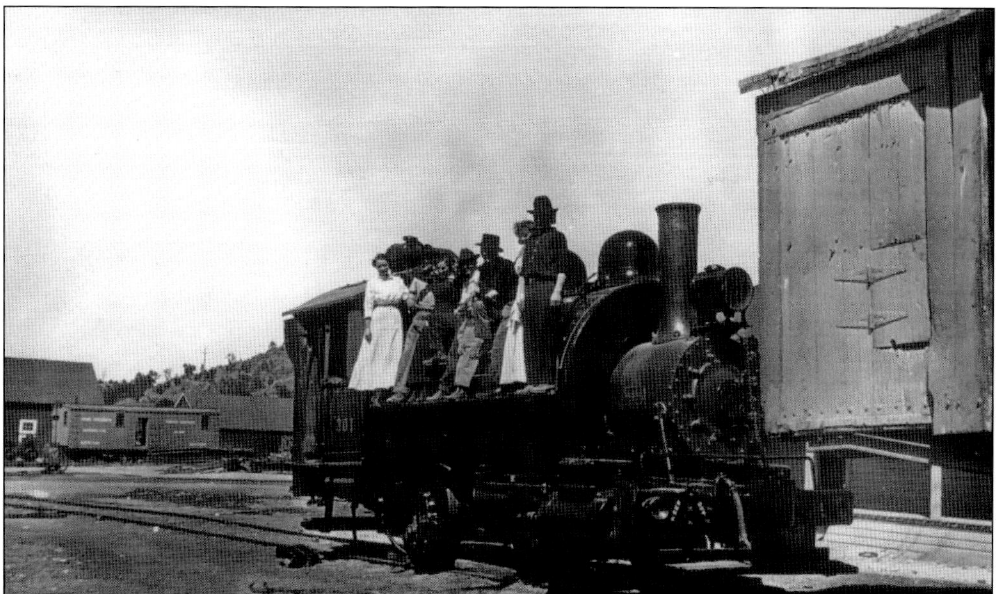

It was not all work. Here, locomotive 301 is being used for photographs taken to show the folks back home. The locomotive is new and shiny in 1907. The railroad car in the background is a crew car. The piece on the right appears to be the back of one of the steam shovels. (Newitt.)

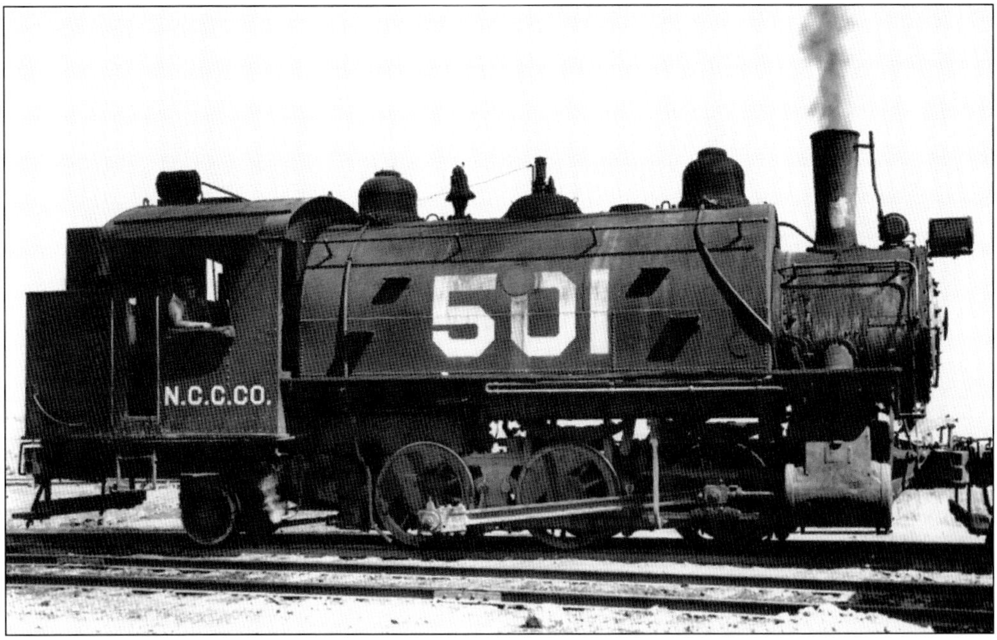

Locomotive 501 was built by the Baldwin Locomotive Company in January 1917. A 0-6-2 locomotive, it was almost twice as heavy as the original dinkies. The water tank is located on the boiler and marked with the 501's number. The small bunker behind the cab carried the coal. The locomotive was used until 1951 and was then scrapped. (Chappell.)

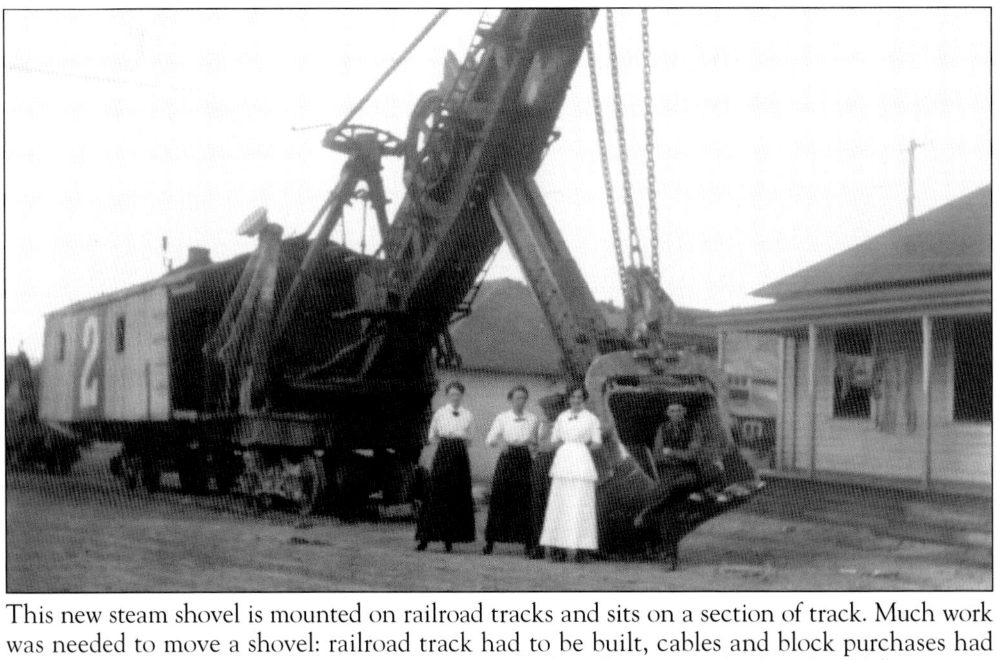

This new steam shovel is mounted on railroad tracks and sits on a section of track. Much work was needed to move a shovel: railroad track had to be built, cables and block purchases had to be attached to, chains and slings had to be rigged, and so on. Early shovel models were not self-propelled; rather they would use the boom to maneuver. (Newitt.)

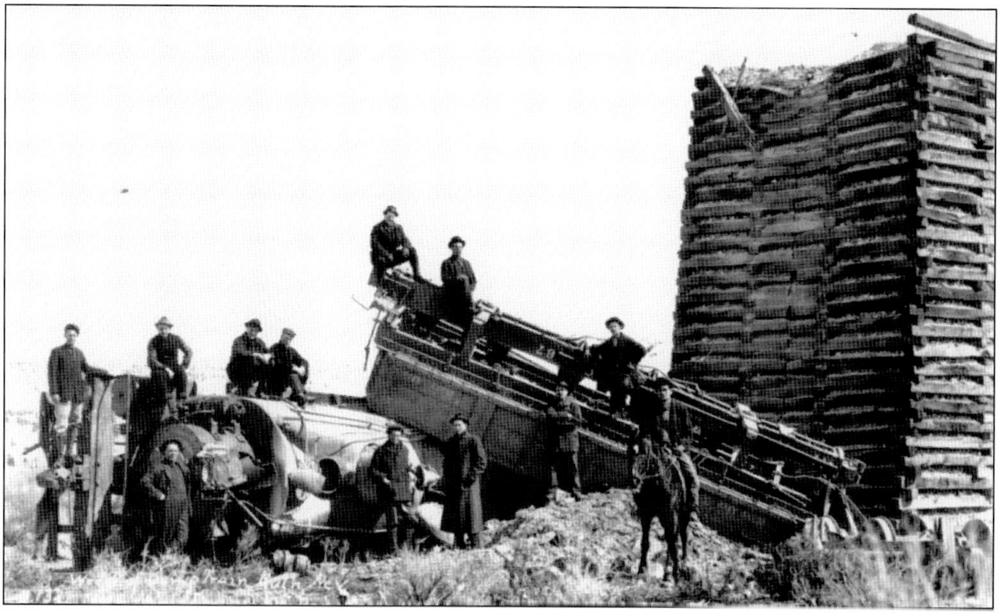

Working at the copper mines was dangerous work that could have fatal consequences. This was a dump train that ran off the end of the track. The engineer and fireman were killed in the wreck. That's a dump car lying upside down on top of the locomotive. The photograph is dated March 16, 1917. (Novich.)

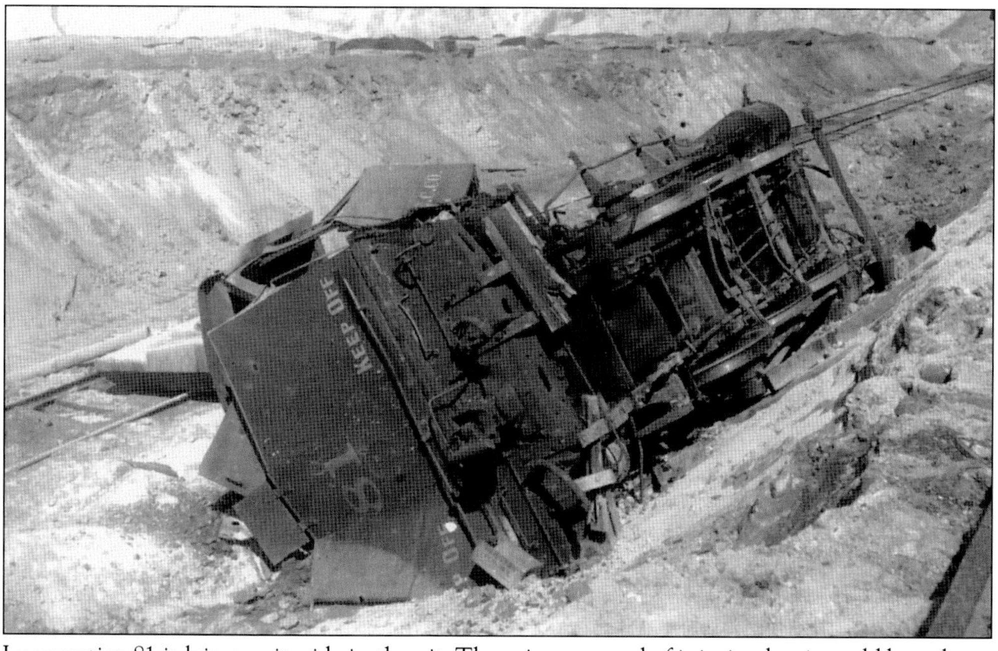

Locomotive 81 is lying on its side in the pit. There is no record of injuries, but it could have been a lot worse. Underneath the rear of the locomotive is a Hercules powder box. Locomotive 81 was pushing a car that also wrecked and is visible above the locomotive. Locomotive 81 was repaired and went back to work until it was scrapped in 1951.

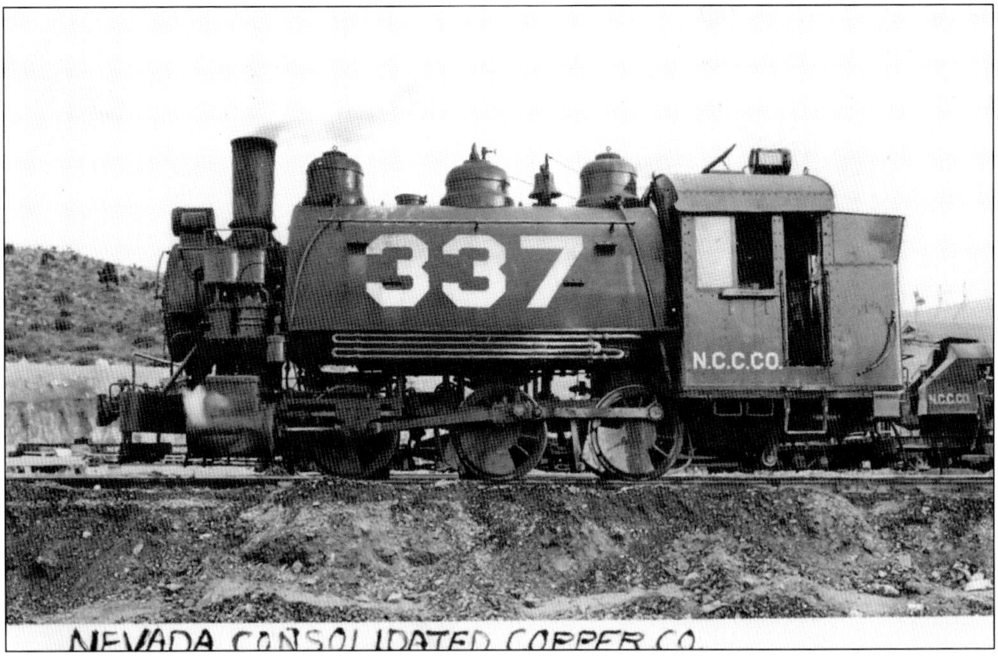

Purchased in October 1909 as part of an order of five locomotives for heavier motive power in the pit, locomotive 337 was the first locomotive of this class. It was a 0-6-0 locomotive. All the locomotive's weight was carried on the drivers, and it weighed 116,300 pounds. It was scrapped at McGill in 1951. (Novich.)

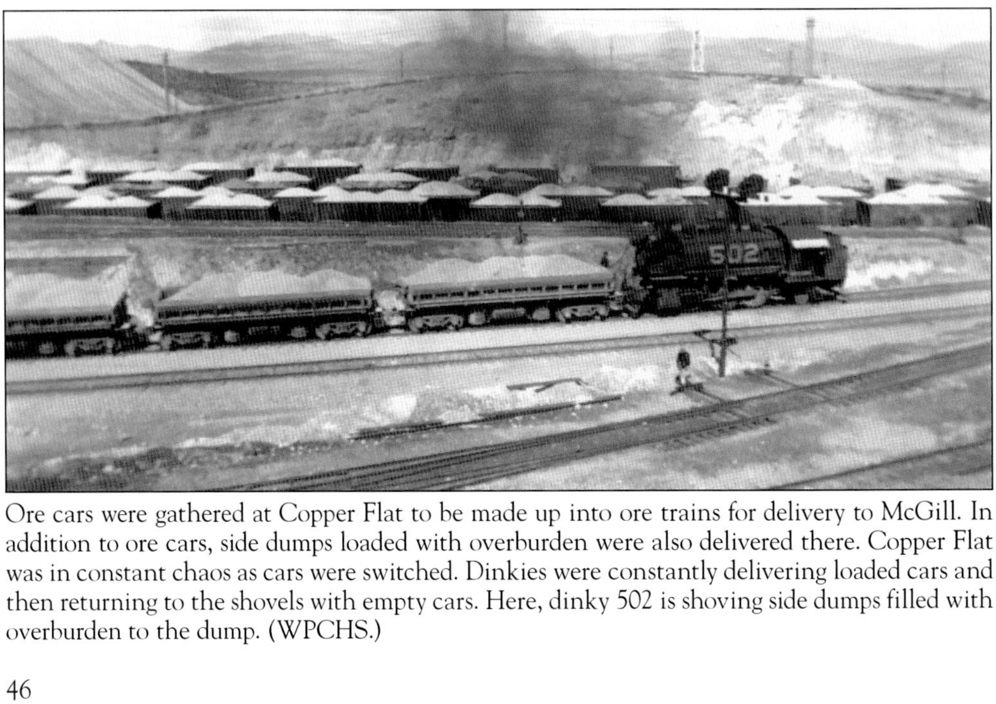

Ore cars were gathered at Copper Flat to be made up into ore trains for delivery to McGill. In addition to ore cars, side dumps loaded with overburden were also delivered there. Copper Flat was in constant chaos as cars were switched. Dinkies were constantly delivering loaded cars and then returning to the shovels with empty cars. Here, dinky 502 is shoving side dumps filled with overburden to the dump. (WPCHS.)

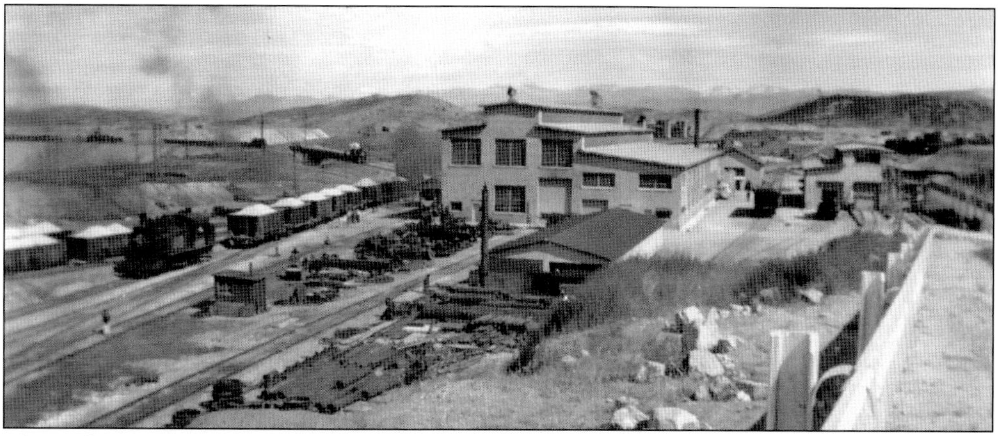

This is the mine's Copper Flat shop where repairs to keep the equipment in operation were made. Dinky 89 is moving to couple onto an ore train. In the background, another dinky is approaching with more cars. All of this is gone now, except for a few ore cars in the Nevada Northern Railway Museum's collection. (WPCHS.)

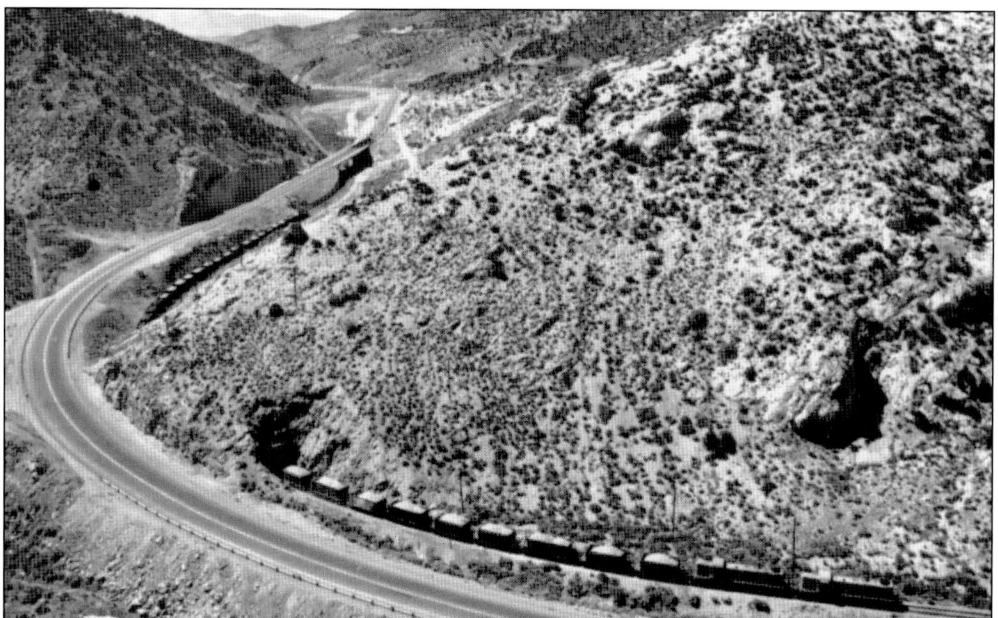

Diesel locomotives have replaced steam locomotives by the time this ore train exits tunnel No. 1. It may not look like it, but the track from the mine to Ely was (and is) a mountain railroad. From the mine, the railroad dropped 526 feet in about seven miles. The steepest section was a three-percent grade with sections that were one- and two-percent grades. (WPCHS.)

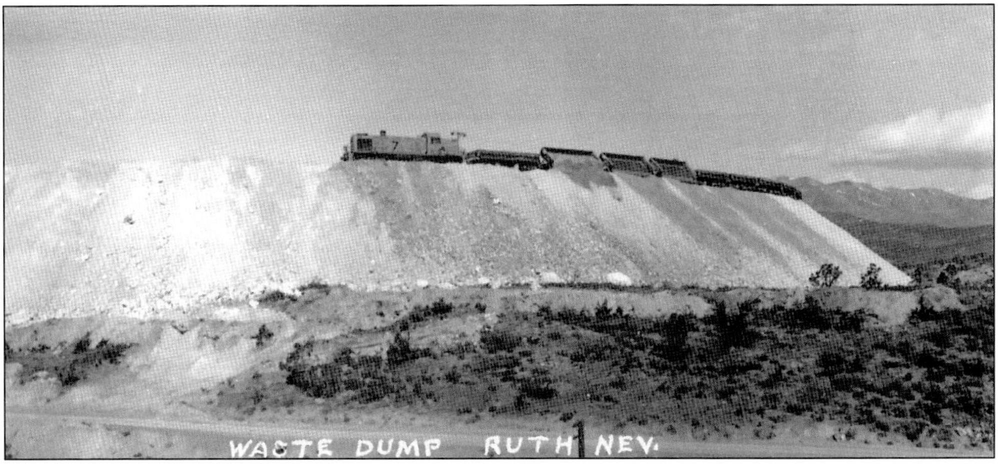

Diesels took over for the steam locomotives in 1951. Here, locomotive 107's train is unloading overburden on one of the waste dumps. Locomotive 107 was built January 1950. It was transferred to KCC Utah in 1978 and scrapped at Industrial Salvage & Metals Company in January 1984. (Novich.)

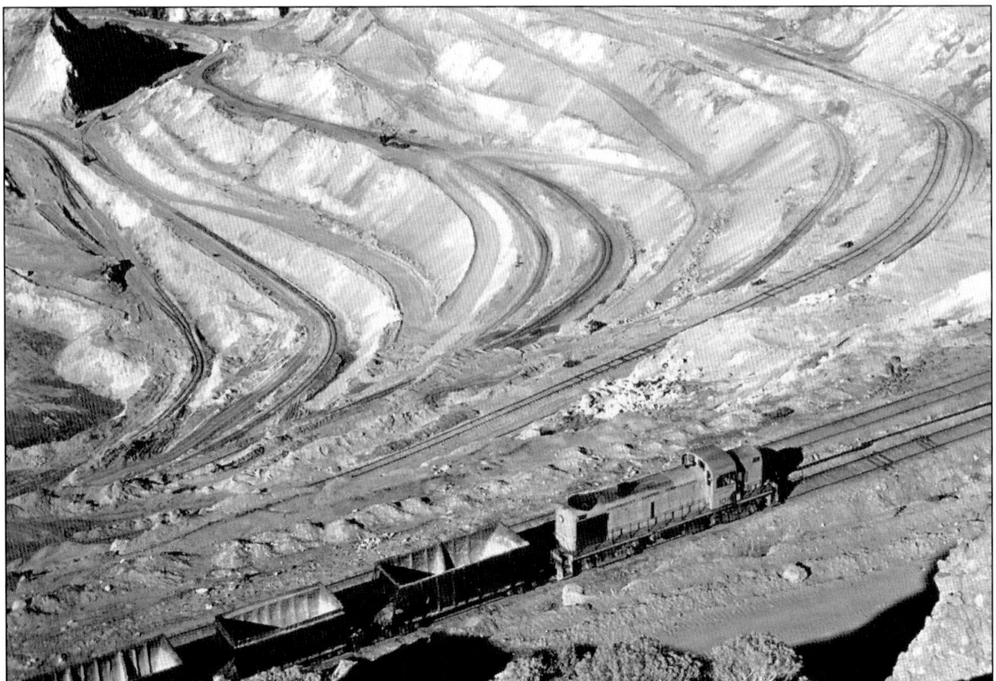
Locomotive 101 with a train of empty ore cars is beginning its trip into the pit. More than 19 miles of track spiraled throughout the pit. Once the ore cars were loaded, they were taken back to Copper Flat to be organized into trains for their journey to McGill. (Swanson.)

Three

Delivering and Smelting a Mountain

Mining and loading the copper ore into the railcars was only the beginning of the process. The ore need to be transported to the concentrating mill and smelter in McGill. There, the ore would be turned into blister copper.

The choice of McGill over the Georgetown site, which adjoined the Nevada Northern Railway yards at East Ely, occurred in June 1906. To process the copper ore, the copper mines joined together to form the Steptoe Valley Smelting & Milling Company, which would build the mill and smelter on William McGill's ranch.

In mid-October 1906, a small tent city formed at what was to be the site of the mill and smelter. By mid-November, construction gangs were building the mill, barracks, mess halls, offices, warehouses, homes, and an electric generating plant. The first delivery of ore to McGill was April 15, 1908. In 18 months, a complete processing plant had been constructed where there had once only been sagebrush.

The Nevada Northern Railway, Nevada Consolidated Copper Corporation, and Kennecott Copper Corporation (all owned by the same corporate parent) served as a steel-wheel conveyer belt to deliver the Ruth copper ore to the mill and smelter. On April 25, 1978, T.J. Lani, a 36-year veteran engineer, used locomotives 101 and 109 to haul the last ore train to the mill, thereby ending 70 years of ore train operations.

Smelting continued at McGill fueled by ore from Utah, Arizona, and other operations in Nevada, delivered by the Nevada Northern Railway. But by the 1980s, higher costs associated with wages and environmental compliance combined with a lower-grade ore signaled the end of Kennecott's operations in White Pine County. The end of operations came on June 15, 1983.

Demolition of the facilities at the mill and smelter site started in 1989. By 1990, most of the plant was gone. On September 4, 1993, explosives toppled the 750-foot smelter stack, announcing the end of copper smelting in White Pine County with a bang.

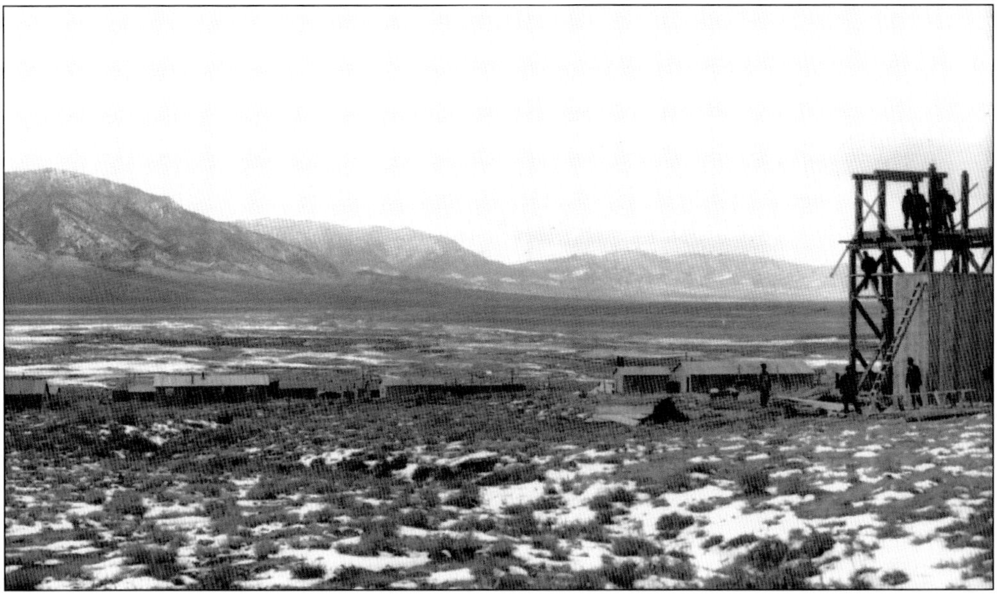

In October 1906, construction is proceeding at what was originally called Smelterville. The name was eventually changed to McGill. Most of the construction at this time was from wood. White Pine County had a small lumber business, but the vast majority of the lumber was delivered to the site by the railroad. (USHS.)

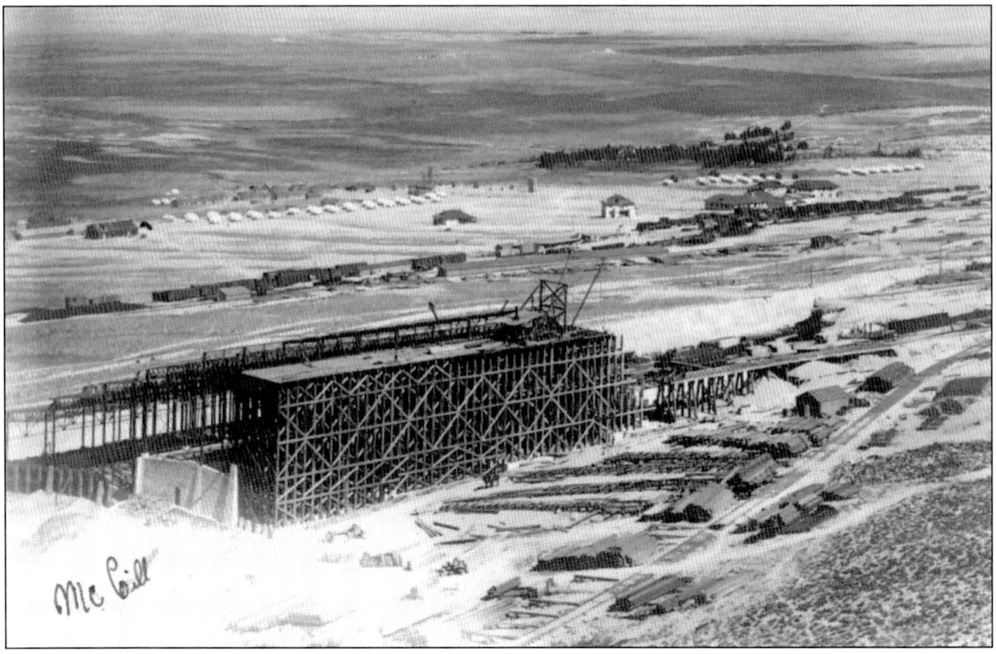

McGill is booming in this photograph. In the foreground, the concentrating mill is under construction. Materials are stockpiled along the railroad track serving the site. In the center is another rail yard filled with boxcars. Above the mill, large buildings used as company offices and housing for company officials are visible. In the background to the left and right, two tent communities are visible. (Novich.)

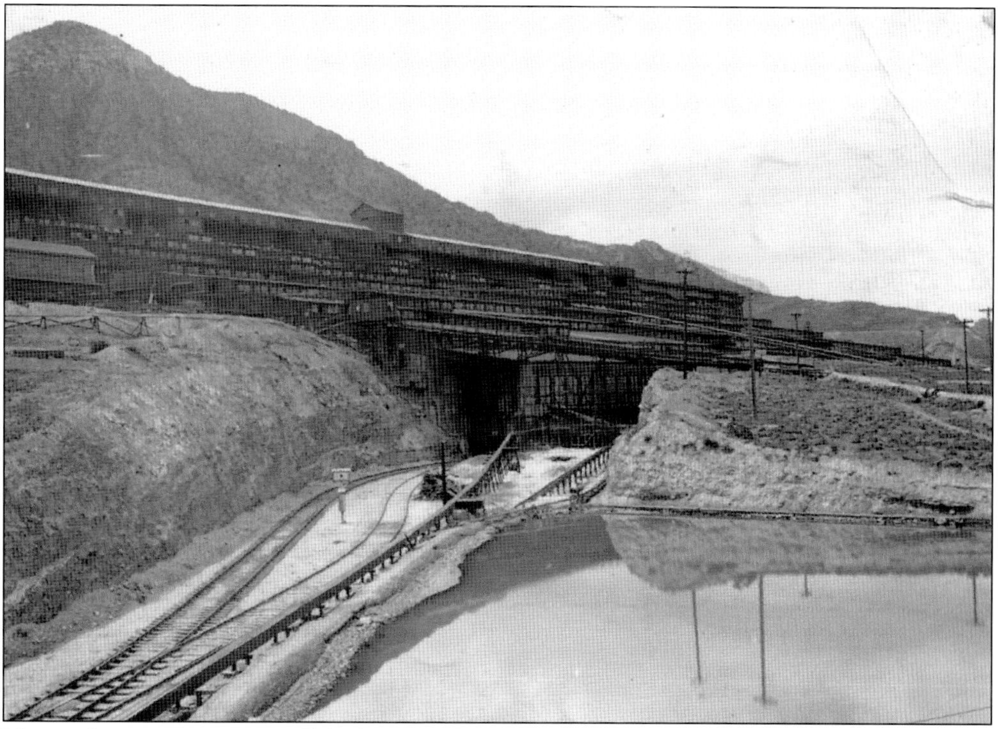

Here is the concentrating mill looking southeast. It could concentrate over 100,000 tons of ore per month. Trains arrived frequently to fill its ore bins. Since the ore contained only about three percent copper, it needed to be concentrated before it went to the smelter for refining into blister copper. (Novich.)

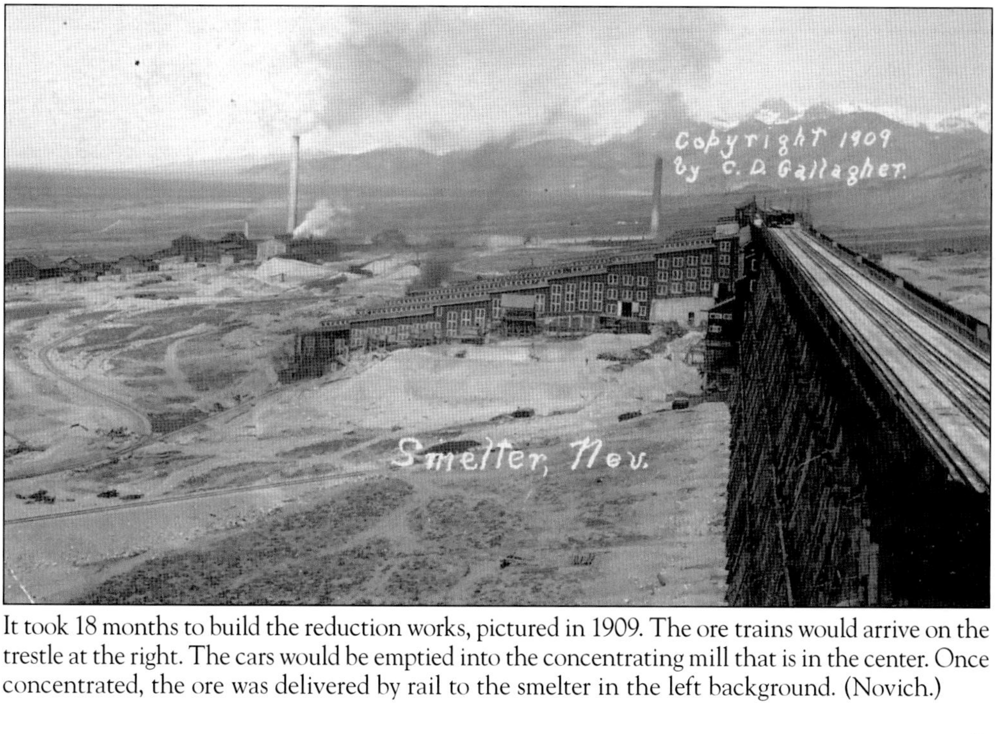

It took 18 months to build the reduction works, pictured in 1909. The ore trains would arrive on the trestle at the right. The cars would be emptied into the concentrating mill that is in the center. Once concentrated, the ore was delivered by rail to the smelter in the left background. (Novich.)

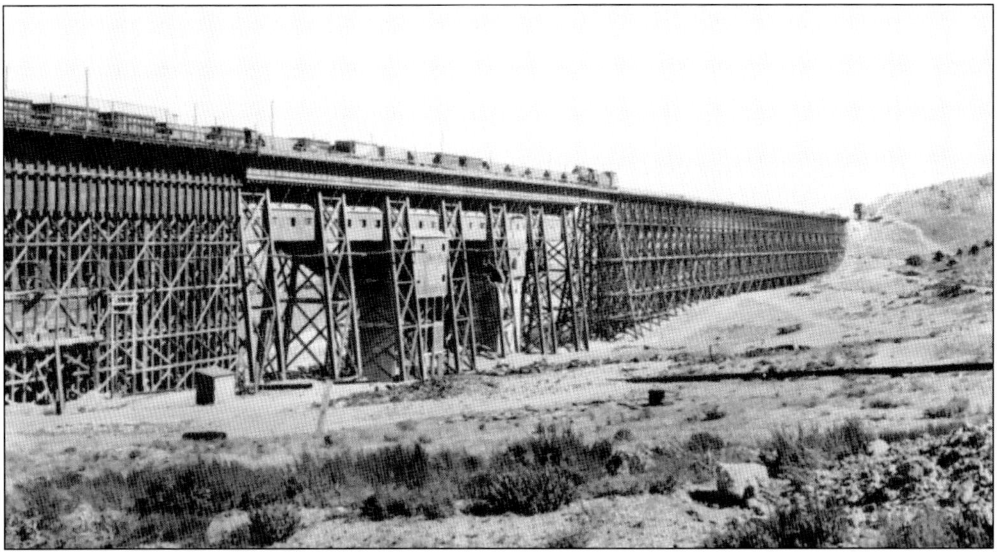

The McGill Trestle was 1,720 feet long and 109 feet tall. It was constructed of almost a million and half board feet of lumber set on concrete piers. The trestle was about 70 percent wood with the remainder built with structural iron. It took 70 tons of bolts, nuts, and washers to tie the trestle together. Ore bins with a capacity of 12,000 tons were located underneath the trestle. At the time it was built, it was considered highest double-track trestle in the world. It was destroyed in the devastating fire in 1922. When the mill was rebuilt, instead of a trestle, an earthen fill was constructed for railroad access to the mill. (Above, NHS; below, Novich.)

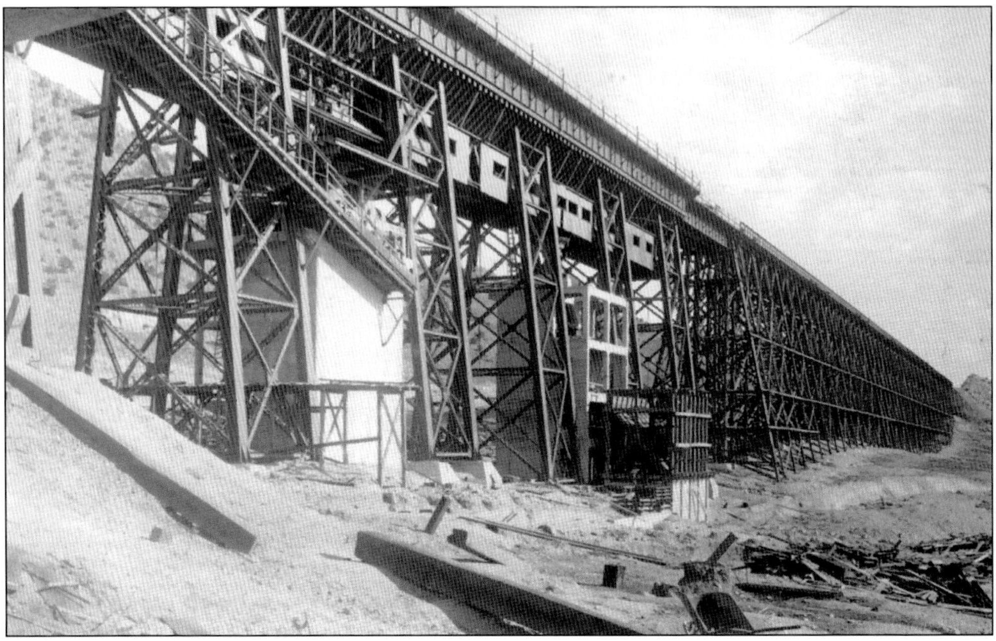

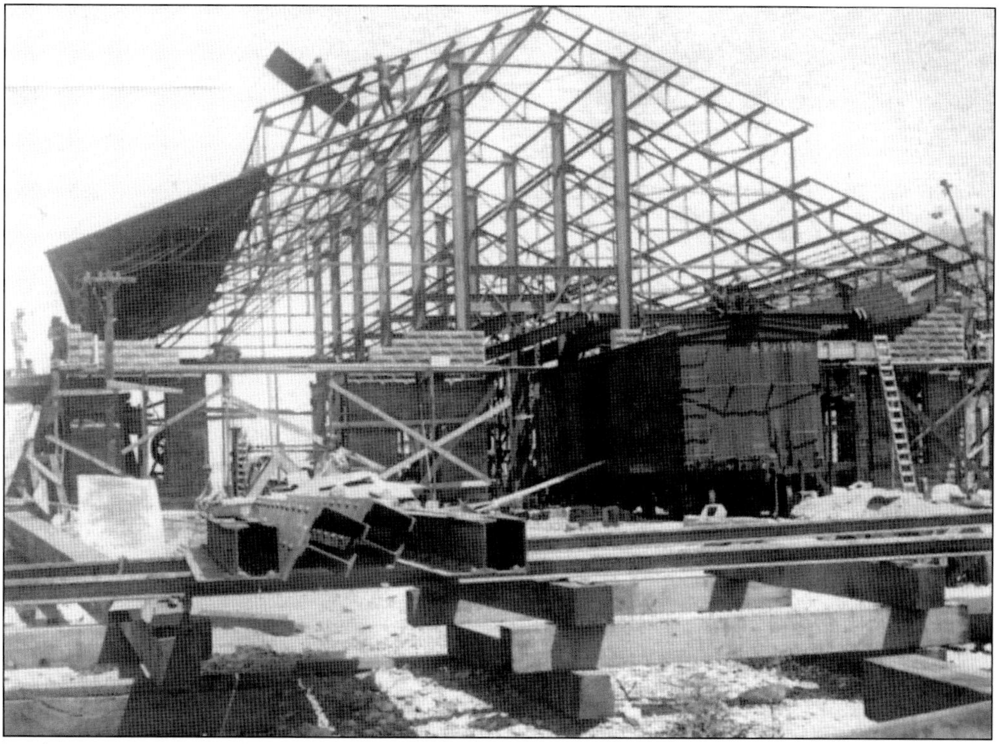

Under construction at the smelter is the machine shop. To give an idea of the scale of the building, in the right-center is a railroad boxcar; it is dwarfed by the building. The building had a steel frame, and the walls were cinderblock faced with what appears to be cut stone. (Novich.)

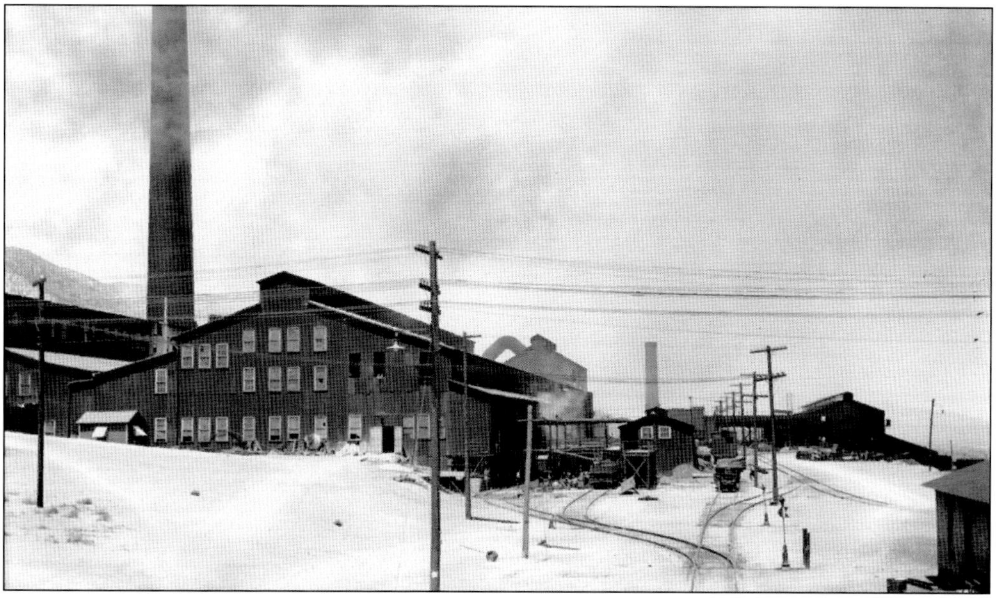

Located north of the mill was the smelter where blister copper was produced. Copper that is about 98 percent pure is known as blister. After smelting, as the almost-pure copper cools, sulfur dioxide gas escapes and causes a broken appearance, known as blisters, on the surface of the copper ingots. Ingots were loaded into boxcars for delivery. (NHS.)

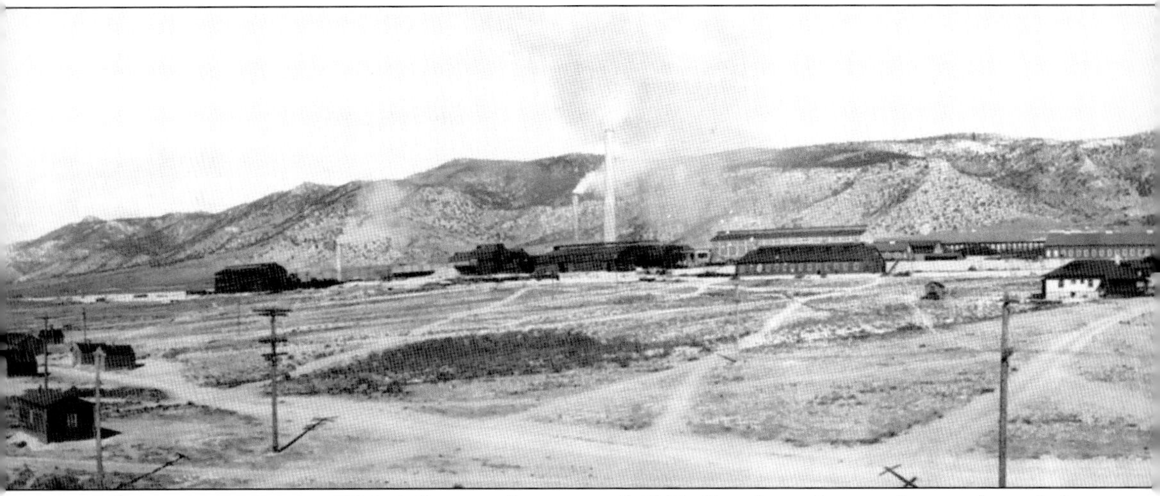

This panoramic view of McGill was taken around 1909. On the right are the trestle and the concentrating mill. The buildings in the center foreground are company offices and housing for the managers. To the left is the smelter. After, being known briefly as Smelter, the town was officially McGill after William N. McGill. Water for the concentrating and milling process

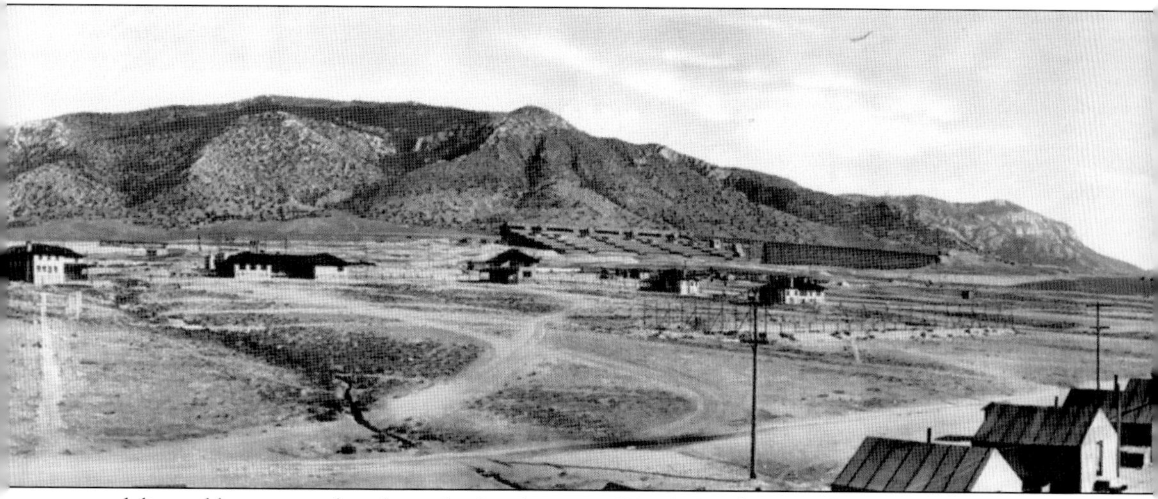

was delivered by an aqueduct from the headwaters of Duck Creek. McGill was a company town that was strictly managed by the copper company. Houses of ill repute and gambling dens were prohibited. The town was segregated by nationality, and sections were named according to the national origins of the residents. (LC.)

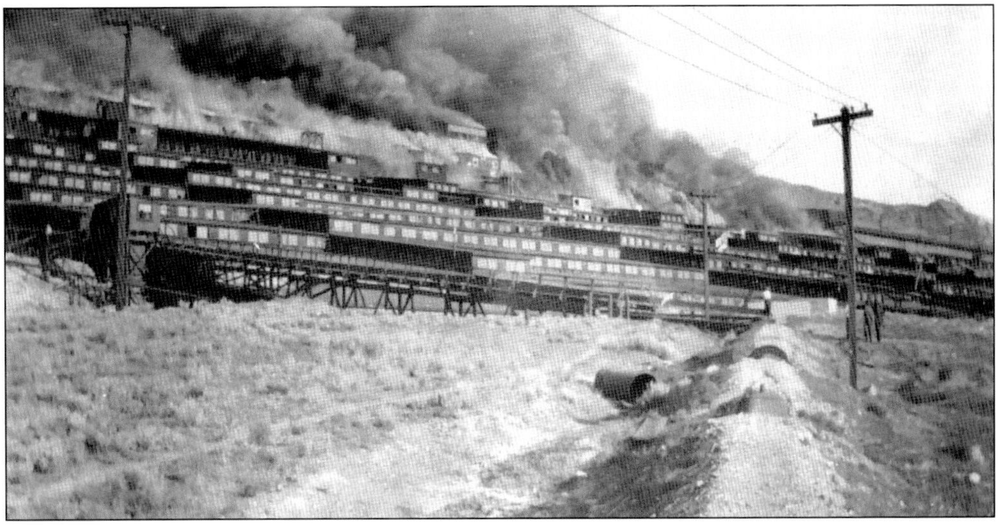

In March 1921, due to the worldwide glut of copper, the McGill mill and smelter were closed, and the workers were laid off for over a year before the McGill facilities would start processing copper ore again. Soon after the factory reopened, disaster struck. On Sunday evening, July 9, 1922, a fire started in the ore bins in the southeast corner of the mill. Strong winds fanned the fire until the entire mill complex was engulfed. The McGill Fire Department, assisted by the Ely Fire Department and company workers, could not stop the fire. The entire seven-acre complex was consumed by the flames. The only part of the complex saved was the concrete foundations. (Below, Novich.)

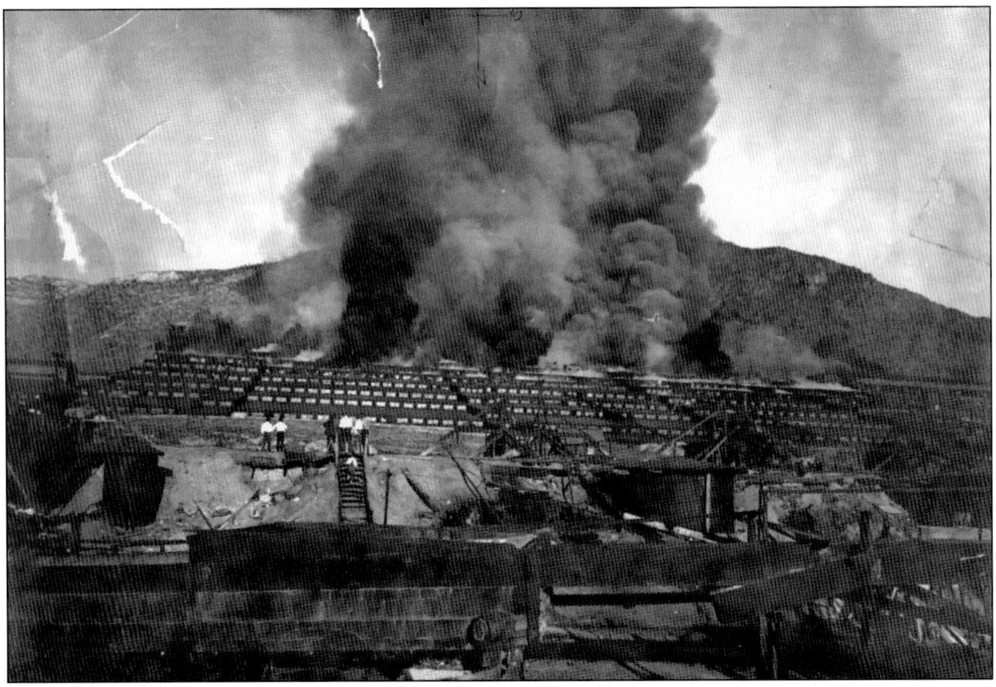

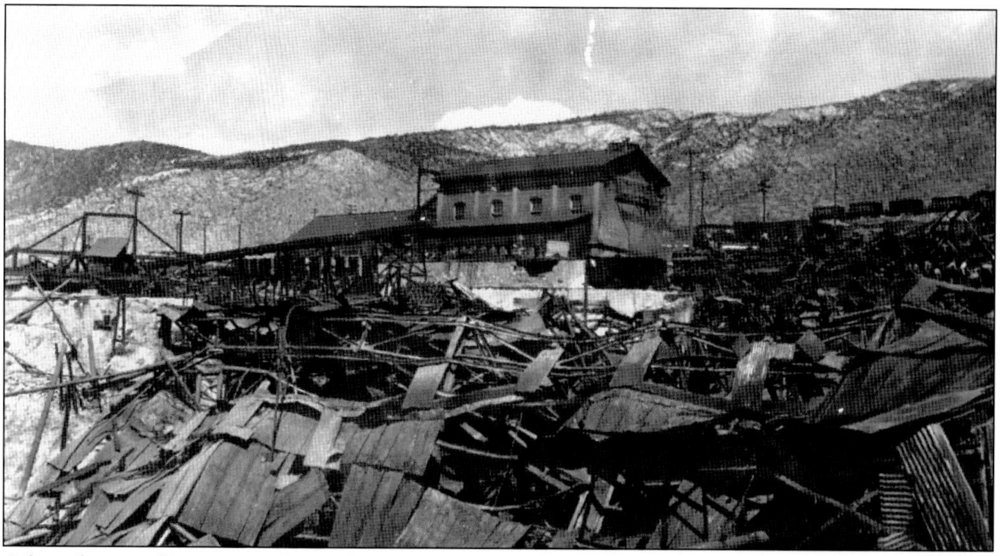

After the conflagration, the mill is gone. The repercussions of the fire rippled through the communities. Without the mill, there was no need for the copper mine. With no copper mine and no mill, the railroad was superfluous. Following on the heels of the 1921 depression and closure, this could have been the end of the copper dream.

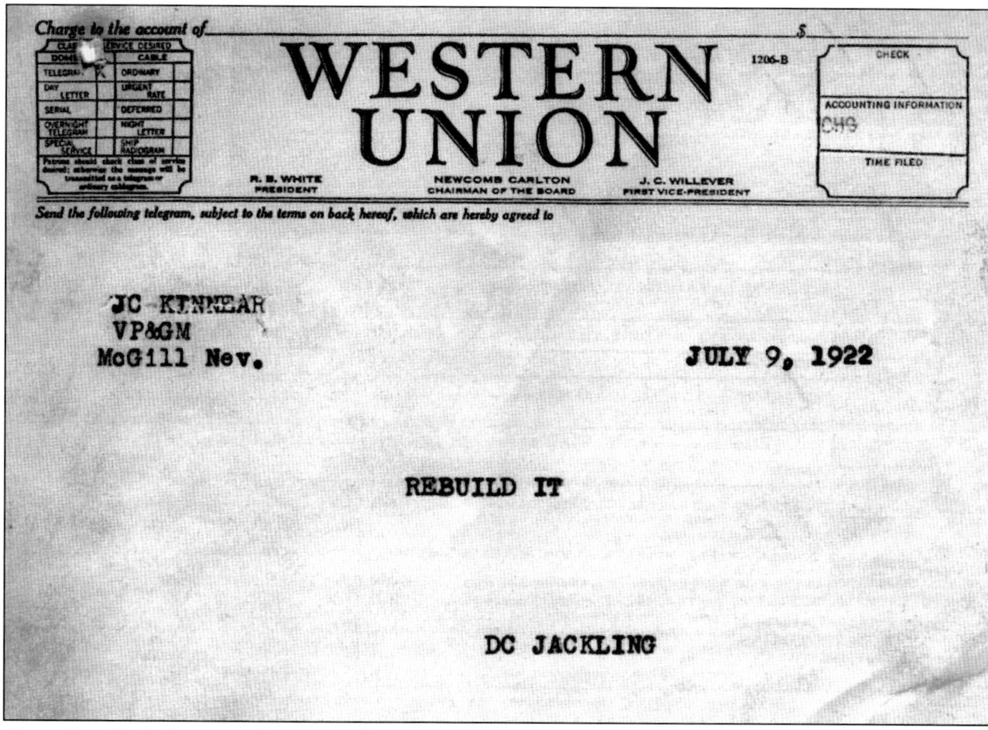

Charge to the account of ______ $

WESTERN UNION

1206-B

CHECK

ACCOUNTING INFORMATION

CHG

TIME FILED

R. B. WHITE, PRESIDENT — NEWCOMB CARLTON, CHAIRMAN OF THE BOARD — J. C. WILLEVER, FIRST VICE-PRESIDENT

Send the following telegram, subject to the terms on back hereof, which are hereby agreed to

JC KENNEAR
VP&GM
McGill Nev. JULY 9, 1922

REBUILD IT

DC JACKLING

Cornelius B. Lakeman, the general manager of the Nevada Consolidated Copper Company in McGill, called a meeting in his house. Attending were mill managers, influential people from Ely, bankers, merchants, and other interested parties. The question was what would happen? A detailed telegram was sent to D.C. Jackling, president of the copper company. The next morning he replied, "Rebuild it." (EERDM.)

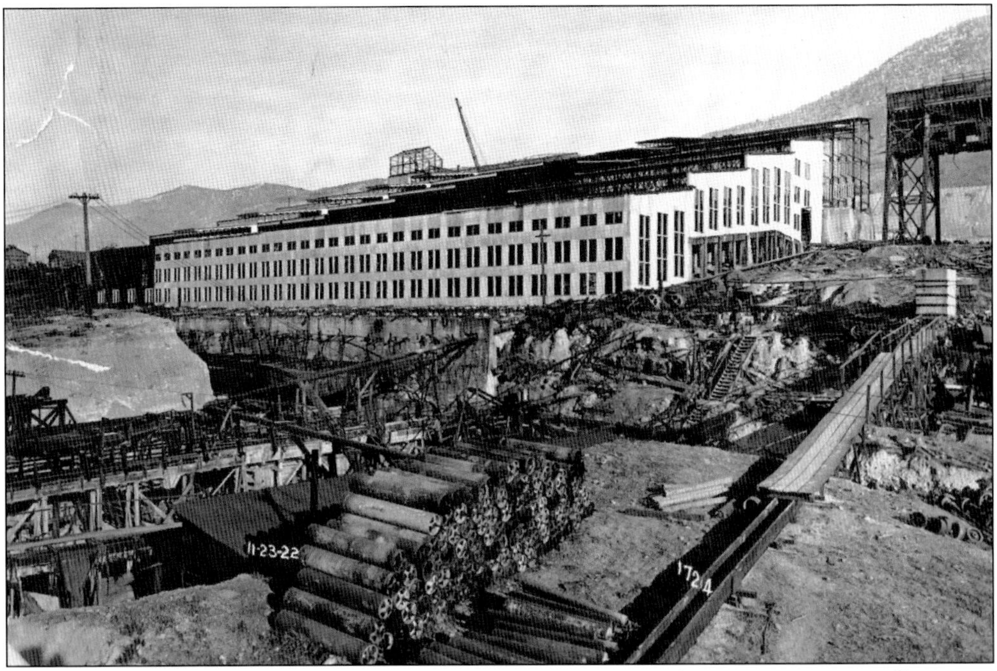

Reconstruction of the mill proceeded at a frenzied pace. In 45 days, a temporary mill was put into operation. The new mill was finished in 523 days. The fire turned out to be a blessing in disguise. Utilizing the latest technology, the new mill increased efficiency, and mill capacity was doubled. These improvements drove down the costs, ultimately making the company more profitable. (Novich.)

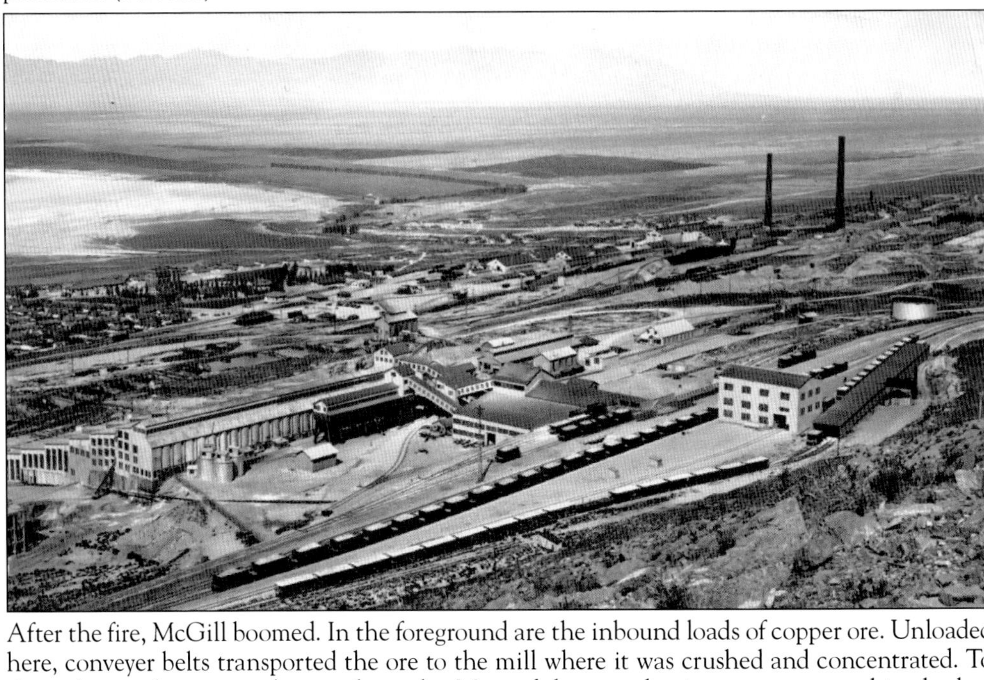

After the fire, McGill boomed. In the foreground are the inbound loads of copper ore. Unloaded here, conveyer belts transported the ore to the mill where it was crushed and concentrated. To the right are the two smelter smokestacks. Most of the complex is gone now, razed in the late 1980s and early 1990s. (NHS.)

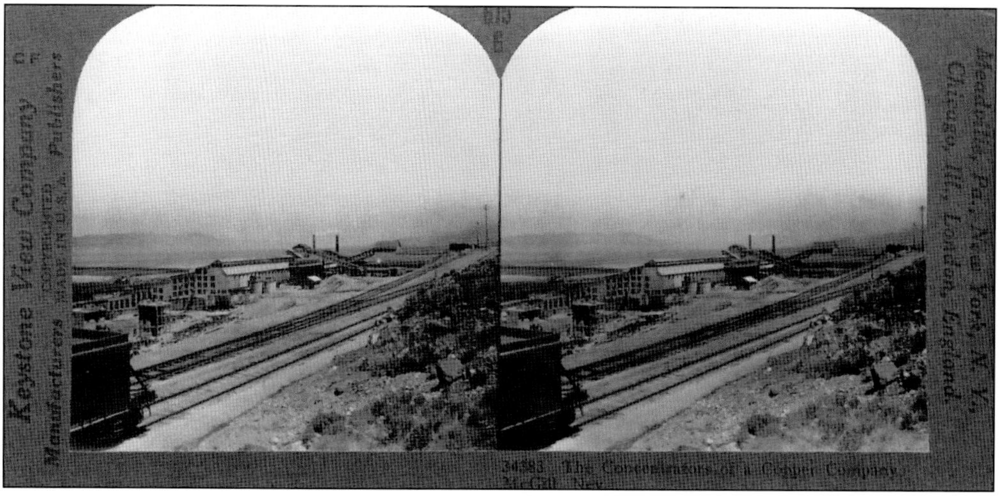

The copper mine and mill were considered an industrial wonder that was to be celebrated. The Keystone View Company of Pennsylvania produced a series of stereographic images of McGill, Ely, and Ruth. This is the only known surviving image from that series. It shows the concentrator in the foreground and the smelter in the background. Stereographic images were viewed with a stereoscope, which gave the perception of 3-D depth. On the back of the card was a printed explanation of what the photograph was about. In this case, the explanation gives an excellent thumbnail sketch of how the copper ore was processed. (Both, Novich.)

615—(34383) Geography Unit No. 18

THE CONCENTRATORS OF A COPPER COMPANY

In these flat-roofed buildings are the machines called *concentrators*. They consist of large slanting boards, which shake continually as a thin stream of water pours over them. This water carries over the boards the "dirt" from the mines, consisting of sand, gravel, and the fine particles of copper ore. The shaking of these boards causes the particles of copper ore, which are heavier, to separate from the grains of sand and earth, which are lighter. The process seems very simple; but the boards must have just the right slant, and the motion must be just right. The earth and sand are carried off by the running water.

After the ore is separated from the sand and dirt, it is taken to the smelters. The tall smokestacks mark the smelters. There the ore is melted in huge furnaces. Much of the ore comes from Ely, which is in the mountains that you see in the distance. Ely resembles Bingham, as it also lies in a cañon which has walls that are masses of copper ore.

Notice the trees and other signs of irrigation in the valley below the works of the copper company.

From McGill we follow the Highway southward to Ely, the chief copper-mining center in Nevada.

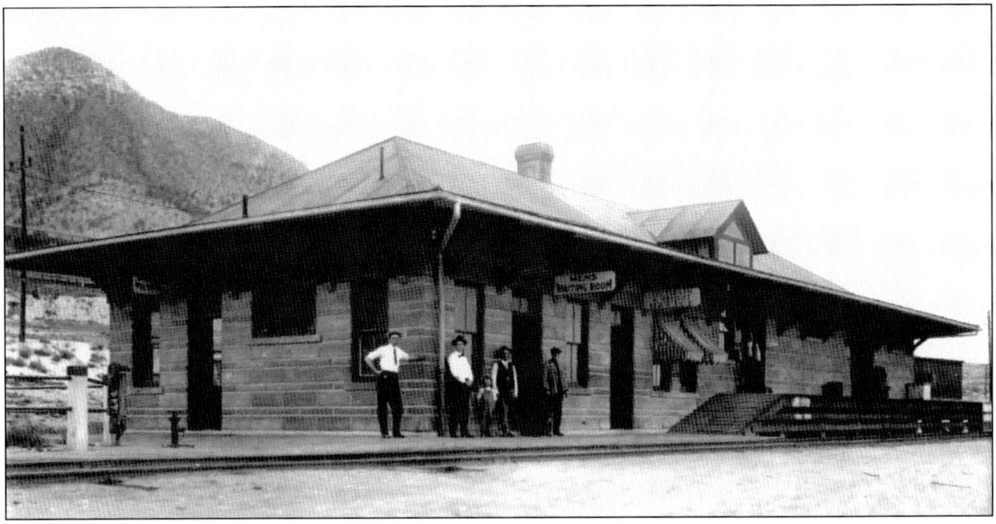

Constructed in 1910, the McGill Railroad Depot was just outside the mill's main gate. The one-story depot was constructed of concrete block with a six-foot-wide wooden platform around half the building. It was used for both passenger and freight service. And just like the East Ely Depot, it had two waiting rooms, one for men and one for women.

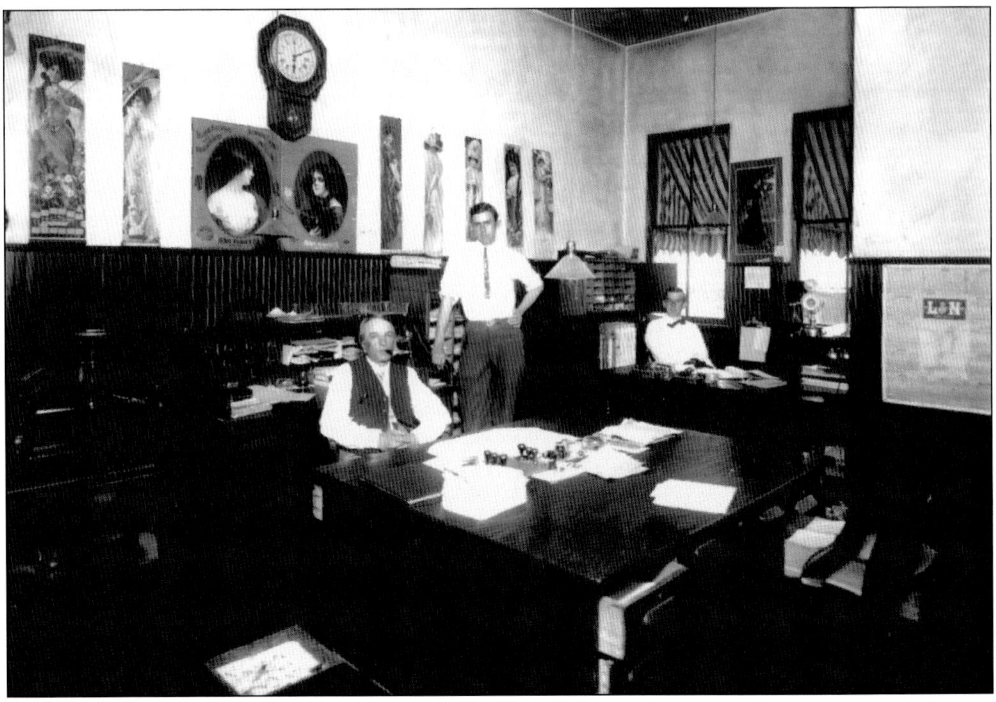

This photograph of the station agent's office in the McGill Depot shows the agent with his two assistants. The individual in the center is William R. Overfelt. The L&N calendar is dated 1913. Above the station agent's head are pin-up girls from the period. The Nevada Northern Railway Museum is restoring the depot and intends to recreate this scene.

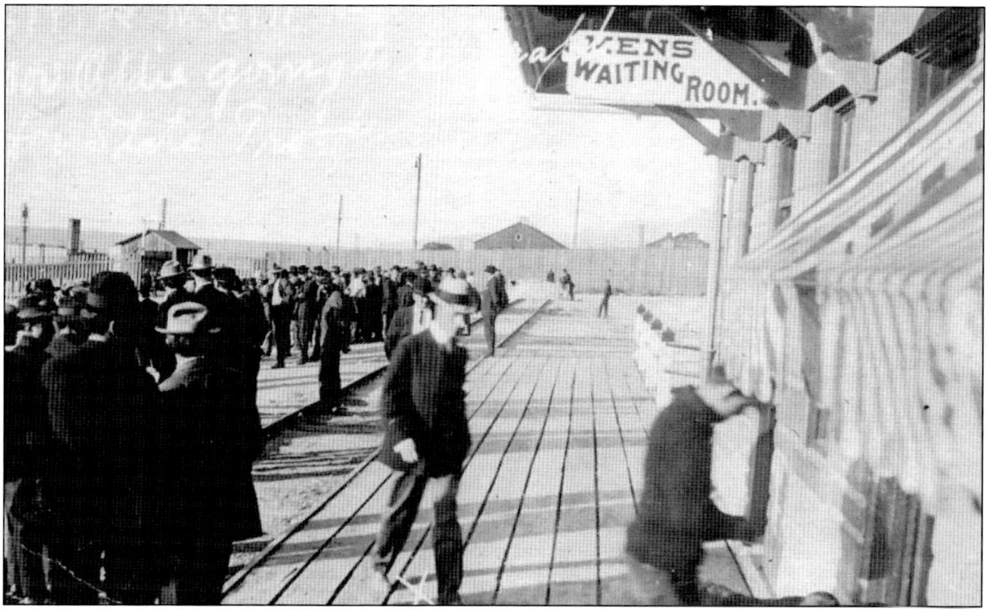

A labor strike was called by the Western Federation of Miners in 1912 and spread to McGill. Several fatalities resulted from conflicts between the strikers and deputy sheriffs. Governor Oddie declared martial law. He offered his services as an intermediary but was turned down by the company. The governor is pictured at the McGill Depot. (Novich.)

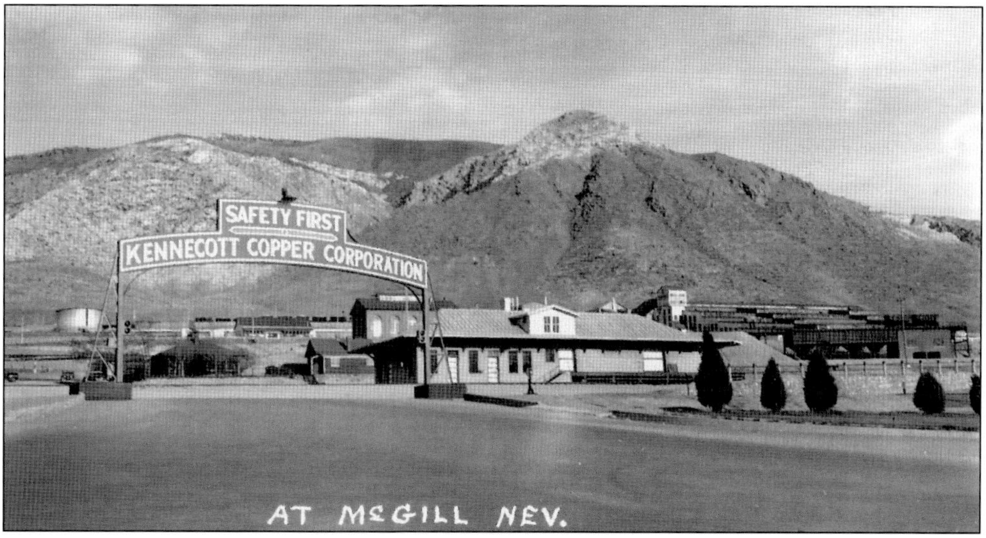

This is the entrance to the concentrating and smelter plant in McGill. The depot is at the center. On the right is the concentrator. All of the buildings and structures visible in the photograph (except the depot, which is currently undergoing restoration) were razed when the plant was closed. (Novich.)

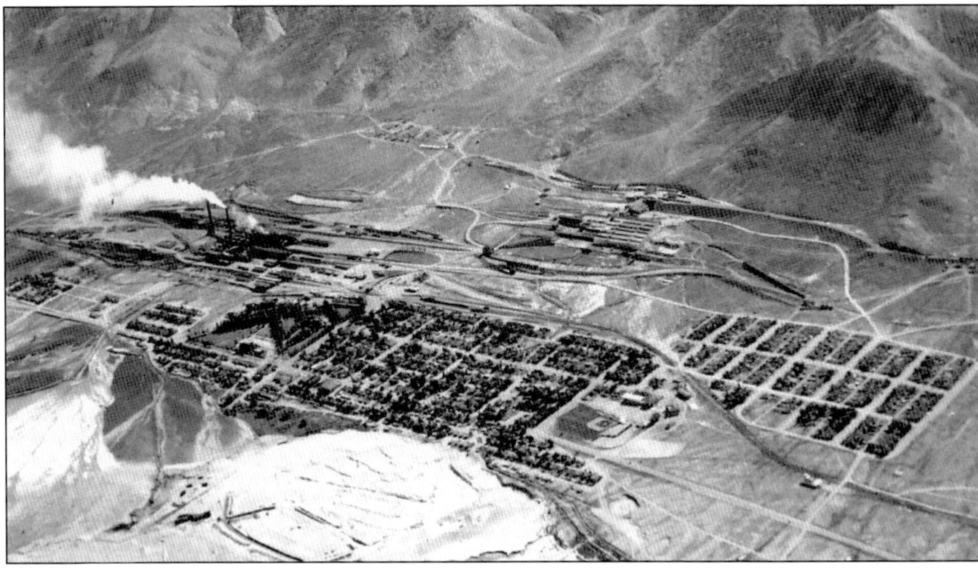

This is an aerial view showing McGill. In the upper right is the concentrator. On the left, the plumes of smoke are from the smelter's smokestacks. In the center, just above the town, is the depot. Below the town are the tailing ponds. The entire plant was served by the railroad. (Novich.)

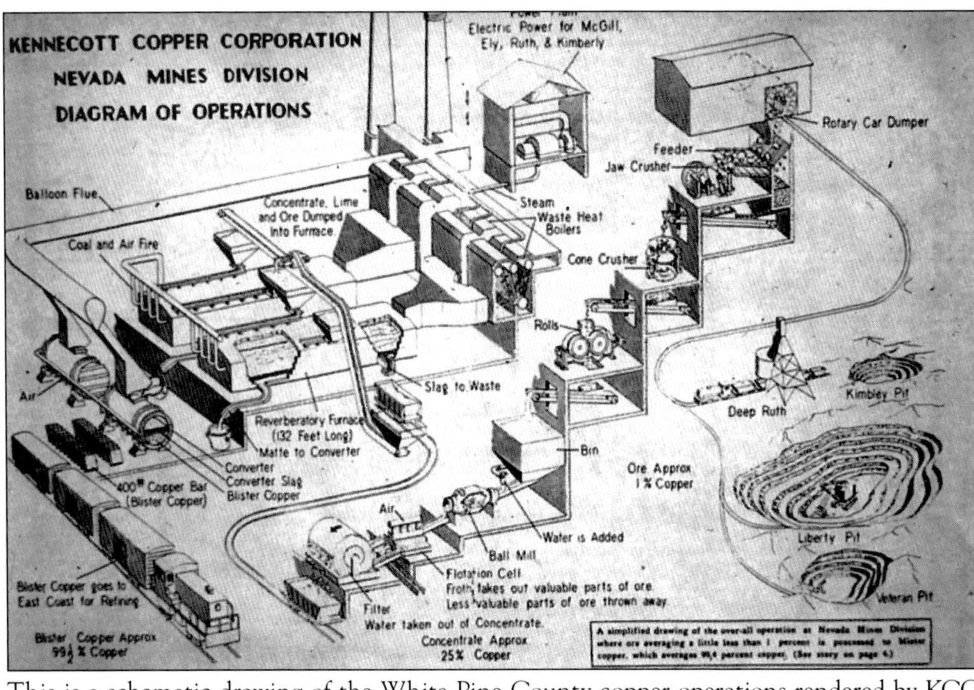

This is a schematic drawing of the White Pine County copper operations rendered by KCC. The drawing shows the mining, refining, and smelting of the copper. It illustrates the roles that the railroad played in copper production from delivery from the pit, to delivery of blister copper to customers.

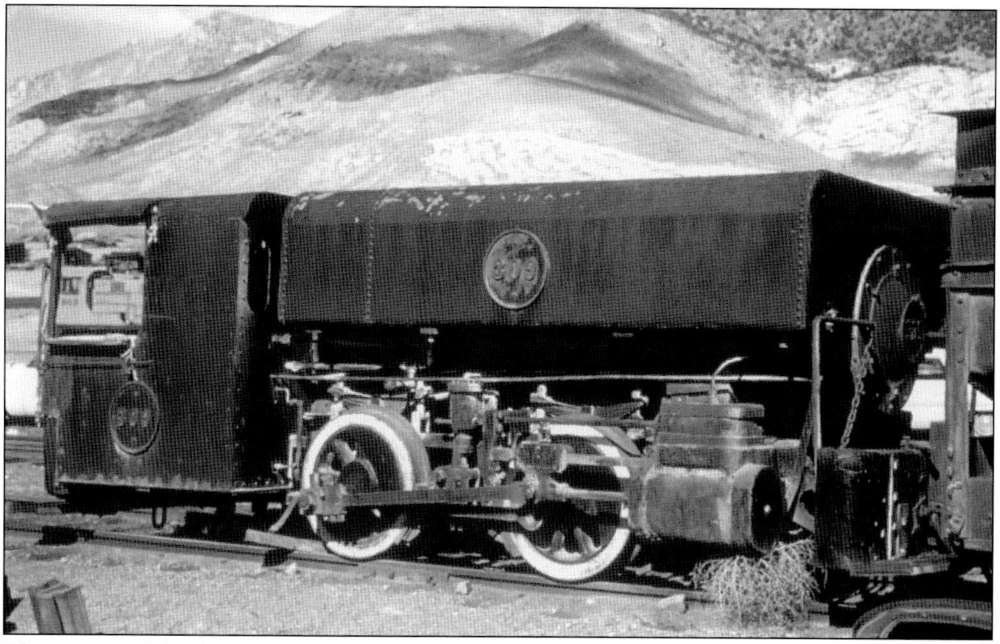

This is one of the locomotives originally purchased by the Steptoe Valley Smelting & Milling Company for use in the smelter. Originally numbered as 3, it was renumbered to 309 when the milling company was taken over by Nevada Consolidated Cooper Company. In December 2010, the locomotive was donated to the museum. (Duke.)

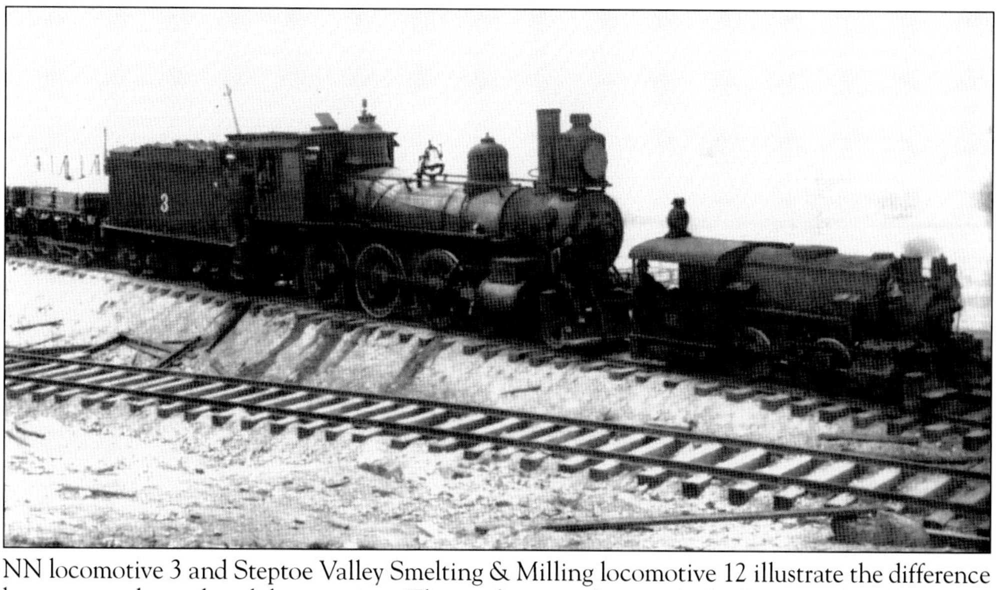

NN locomotive 3 and Steptoe Valley Smelting & Milling locomotive 12 illustrate the difference between tender and tank locomotives. The tender or coal car with the large number three on it carried the coal and water needed by locomotive 3. Locomotive 12 carried its own coal and water in the tank on top. This illustrates why locomotive 12 was called a dinky. (EERDM.)

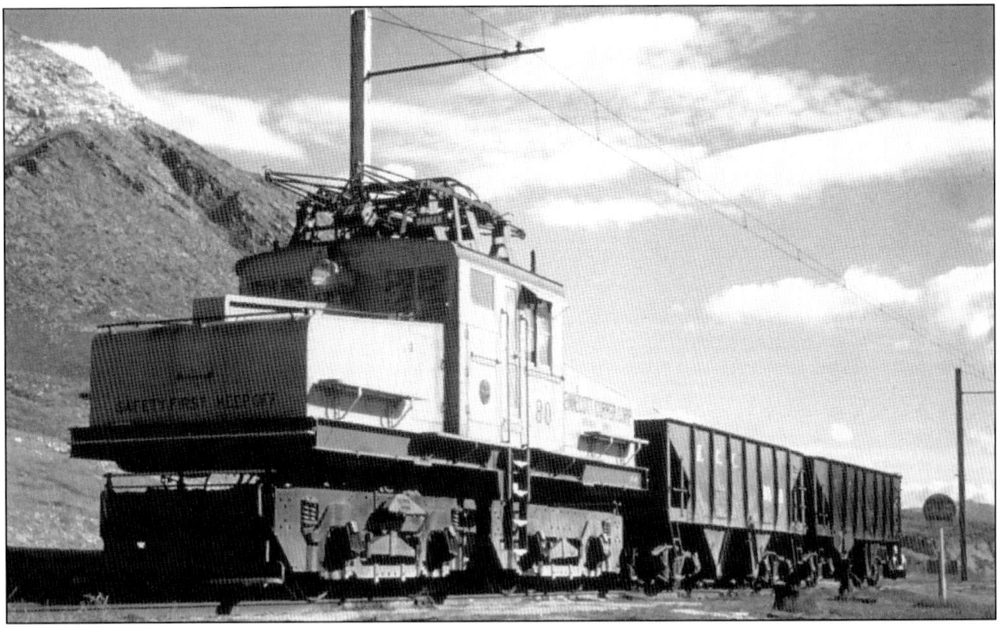

The mill had a small electric railroad. Steeple-cab electric locomotive number 80 is parked with hopper cars. Electric locomotives received power from overhead electric wires. The locomotive and cars still exist and are part of the Nevada Northern Railway Museum's collection. It was rare for a railroad to utilize steam, diesel, and electric locomotives in its operations. (Duke.)

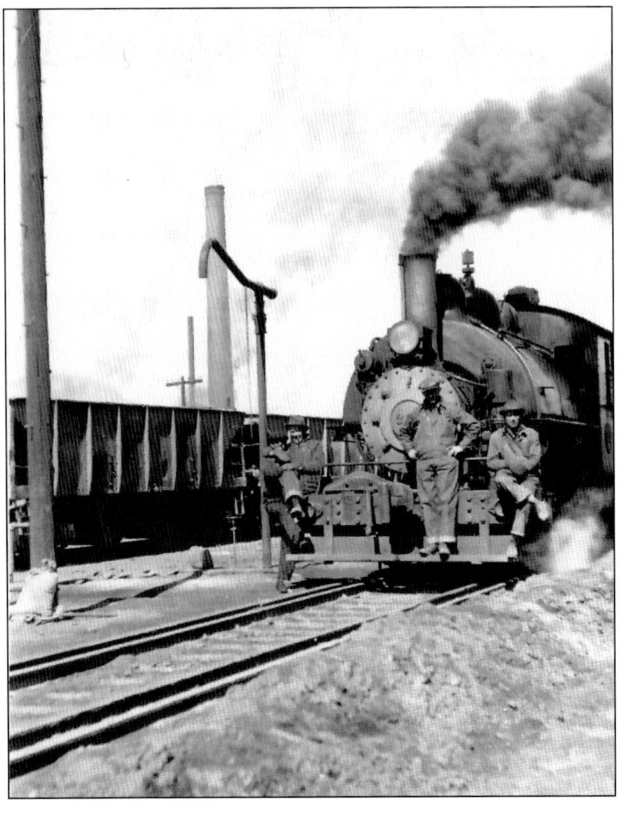

This is one of the 300-class, tank locomotives with its crew mugging for the camera. Tank locomotives had many advantages; they could operate in tight spaces and around sharp curves, and all of their weight was on their drivers for traction. Their need for water was their disadvantage. The tall pipe next to the locomotive was used as a water column to fill the water tank on top of the locomotive. (Gardner.)

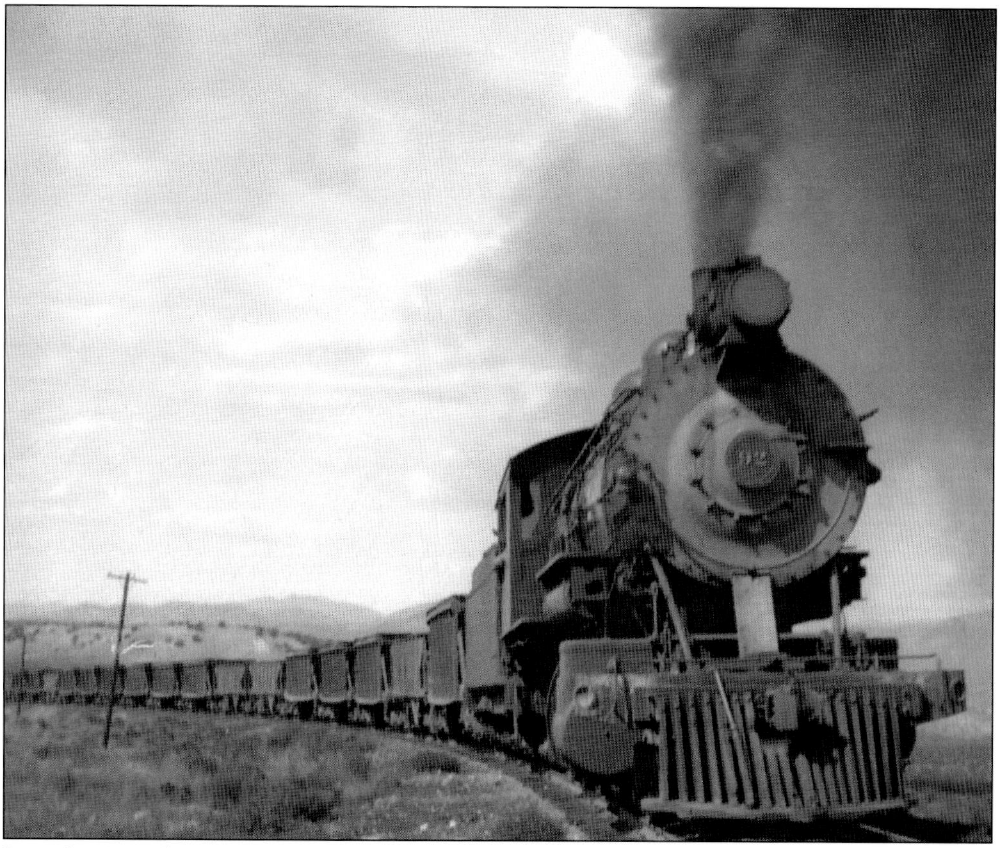

In early 1908, the copper company ordered its first four locomotives for ore train service from the American Locomotive Company's (ALCO) Pittsburgh works. These were, as the *White Pine News* declared, "the 'monster' locomotives" needed to haul the ore trains from Ruth to McGill. Locomotive 92 was the third locomotive in the order. (The first was locomotive 90, and the last was locomotive 93.) With a 2-8-0-wheel arrangement, these locomotives were referred to as consolidations. Locomotive 92 cost $17,585, weighed 187,000 pounds, and was equipped with 51-inch drivers. It hauled ore cars for 43 years until it was displaced by the diesel locomotive, also from ALCO, and scrapped at McGill in January 1952. (Newitt.)

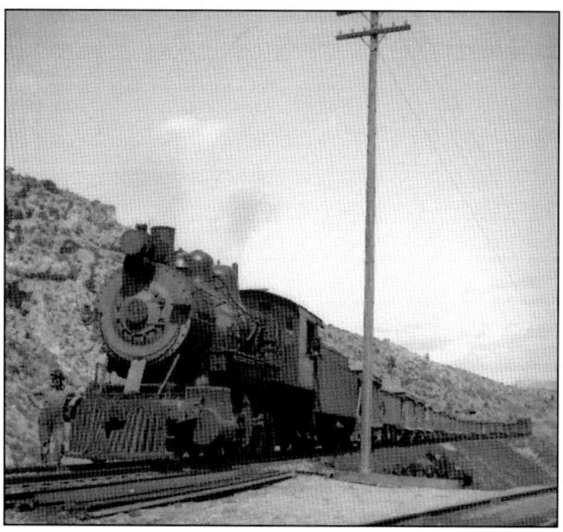

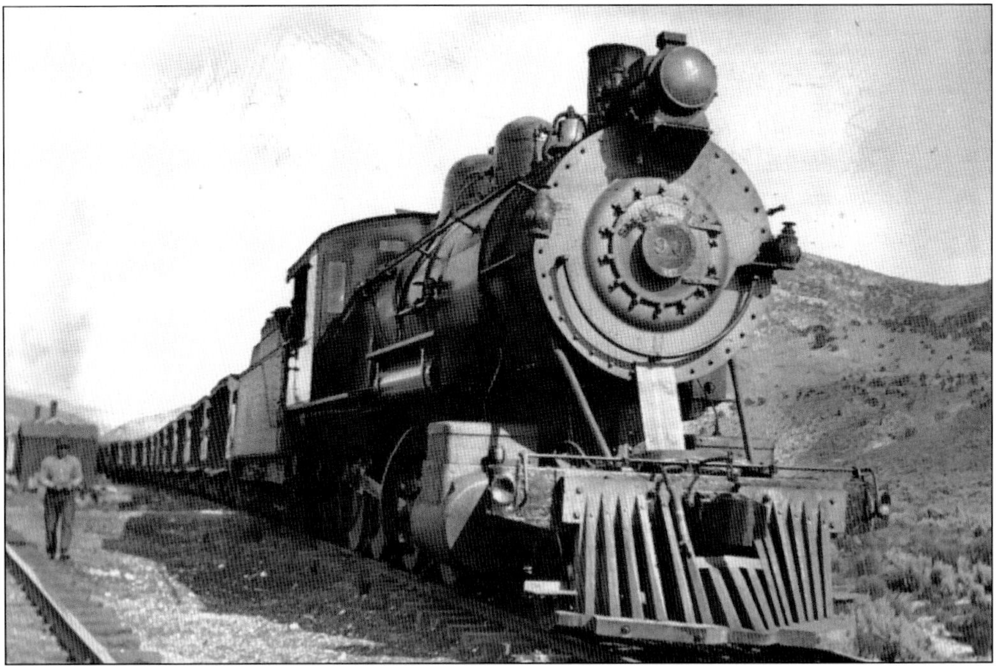

Locomotive 90 has stopped at East Ely after a safe downhill trip from the mine. There, the ore car's retainers were applied. Every car had a retainer valve, which when engaged, allowed the brakes to partially apply. At night, the wheels could be seen glowing red-hot from friction. At East Ely, the retainers were turned off, as they were not needed for the uphill trip to McGill. (Newitt.)

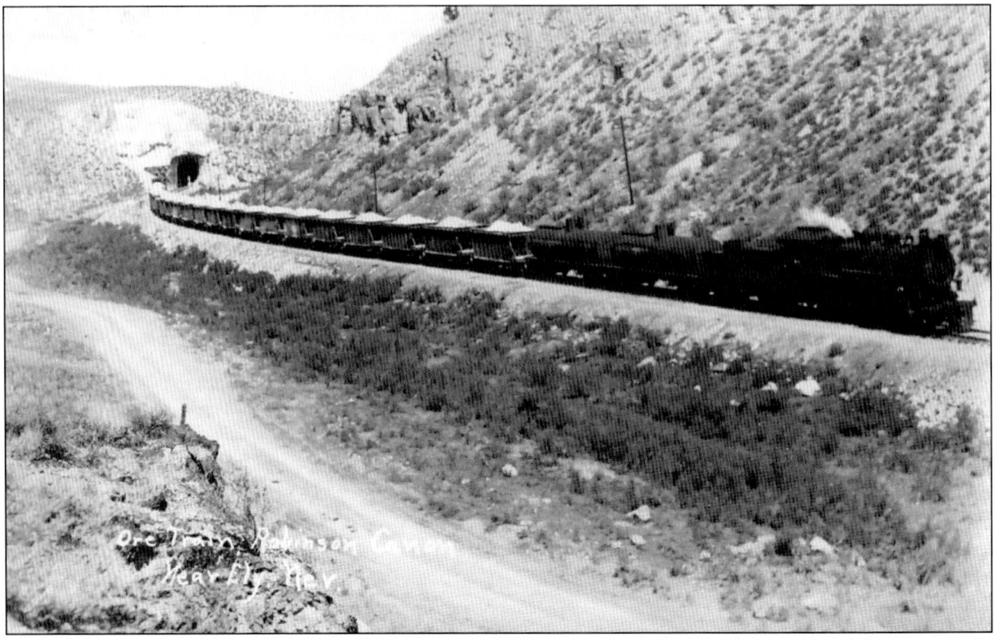

In Robinson Canyon just east of tunnel No. 2 is an ore train. The tunnel was one of three tunnels on the railroad and was daylighted during World War II. The term *daylighting* means taking the roof off a tunnel. The locomotive is one of the 90 series. Behind the locomotive are two water cars that will be filled at East Ely before returning to Ruth. (Novich.)

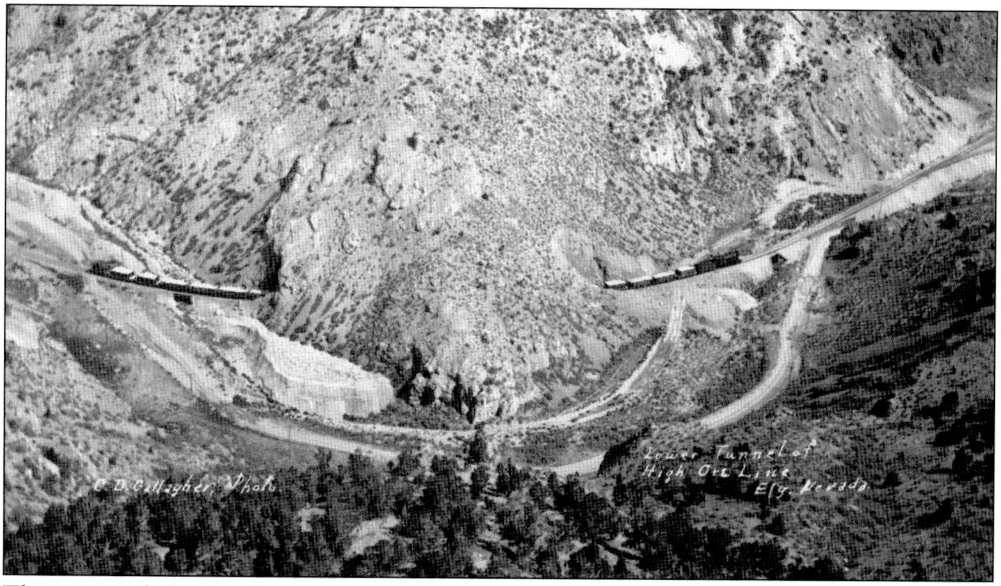

This is tunnel No. 1 with an ore train going through the tunnel. This tunnel still exists and is used by the museum's excursion trains. Growing up in Ely came with a rite of passage—standing in the timber-lined tunnel as the ore trains came through. If an engineer saw an Ely youngster in the tunnel, he would give the thrill-seeker a blast of steam to discourage the stunt. (Novich.)

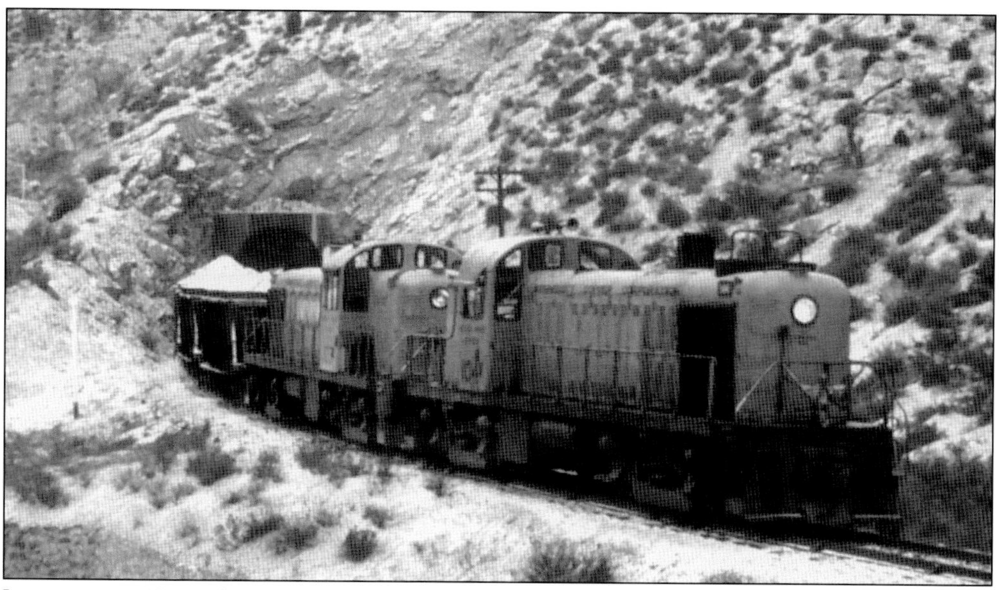

Locomotives 104 and 103 exit tunnel No. 1 with an ore train. After World War II, the railroad dieselized quickly. Locomotive 101 was delivered in 1948. In 1949, locomotives 102–105 and 108 were delivered. In 1950, locomotive 107 was delivered. All were ALCO RS-2s. Locomotive 109, an ALCO RS-3, showed up in 1970 on a transfer from Kennecott's Arizona operations. Locomotives 105 and 109 are in the Nevada Northern Railway Museum's collection. (Duke.)

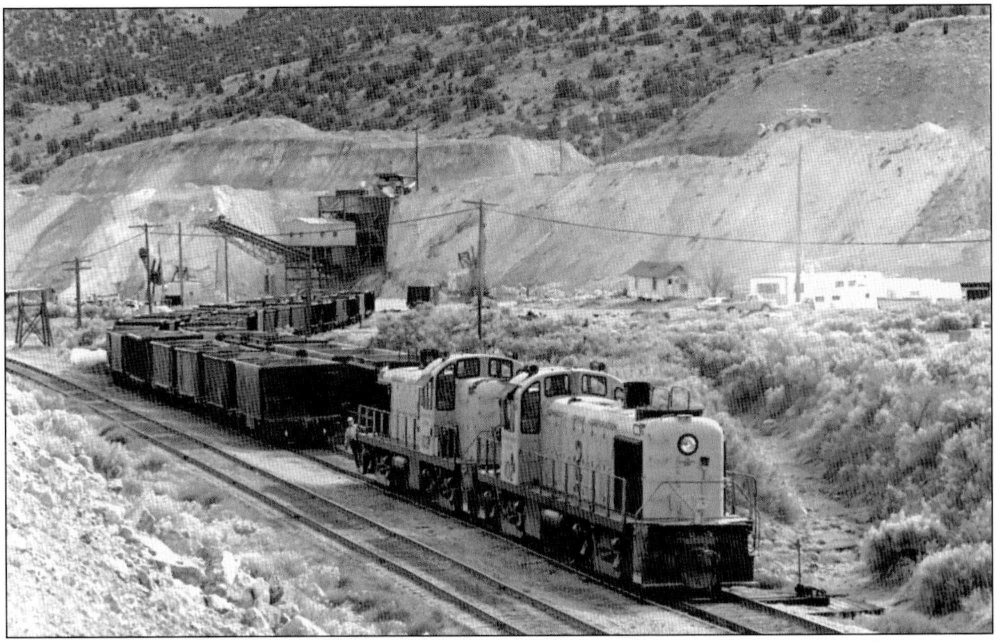

With their train of ore empties spotted for loading at Lane City on November 16, 1977, locomotives 102 and 103 prepare to retrieve 50 loads for delivery to McGill. Museum excursion trains pass this site, but the only thing remaining from this picture is the brakeman's wooden tower visible to the very left. (Benson.)

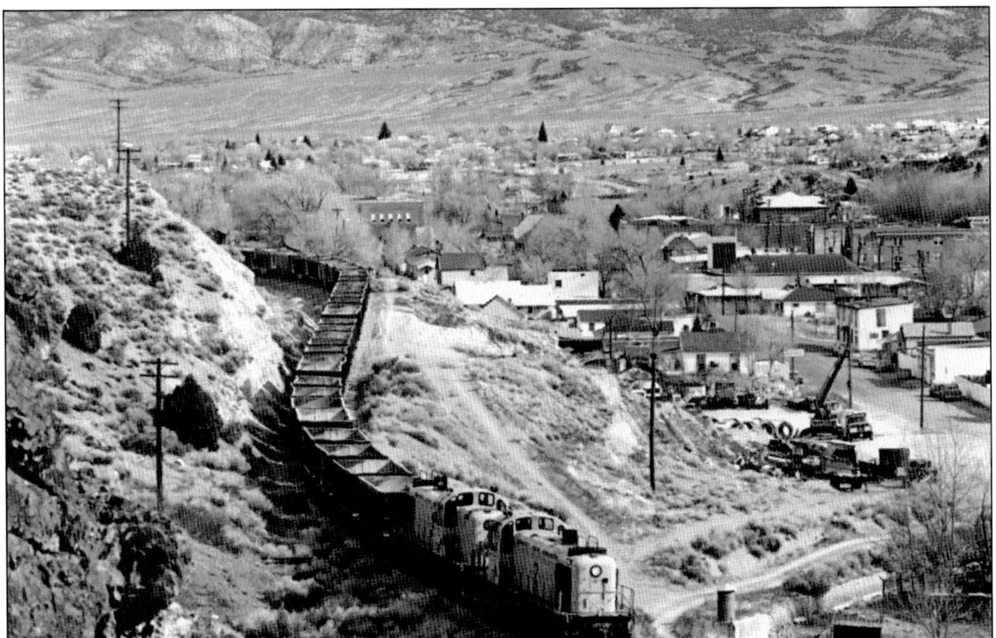

Locomotives 102 and 103 roll a train of mine-bound ore empties above downtown Ely on Wednesday, November 16, 1977. The ore trains ran around the clock day in and day out. After the ore trains stopped, the quiet made it difficult for some of the residents to sleep at night. (Benson.)

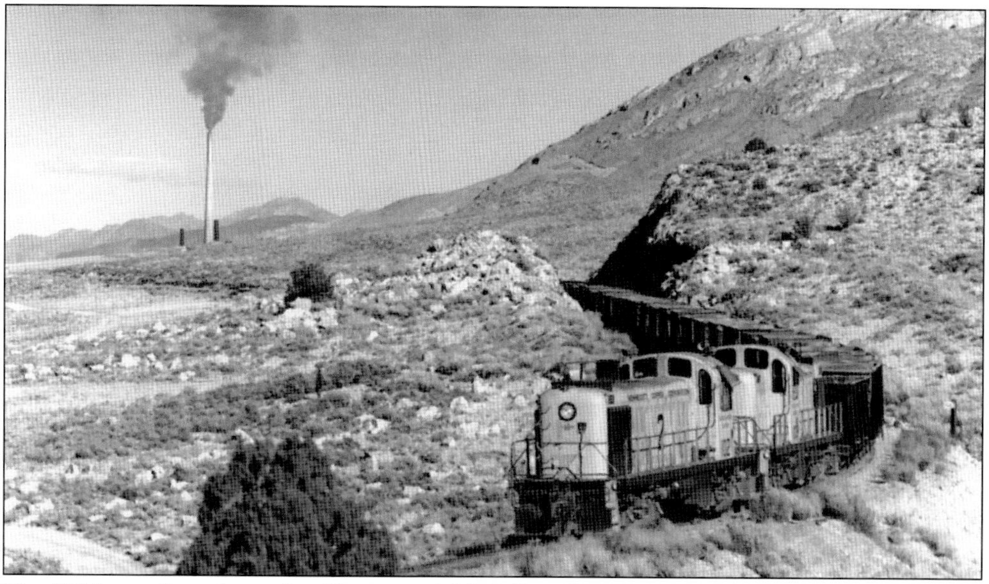

The 750-foot-tall smokestack at Kennecott's McGill smelter towers over locomotives 102 and 103 passing milepost H-6 with a train of empties on November 16, 1977. The smelter emissions were a major source of regulatory misery for Kennecott in Nevada in the late 1970s and were one of the contributing factors to the closure of the facilities. (Benson.)

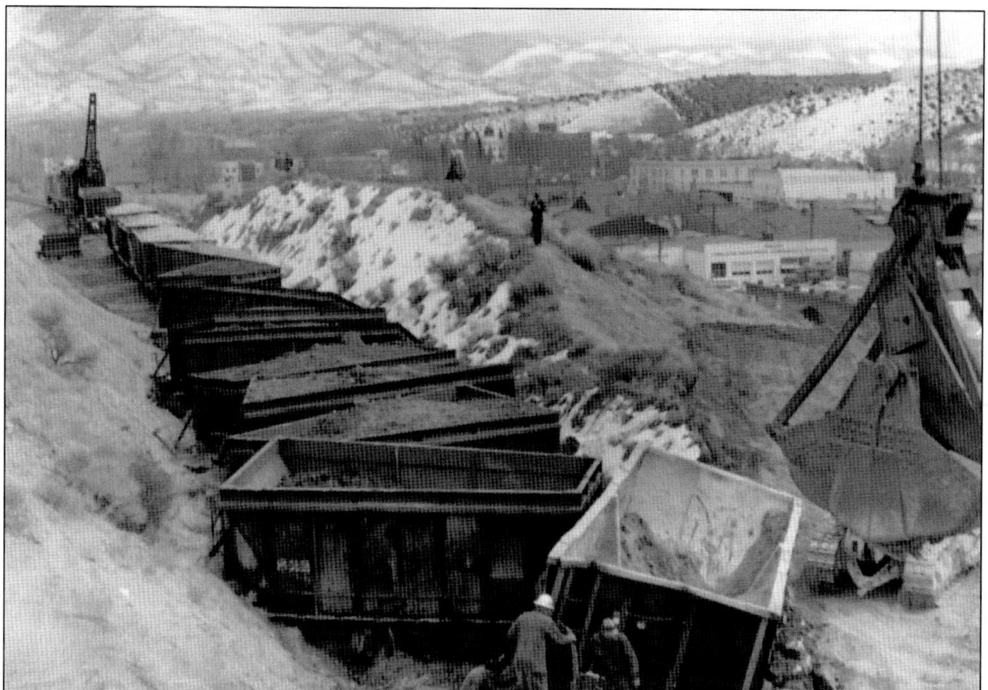

Not all ore trains made it to McGill. This derailment occurred March 20, 1962, on the ore line above Ely. Wrecking crane A is on the left putting cars back on the track. A crane with a bucket is removing ore from the cars to make them lighter. The derailment site is still noticeable, marked by the mounds of ore removed from the cars.

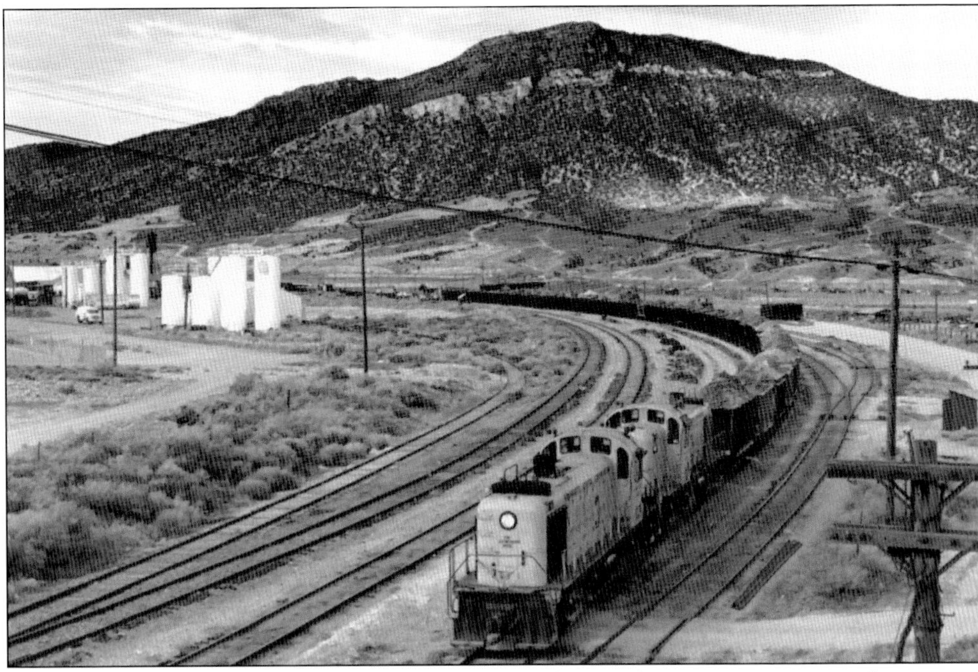

Ore for McGill departs East Ely following a stop for weighing and inspection. Kennecott locomotives 103 and 102 are in charge of 50 eastbound loads on Thursday, November 17, 1977. Above, the view is to the west showing the ore yard. The East Ely yard is further west just beyond the curve. Below, the view shows the train leaving the ore yard. The EAST ELY lettered on the building was a directional aid for airplanes. Both views were shot from the now-vanished Highway 93 overpass. The grade crossing that replaced the bridge shortened the ore yard. (Both, Benson.)

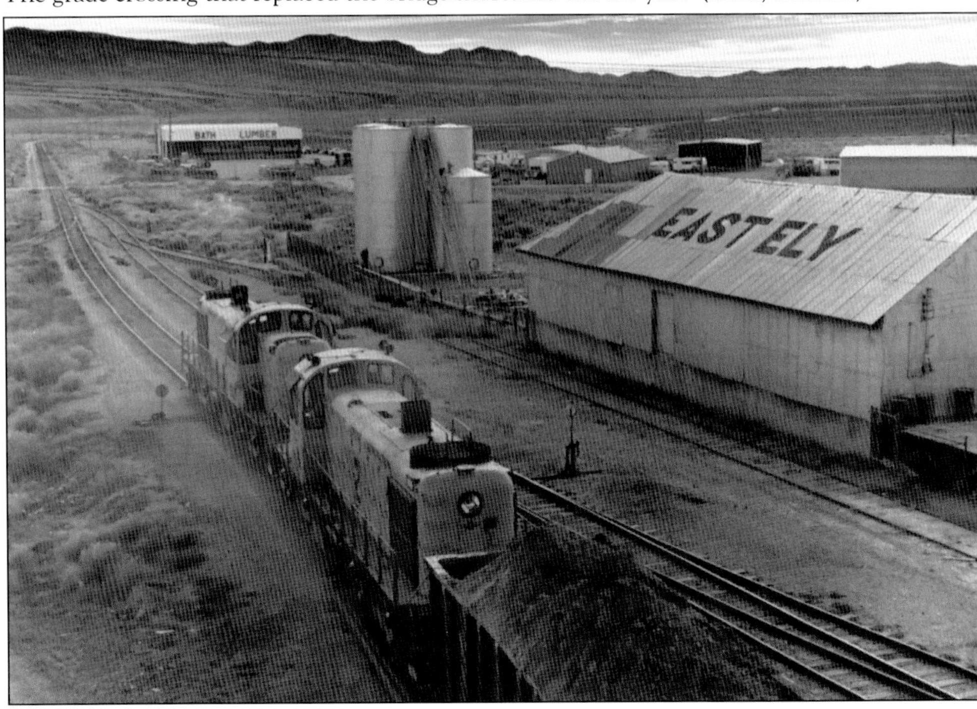

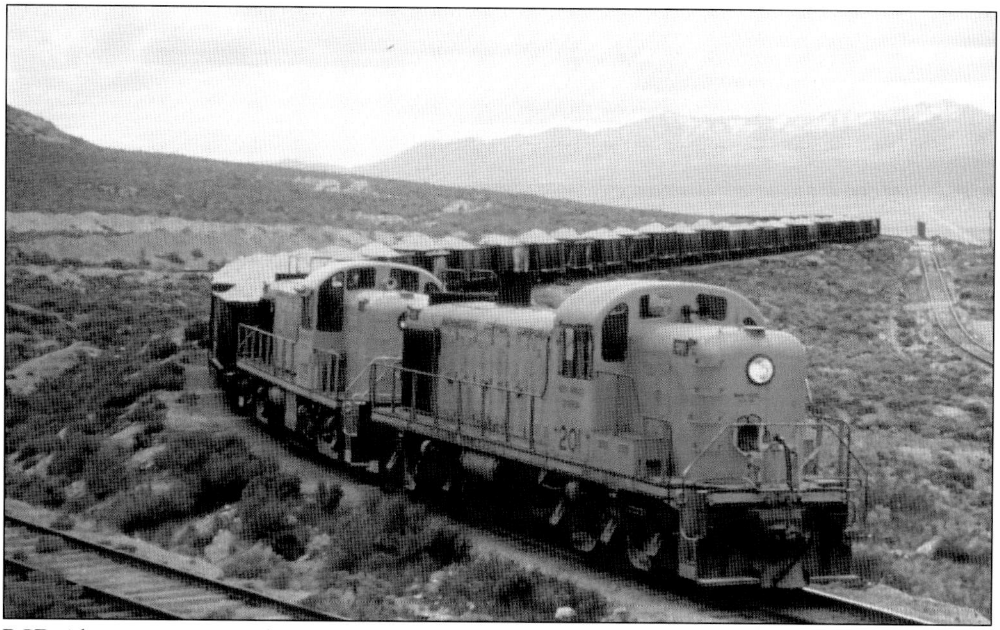

RSD-4 locomotive 201 is leading RS-3 locomotive 109 with a northbound ore train just past the Adverse switch on the Hiline. Kennecott believed in ALCO products, purchasing RS-2s, RS-3s, and an RSD-4. Only 36 RSD-4s were built, and the only survivor is locomotive 201, located at the Northwest Railway Museum in Snoqualmie, Washington. (Duke.)

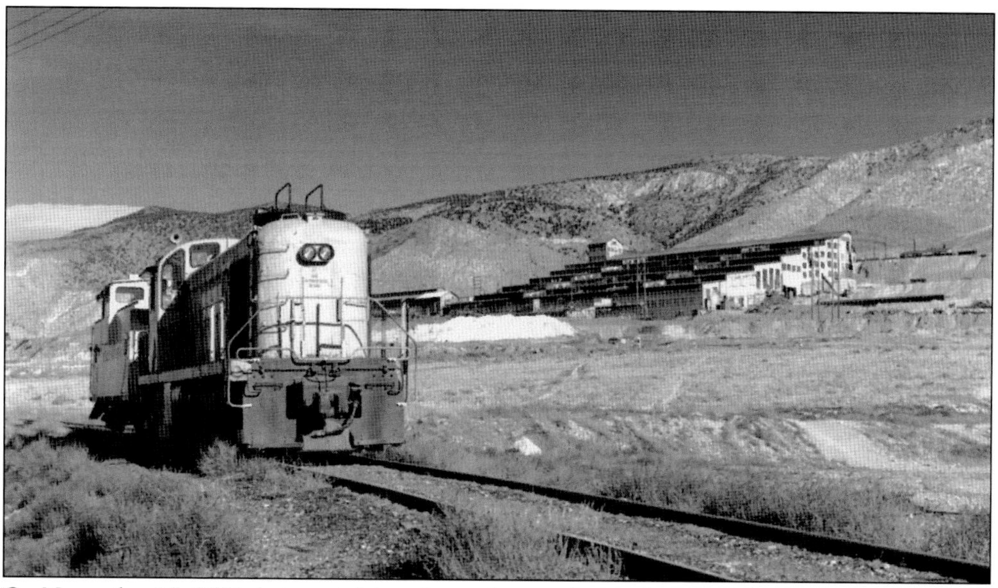

On November 15, 1977, their switching chores done at the smelter, RS-2 locomotive 101 and NN caboose 6 trundle past Kennecott's McGill concentrator on their way back to McGill Junction and the waiting inbound Cobre Local train. In five months, operations at the copper mine would end, and in six years, the milling and smelter operations would also end. (Benson.)

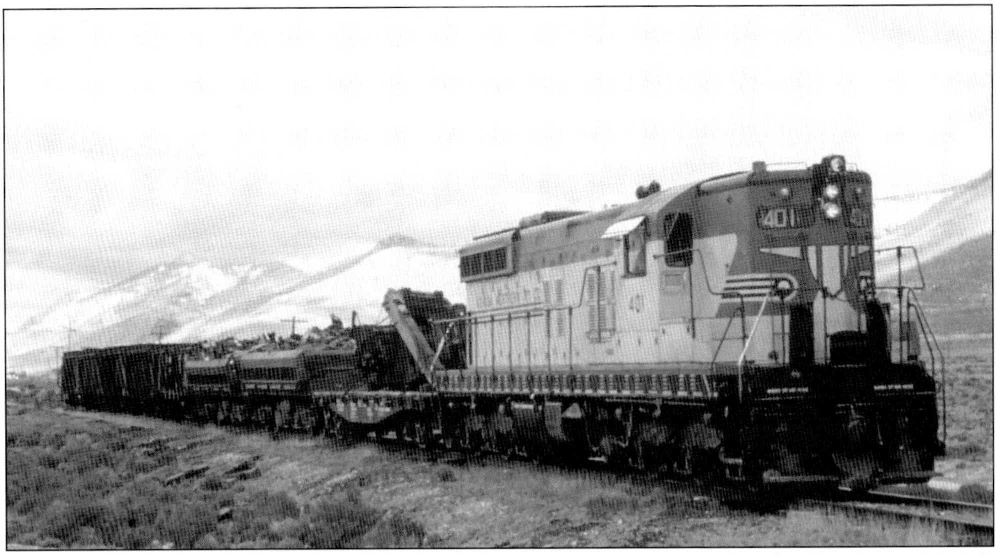

The mill had a constant need for scrap steel, which would be delivered to the foundry at McGill to be melted and cast into mill balls. The balls would then be used at the mill to smash the copper ore as the first stage of milling. Here, locomotive 401 is heading to McGill. (Duke.)

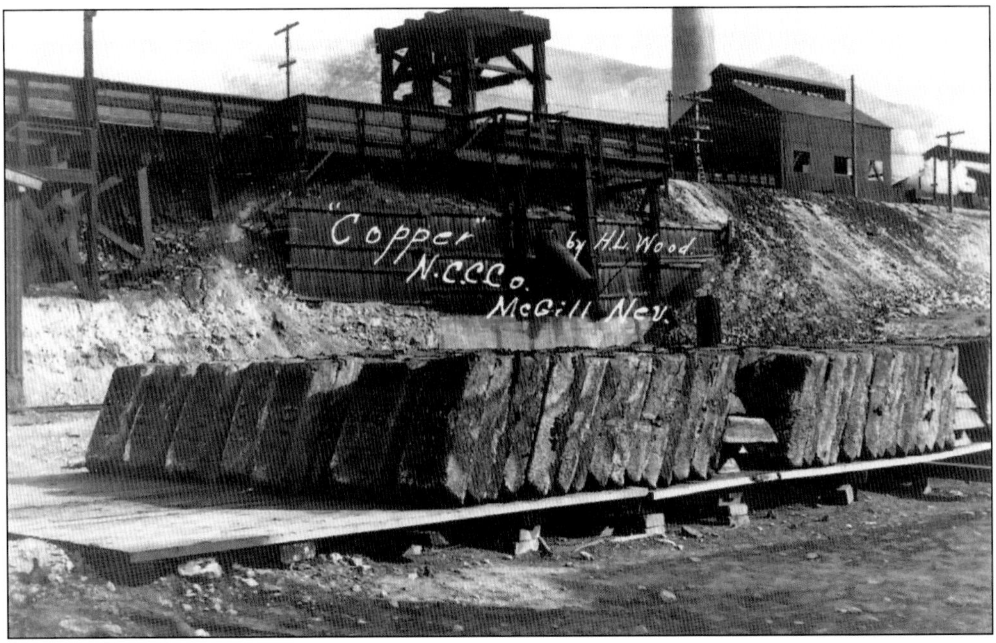

The end product of moving a mountain of low-grade copper ore is blister copper, 98 percent pure copper. Starting with one to three percent copper ore in Ruth, trains ran around the clock from Ruth to McGill feeding the concentrating plant and smelter. The blister copper was shipped to refineries to produce a wide spectrum of copper products. (Novich.)

Four

Freight Service Carries the Goods

Railroading revolutionized society at its most basic levels. Today, every glance at a clock is an echo of this revolution. Steam locomotives were the first invention that did not rely on wind power or animal power—they could operate around the clock. They traveled faster than the sun. In an age before cell phones, radios, telephones, and even the telegraph, the question was, "How do you control two trains on the same track?" The apparent simple solution was with time. In other words, train A will meet train B at Hillsdale. Sounds simple enough, but what happens if the engineers' watches on the two opposing trains did not agree? The result could be a collision. The revolutionary and contentious solution was to standardize time. All clocks in the Pacific time zone would be set to a standard time; now when it was 7:00 a.m. in Ely, it would also be 7:00 a.m. in Reno. The change was controversial, because the railroads were said to be changing God's time.

Railroads made possible the settlement of the interior of the country. Large cities not on the coasts or on rivers, like Las Vegas, Nevada, would not exist without railroads, because it would be impossible to feed and supply interior cities without them.

The Nevada Northern Railway single-handedly made the development of the copper industry possible in White Pine County. Without the railroad, there would be no way to move the ore from the mines to the mill; the railroad delivered 200 million pounds of ore to McGill in just one month. That could not have been done with animal or wind power.

From 1906 until the early 1930s, everything needed in White Pine County came by the Nevada Northern Railway. As roads were built and trucks and airplanes improved, freight left the rails. The end of smelting in McGill was the final nail in the coffin for the railroad. And on June 21, 1983, the last train tied-up at East Ely, ending 78 years of freight service.

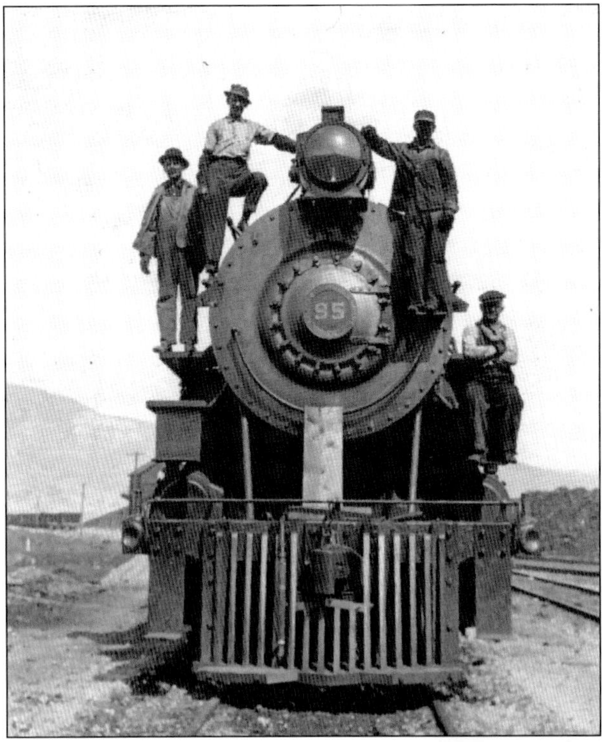

In the visitor center of the Nevada Northern Railway Museum, a sign states, "Railroads are people serving people." The steam locomotives thrill visitors, but none of this would matter without people. The engine crew shows their pride in locomotive 95. Chances are, all the men in photograph at left immigrated to Ely to work on the railroad. Below, after 66 years, there's not much ticking—other than the clock—as Nevada Northern chief dispatcher Jack Whitehurst reflects on the company's fortunes at the East Ely dispatcher's office on September 16, 1976. One train a week was the best the railroad could offer then. The federally enforced shutdown of the McGill smelter was especially hard to swallow; news came during the recession-wracked summer of the bicentennial. (Left, Novich; below, Benson.)

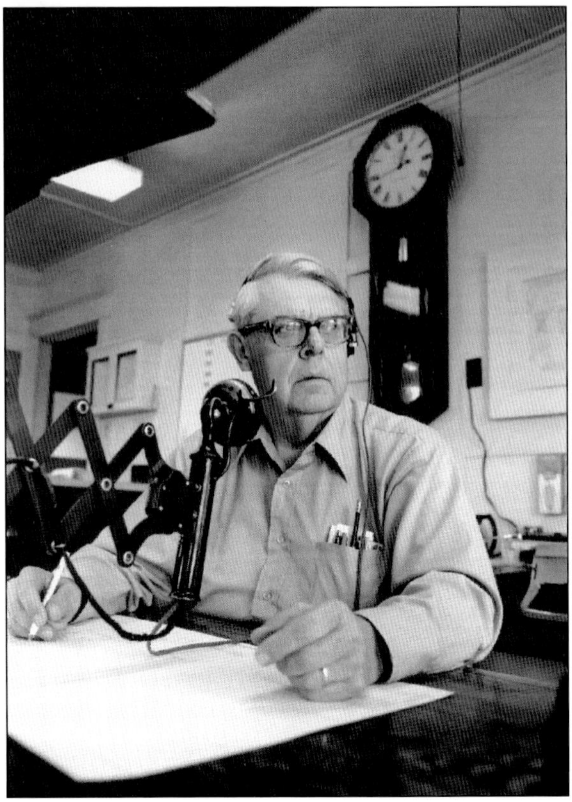

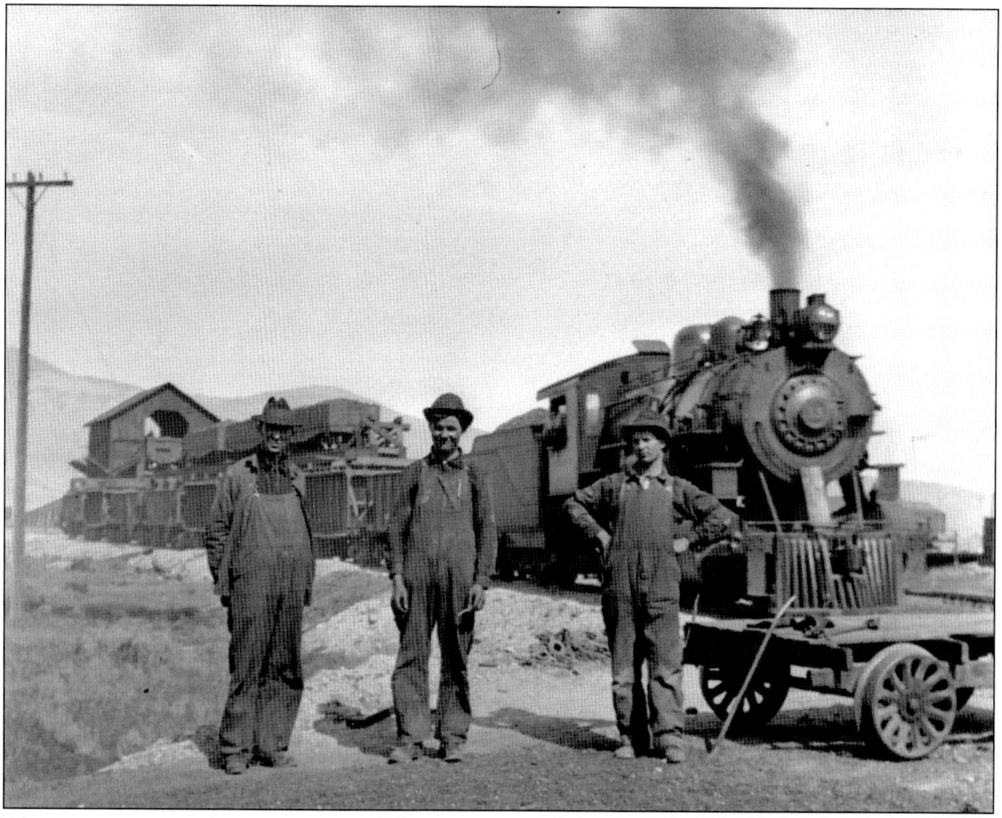

The men are part of a section gang. They maintained the track by hand. Their tools are on the little four-wheel pushcart, which they pushed on the track. In the background is the original coal-loading tipple. Coal cars were pushed up the tipple track and dumped into bins; the coal was loaded into the locomotives. (Newitt.)

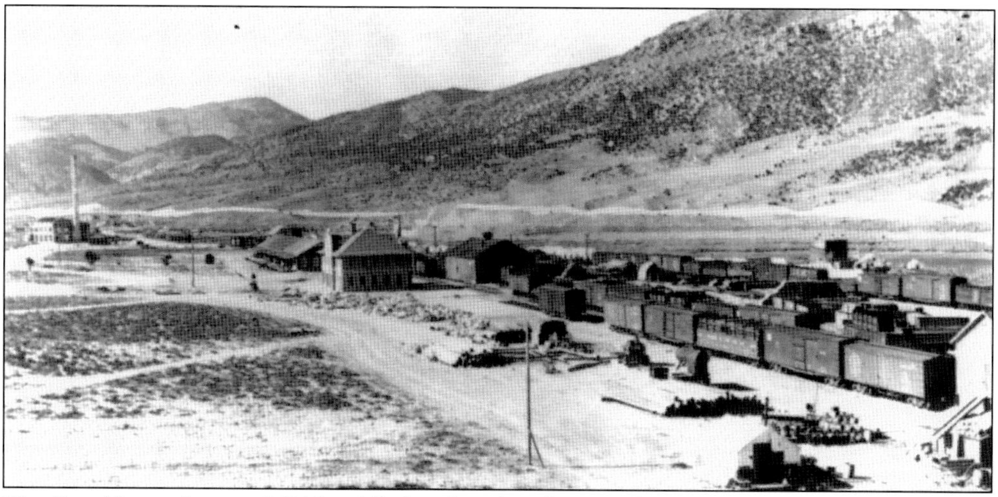

The East Ely yard around 1910 is filled with railroad cars. The East Ely Depot is in the center, and the first engine house is to the right. Behind the depot is the freight house, and to the far left is the electrical power plant. The white line across the center of the photograph is the newly built ore bypass track. (WPCHS.)

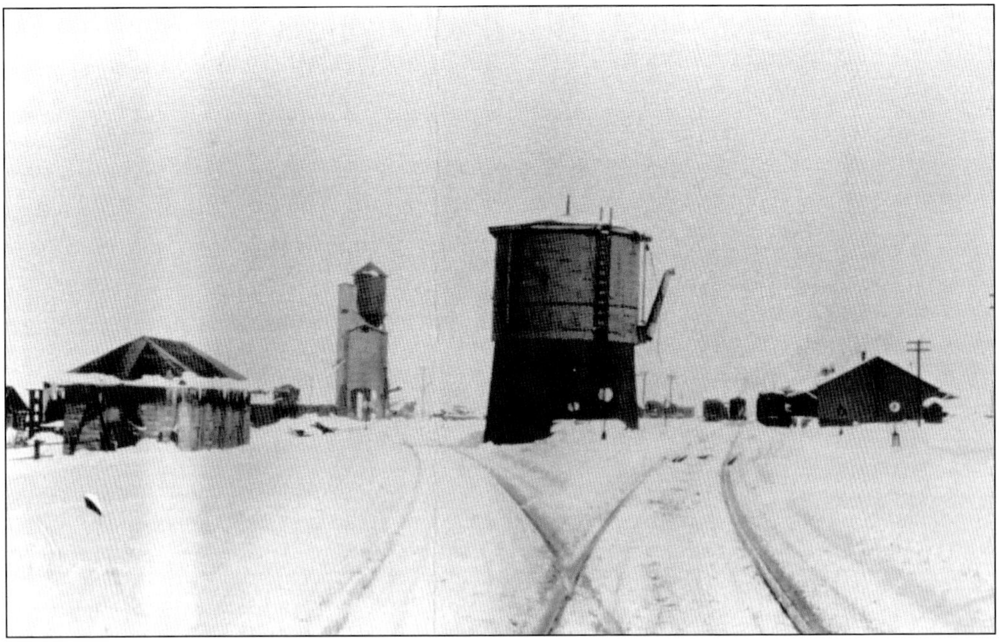

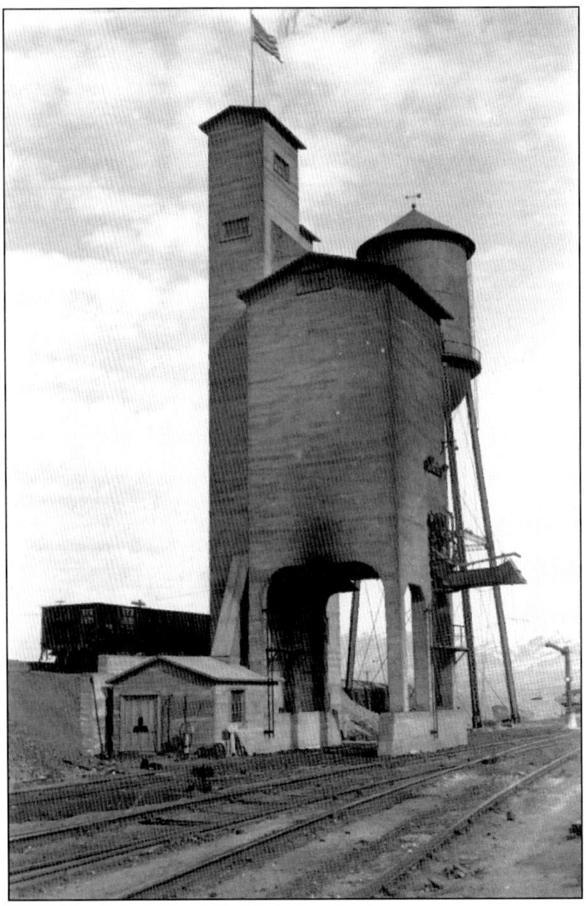

Pictured is the west end of the East Ely yard looking east on a cold, wintery day. Directly in front is a water tank for the steam locomotive tenders. The building on the left is the pipe shop, and in the distance is the coaling tower and another water tank. The freight barn is to the right. (EERDM.)

Built in 1917, the concrete coaling tower is located in the East Ely yards and still exists. The coal cars on the left dump their coal into a hopper under the track. The coal was then loaded into buckets inside the building that delivered the coal to the top of the tower and dumped it into a concrete hopper. A locomotive's tenders were then filled under the tower.

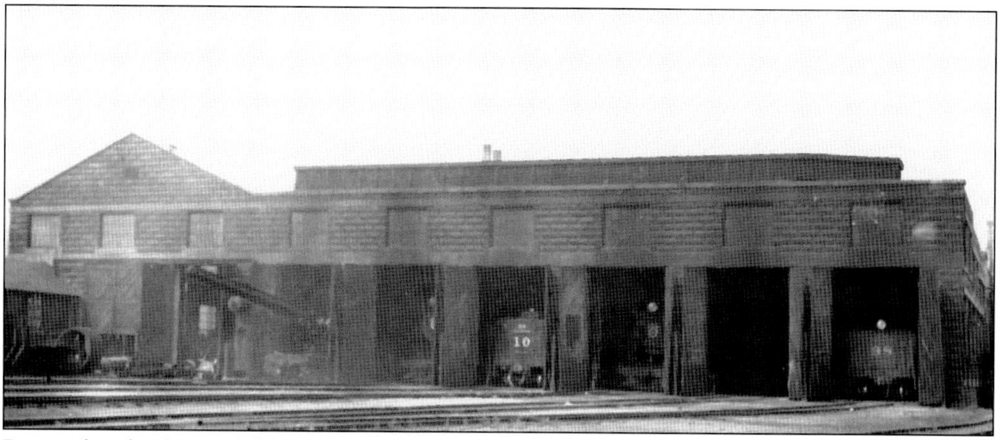

Pictured is the front of the current engine house at East Ely; it could hold 12 locomotives. Even though the building is rectangular, it was still referred to as the roundhouse. To the left under the peaked roof is the machine shop where locomotive repairs and maintenance were done. Built in 1907, the buildings are still in use. (Bechtold.)

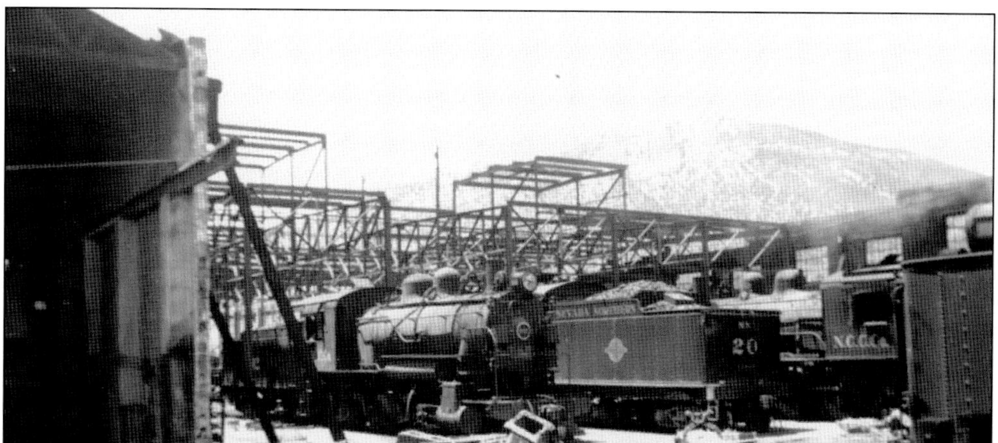

In the summer of 1941, major improvements were made to the machine shop and engine house buildings. The wooden doors were replaced with metal rollup doors, and the roof was rebuilt to incorporate skylights. The construction and the improvements did not stop the railroad from using the engine house; locomotives occupying the engine house stalls are visible. (WPCHS.)

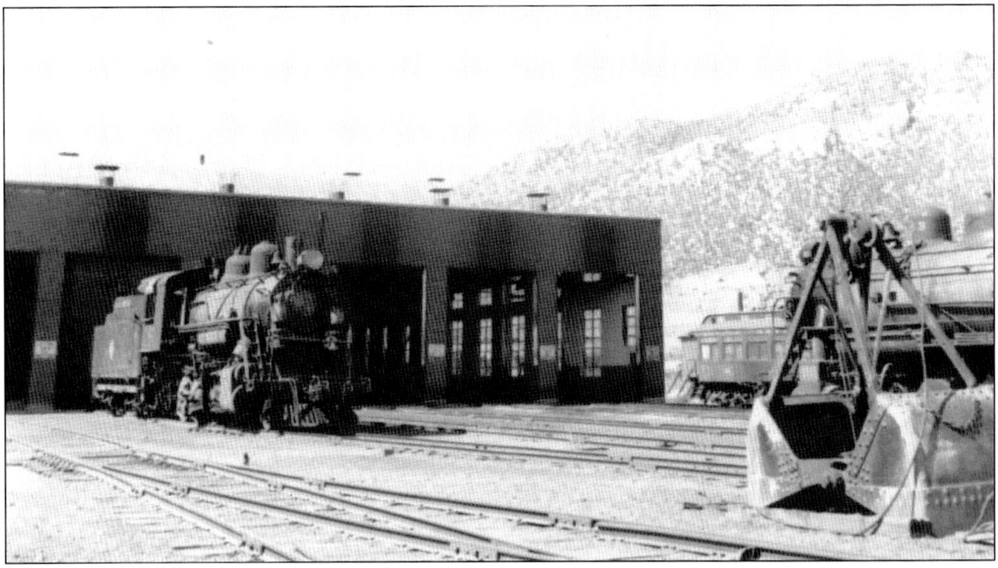

The objects on the roof are smokejacks. The smokestack of a locomotive is placed directly under the smokejack so the smoke vents through the roof. Locomotive 81 is on the left, and the front of locomotive 93 is on the right; both locomotives are still stored in the engine house.

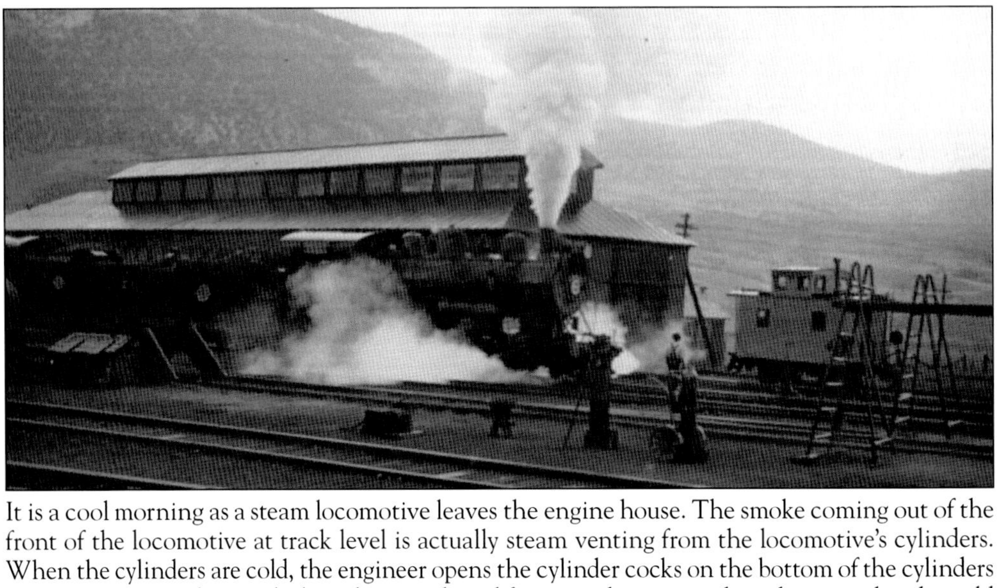

It is a cool morning as a steam locomotive leaves the engine house. The smoke coming out of the front of the locomotive at track level is actually steam venting from the locomotive's cylinders. When the cylinders are cold, the engineer opens the cylinder cocks on the bottom of the cylinders to vent any water that might have been gathered from condensation when the steam hit the cold cylinders. (Chappell.)

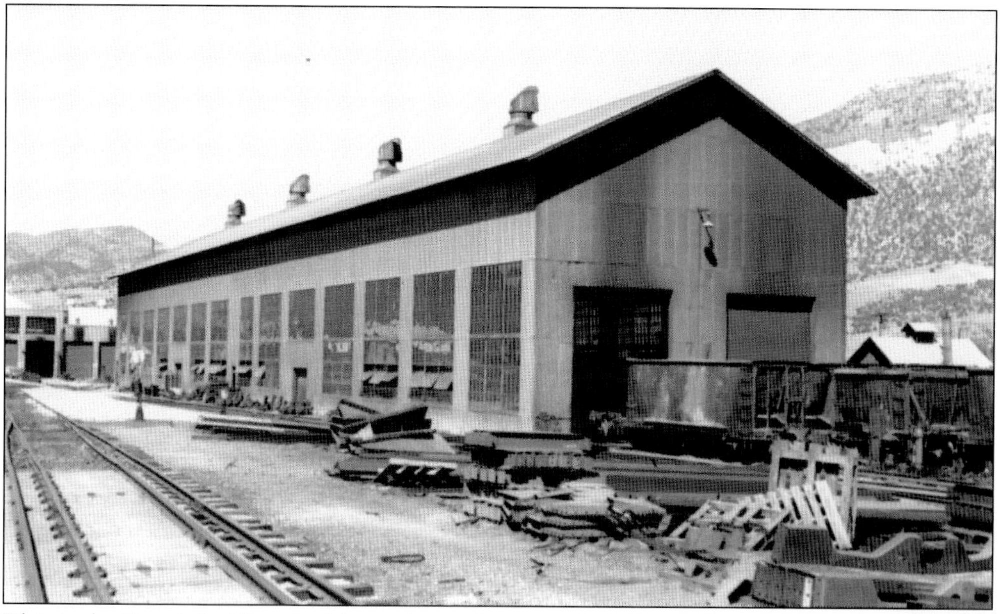

This is the Repair In Place building—better know as the RIP building—in 1968. Ore cars led a rough existence. They were banged with shovels, boulders were dropped into them, and the wear and tear of running back and forth between Ruth and McGill was substantial. Before the construction of the RIP building, cars were repaired outdoors year round. (Sundance.)

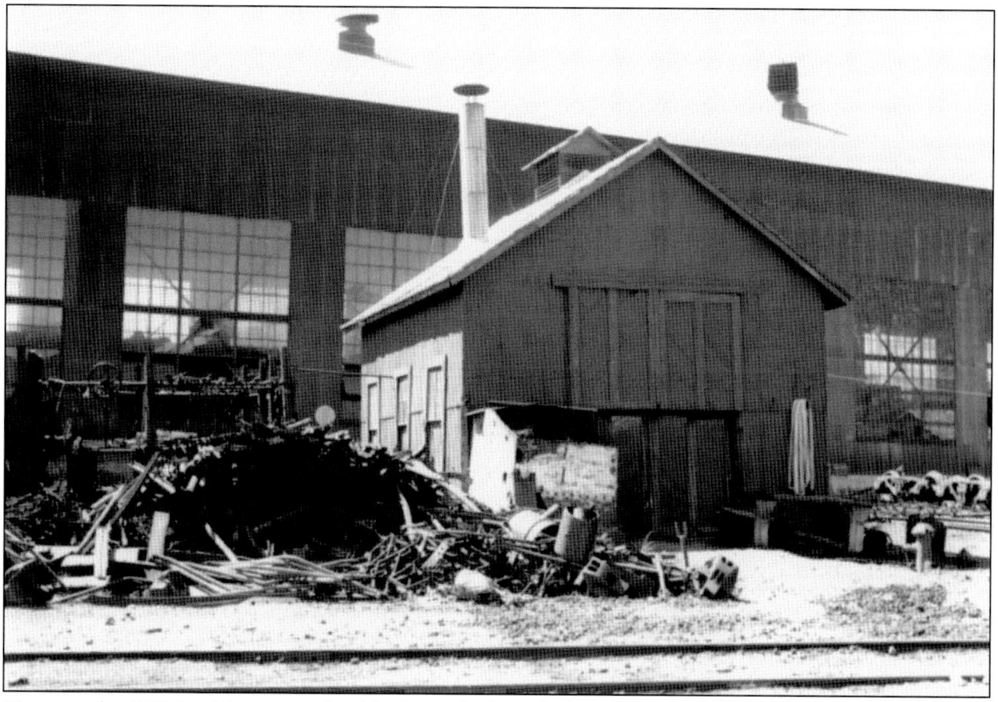

Next to the RIP building was the blacksmith shop, located amidst a mountain of supplies used to repair the ore cars. Here, parts were straightened, mended, or newly fabricated. On the verge of collapse in 2010, the interior structure of the building was restored by the Nevada Northern Railway Museum. (Sundance.)

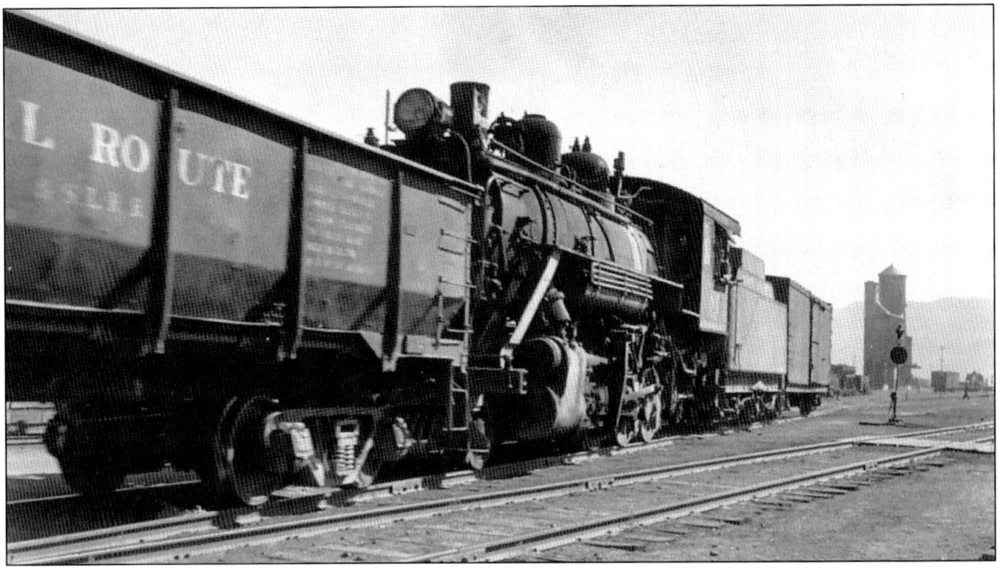

The East Ely yard was a busy place. Here, locomotive 81 is switching in the yard. Notice the switch lamp on the switch stand. All switch stands would have switch lamps, which needed to be lit every evening and extinguished every morning. In the background is the coaling tower. (Novich.)

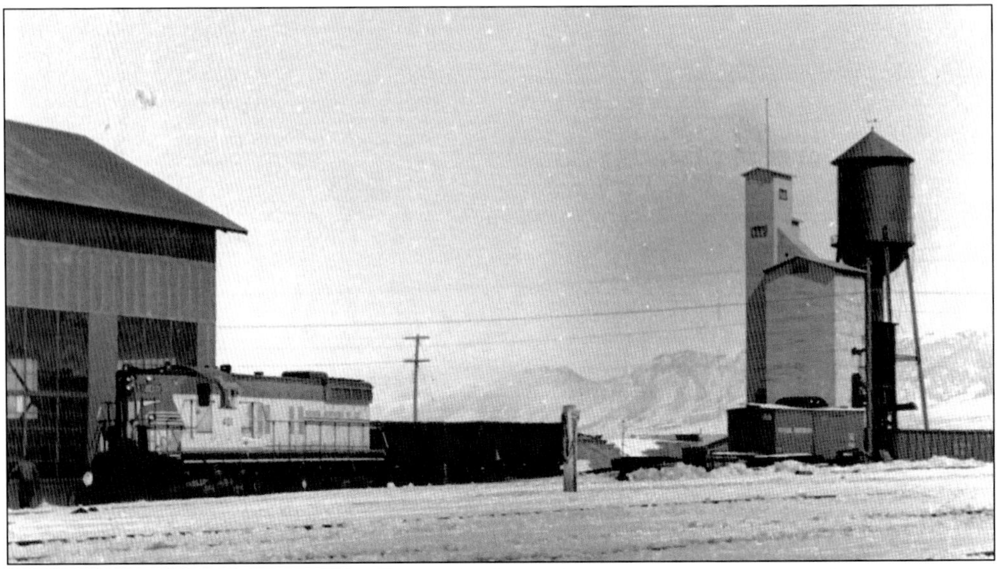

The locomotives have changed, but the work of switching continues the same. Locomotive 401 is moving two hopper cars. Between the hopper cars and the coaling tower is a view up Steptoe Valley. At the bottom of the mountain slope is McGill. The coaling tower is now used to store sand, which provides traction on slippery, wet rails.

Crewmen exchange pleasantries on a chilly November day as locomotive 101 pauses for fuel at East Ely in 1977. The ALCO RS-2 has just arrived with the railroad's Cobre freight train and still has to make a quick roundtrip to Copper Flat before calling it a day. (Benson.)

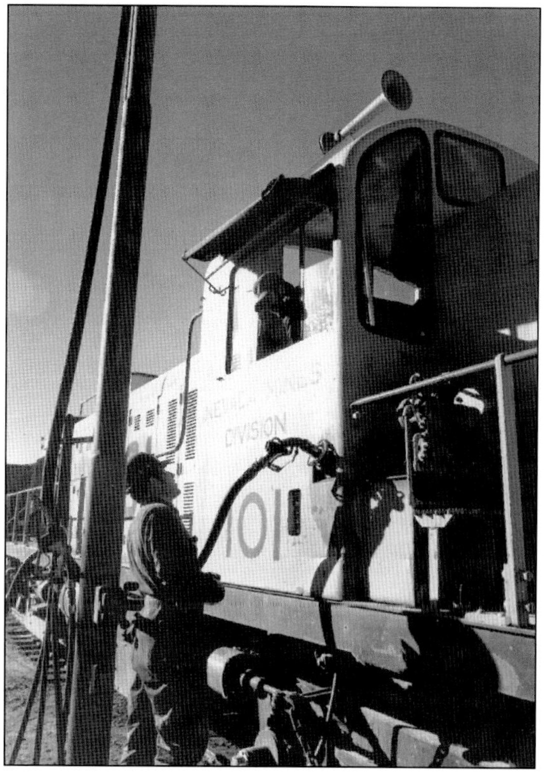

The days of copper have ended. Next to the coaling tower is the last train from McGill. It consists of locomotive 801, a Baldwin VO-1000 built in December 1942, and locomotive 802, a Baldwin S-12 built June 1952. Behind the Baldwins are the two electric locomotives (80 and 81) and string of ore cars. The locomotives will be shoved into the engine house.

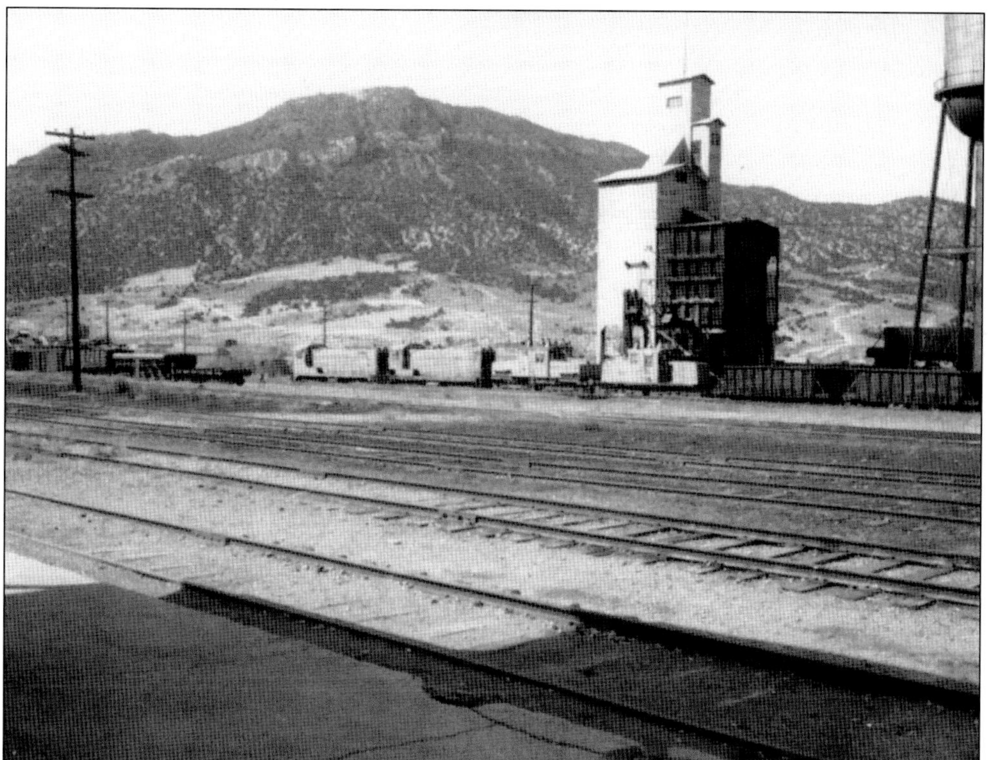

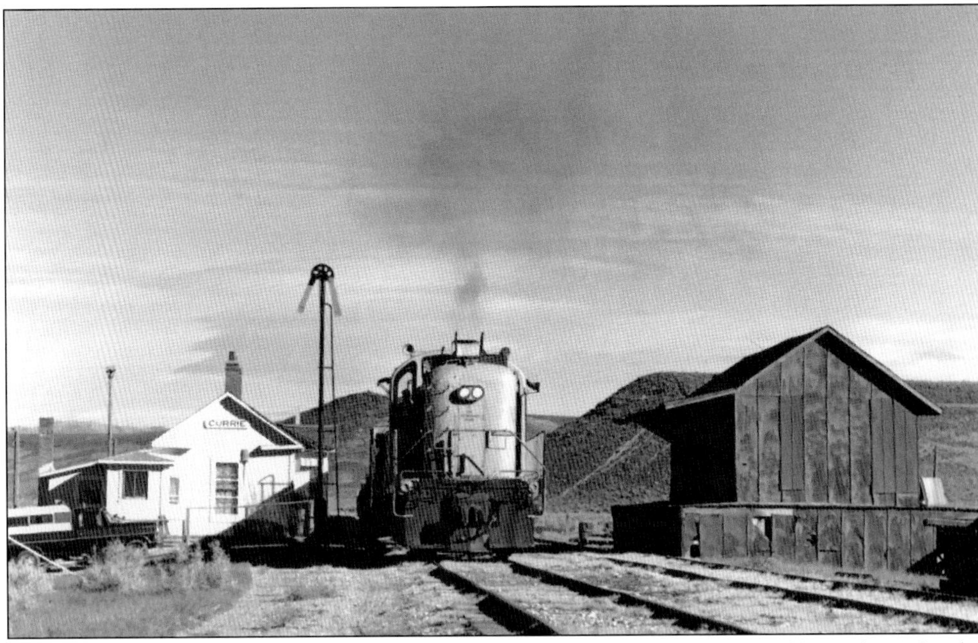

This photograph shows train time at Currie on November 15, 1977, as the southbound NN freight, behind locomotive 101, rattles the depot windows. The depot still stands at Currie long after the adjacent freight house was removed. It is no longer an open office, the train order boards are no longer used, and the station is now home to a section boss. (Benson.)

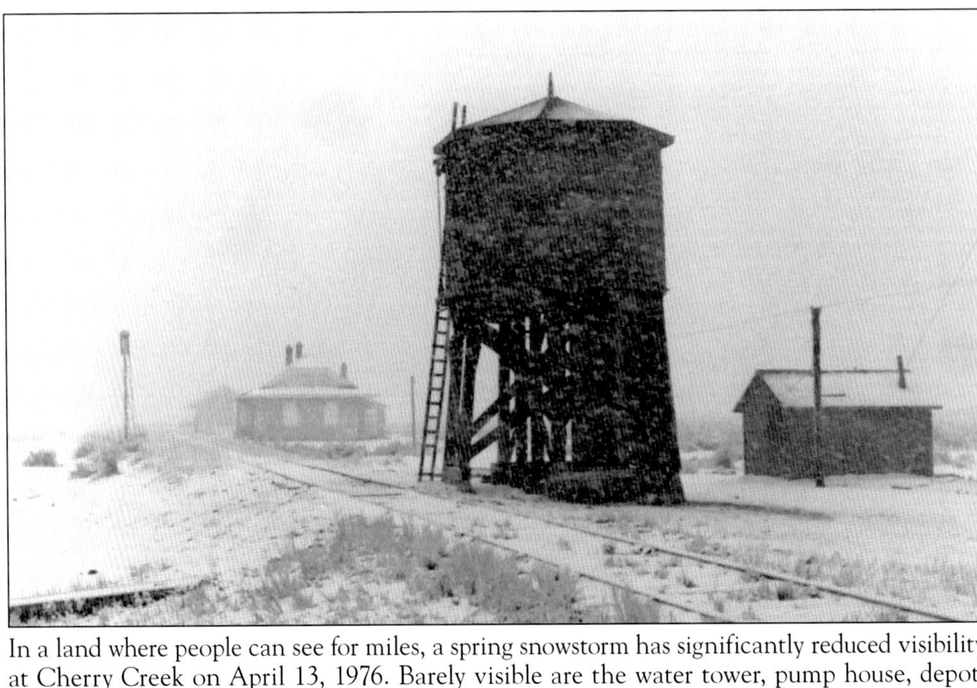

In a land where people can see for miles, a spring snowstorm has significantly reduced visibility at Cherry Creek on April 13, 1976. Barely visible are the water tower, pump house, depot, train order semaphores, and the freight house. The snow symbolized an uncertain future for the Nevada Northern, where the past would remain happily frozen in time into the 20th Century. (Benson.)

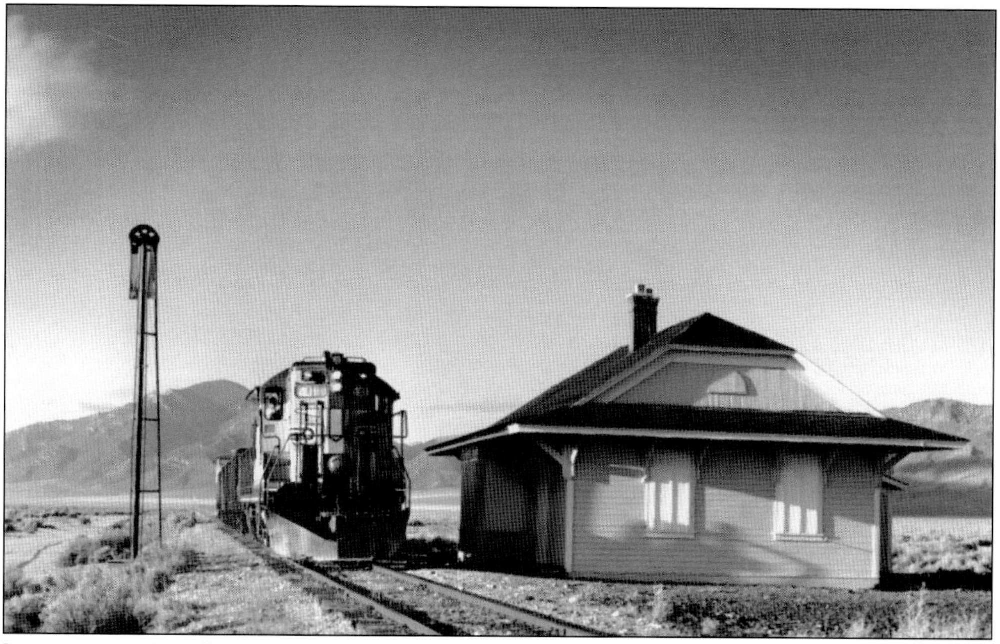

Locomotive 401 rolls northbound past the Cherry Creek station on September 17, 1976. With mining operations closed due to pollution issues in McGill, freight service is down to on-call only, with one train a week on average. Three gondola loads of scrap separate Nevada Northern's handsome diesel engine and the yellow caboose 6. (Benson.)

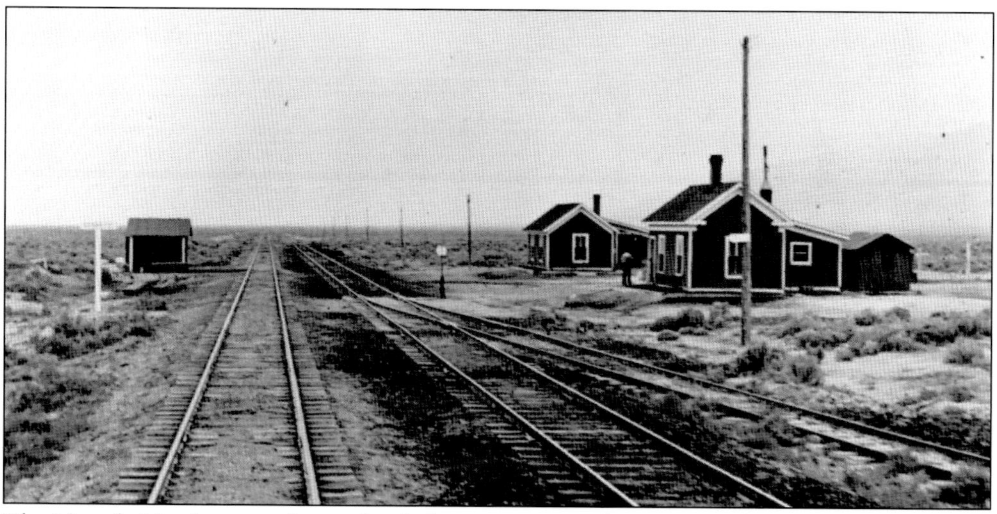

The Nevada Northern track was divided into sections of approximately 20 miles. Within the sections was a tiny community where section workers lived. This is Goshute, Nevada, located 60 miles north of Ely and 71 miles south of Cobre. The buildings on the right were the homes for the workers, and the shed on the left was for their speeder.

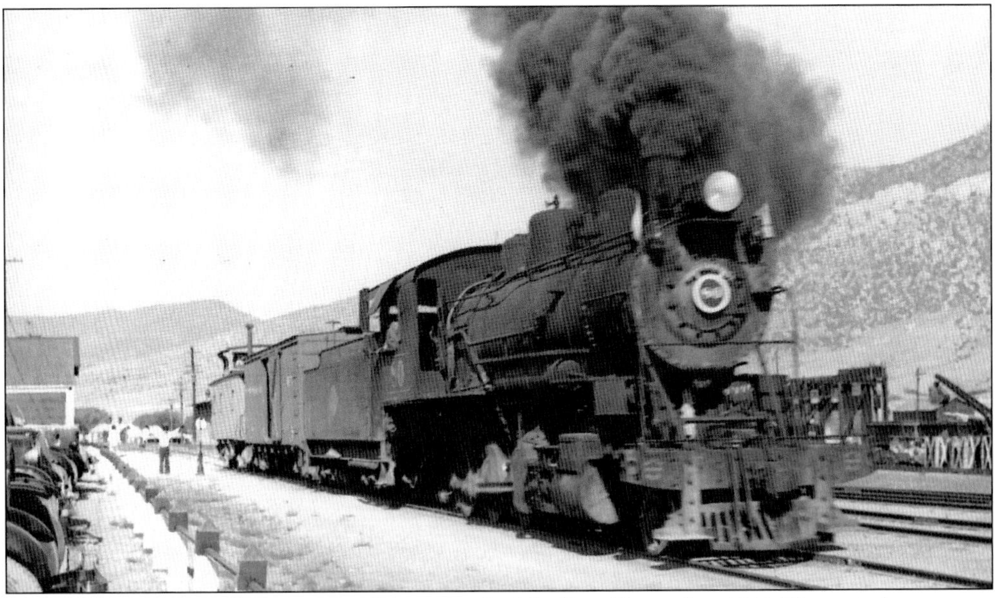

Locomotive 80 is switching cars on the west end of the East Ely yard in 1941. The switchman near the caboose is preparing to give the stop signal. Workers' automobiles line the fence. Within six months of this photograph, the country will have plunged into World War II, and the railroad will move record amounts of copper ore. (Bechtold.)

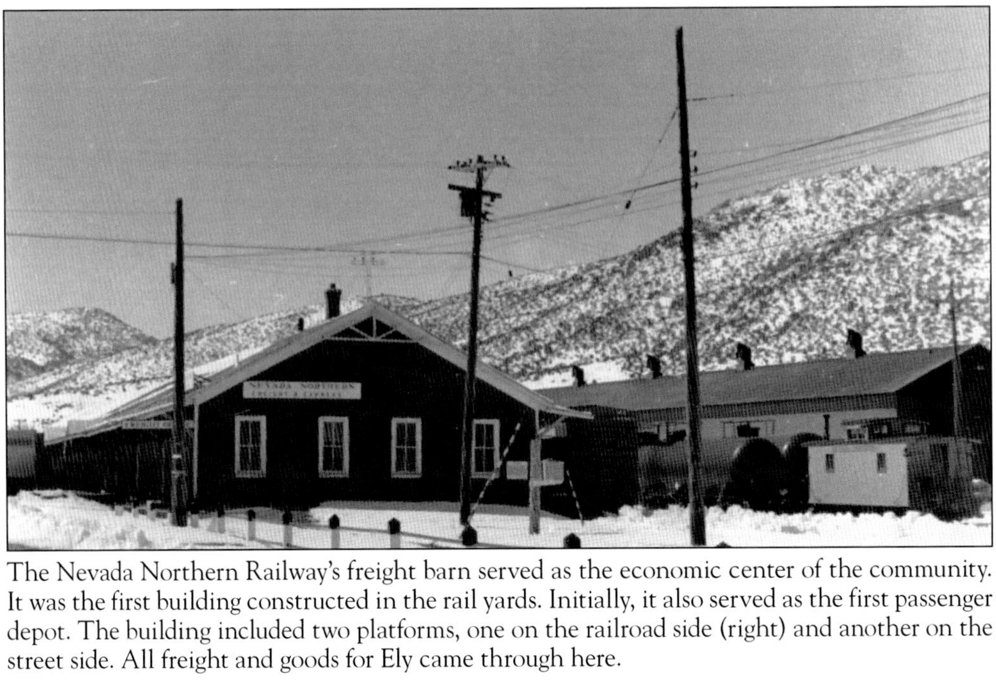

The Nevada Northern Railway's freight barn served as the economic center of the community. It was the first building constructed in the rail yards. Initially, it also served as the first passenger depot. The building included two platforms, one on the railroad side (right) and another on the street side. All freight and goods for Ely came through here.

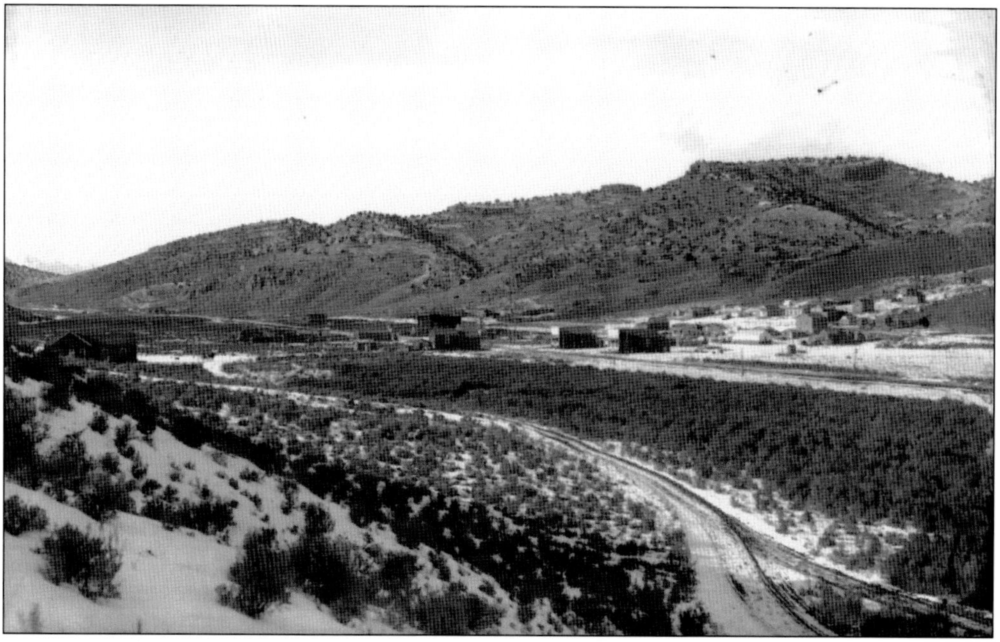

Lane City is between Ely and Ruth. Originally named Mineral City, it was settled in 1869. The name was changed when Charles Lane purchased the Chainman Mine in 1896. He invested heavily and installed a water ditch, power plant, and cyanide mill, which didn't work. It was thought Lane City would boom with the copper mines. But the mines built their own towns, and Lane City died. (USHS.)

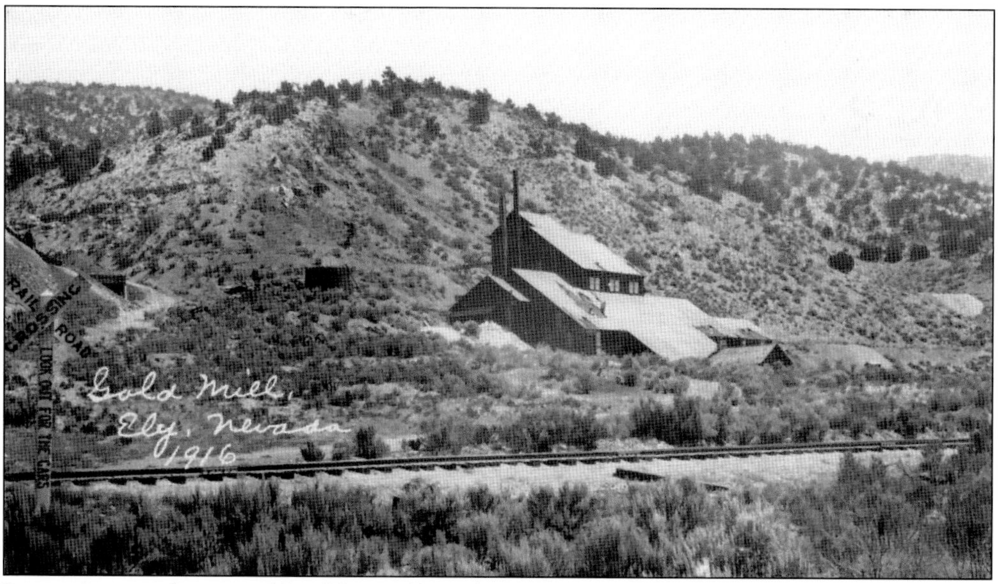

Pictured is an unknown gold mill located in Robinson Canyon. The access road crosses the railroad tracks on the left. The lettering on the crossbucks—"LOOK OUT FOR THE CARS"—refers to the railroad cars. Before the automobile, railroad cars were generically referred to as cars. With the advent of the automobile, the lettering would be changed to read, "WATCH OUT FOR TRAINS." (Novich.)

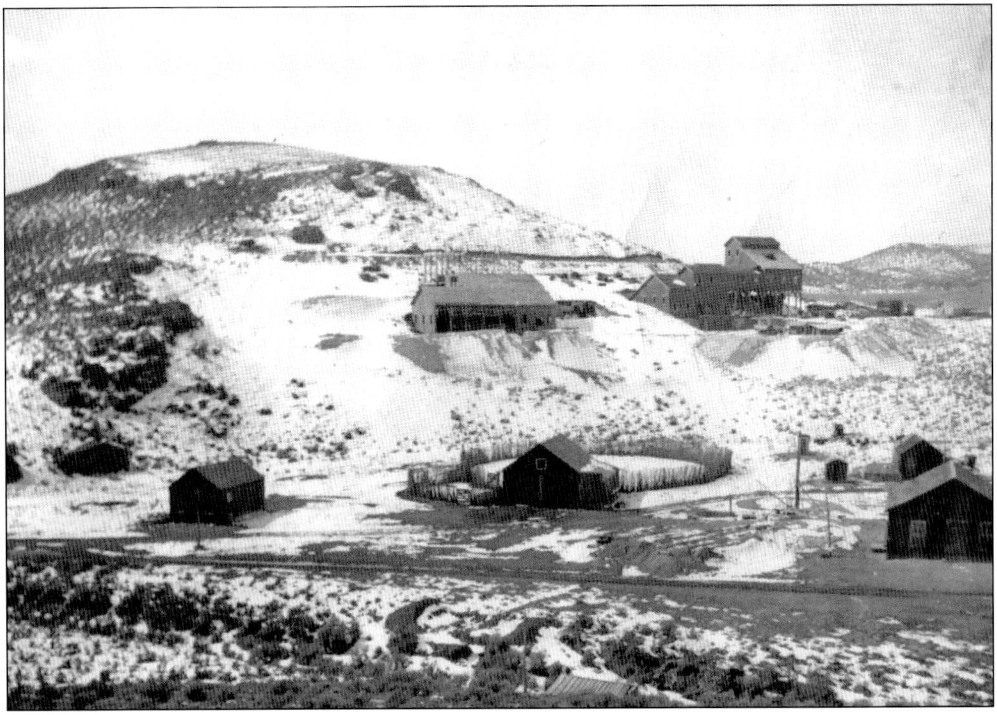

Keystone, Nevada, was the headquarters of the New York-Nevada Copper Company; one of the pioneer companies in the district. When it went bankrupt, Mark Requa purchased its claims and formed the Nevada Consolidated Copper Company. The mine was named Keystone for the equipment used there, which was purchased from the Keystone Manufacturing Company. (WPCHS.)

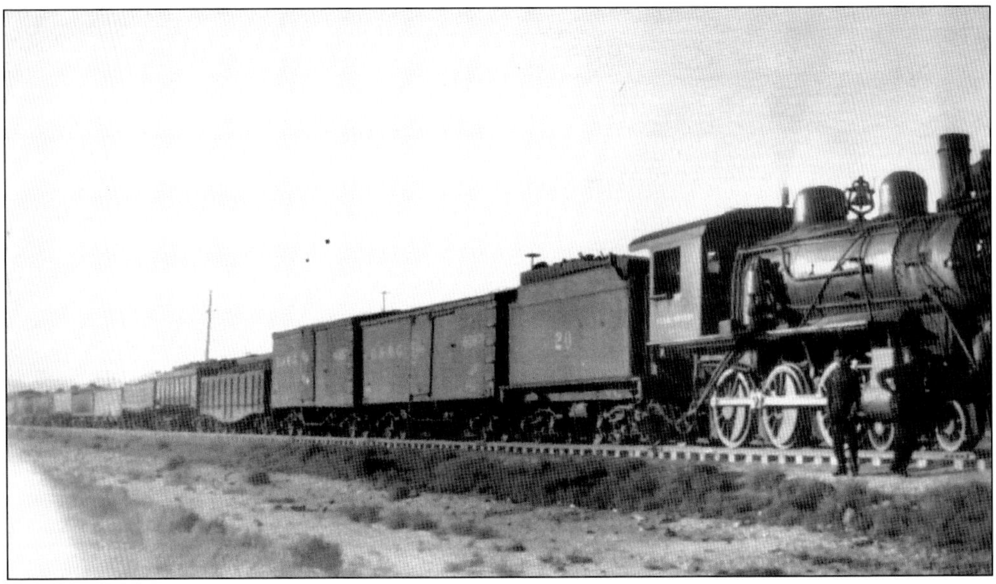

Locomotive 20 is a mixed-service model with a 4-6-0 wheel arrangement. Referred to as a 10-wheeler, the locomotive had four pilot wheels to guide it around curves, six driving wheels, and no wheels to the rear of the drivers. Mixed-service locomotives were used in both passenger and freight service. (Newitt.)

Standing next to their caboose are the conductor and brakeman. The conductor was in charge of the train, and the brakeman would couple and uncouple cars and serve as a flagman to protect the rear of the train. The crew would also watch the train, looking for any hotboxes and equipment that may be dragging. The caboose served as their office and home. (Newitt.)

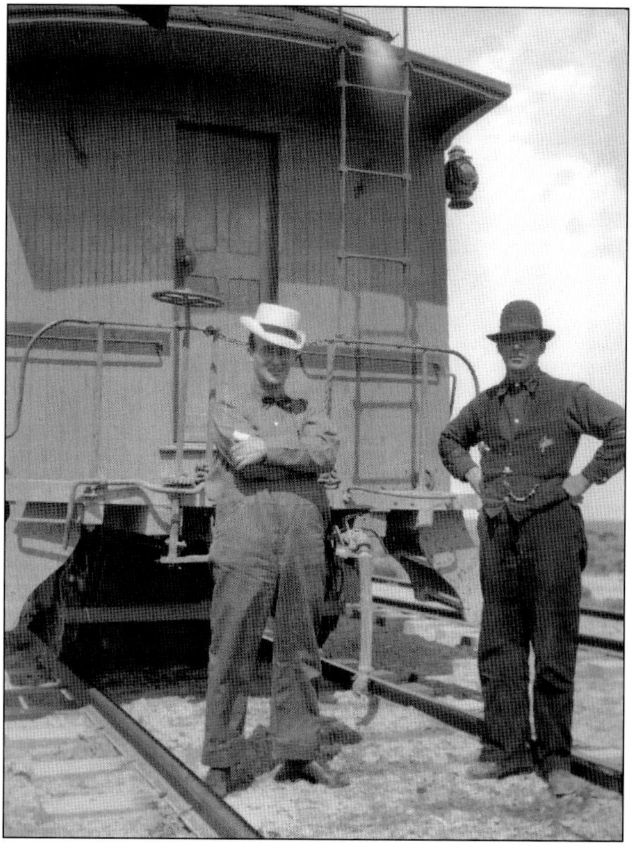

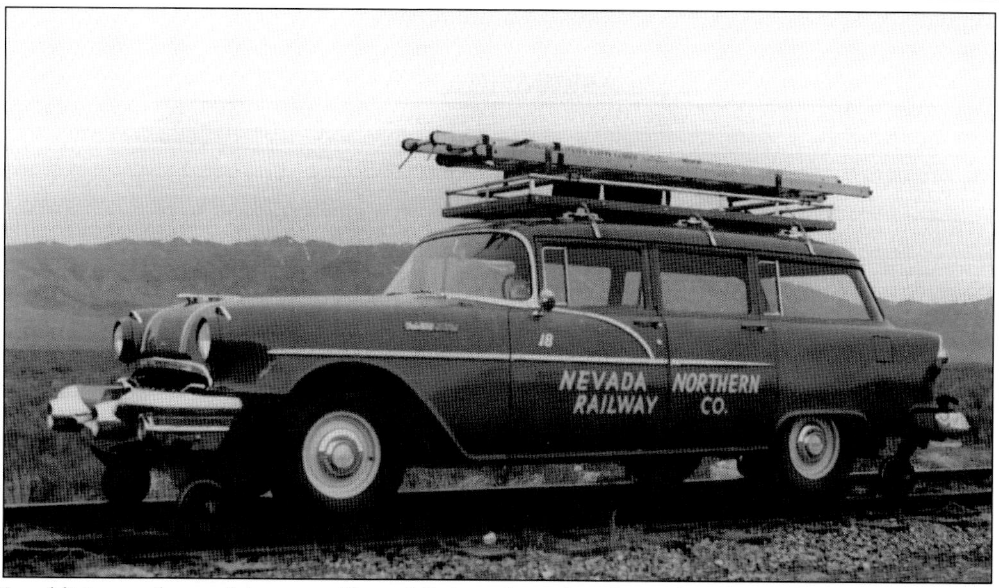

In addition to the track between Ely and Cobre, the railroad was also responsible for maintaining the telephone and telegraph lines that paralleled the tracks. The maintenance crews rode in style in hi-rail 18. A modified station wagon, it had hi-rail wheels that allowed for travel by rail; the wheels could also be retracted so that the vehicle could run on the highway. (Chappell.)

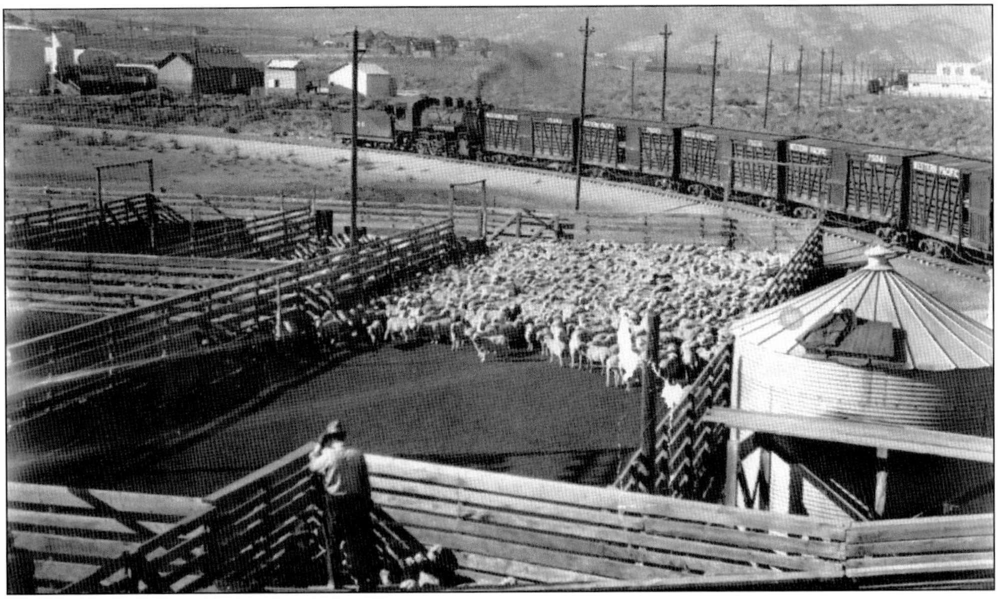

It is fall sheep time, and locomotive 96 has taken a break from its ore train duties. It is now moving stockcars at the sheep pens of the Ely stockyards. Sheep from the McGill and Adams Ranch were brought to Ely for loading into Western Pacific (WP) stockcars. Once all the sheep were loaded, the train headed north up Steptoe Valley to the Nevada Northern's connection with the WP at Shafter, Nevada. Once at Shafter, the sheep will continue their journey to market. Standing next to the long train are the engineer, the fireman, and the head brakeman. (Both, WPCHS.)

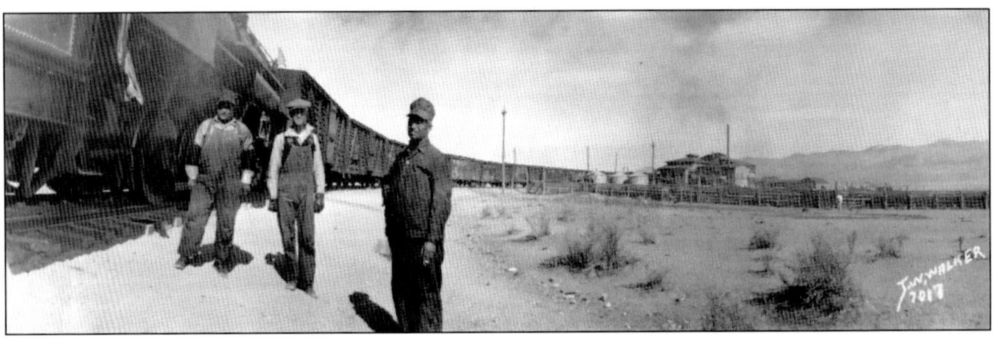

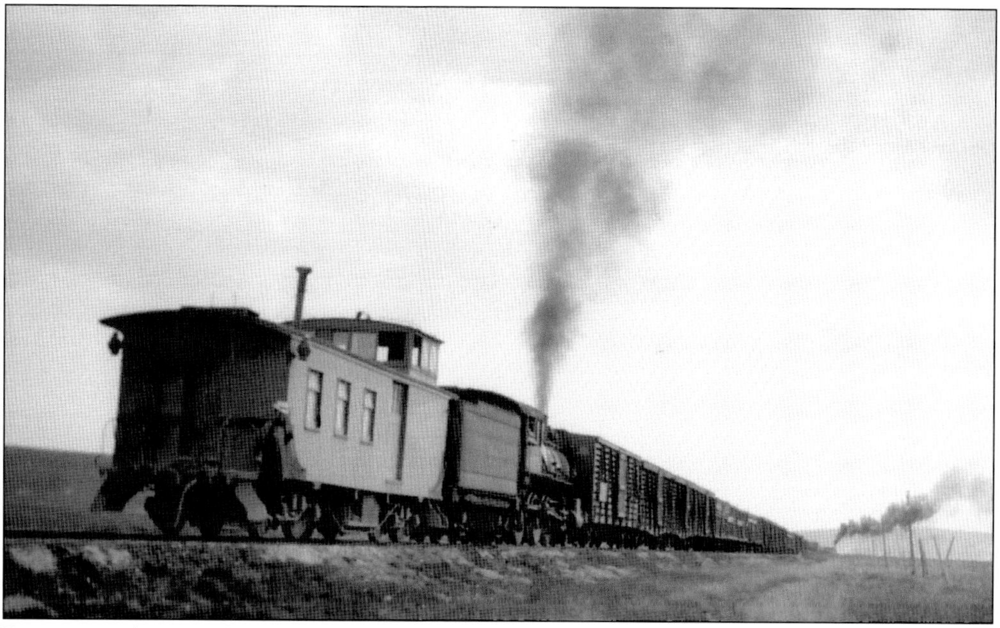

Bringing up the rear of a stock train is one of the early NN side-door cabooses, so named for the door on its side. The doors were eventually removed by the railroad. A helper locomotive, also known as a pusher, just in front of the caboose means the train must have been heavy. (Newitt.)

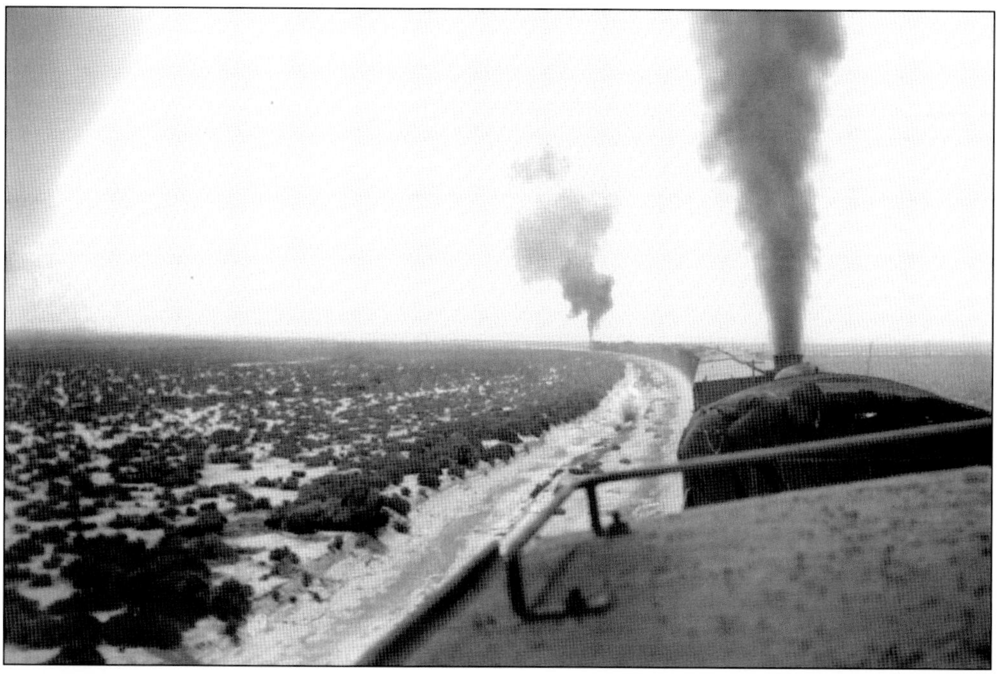

In this photograph taken from the caboose's cupola, the plume of the lead locomotive in visible in the distance. The pusher in front of the caboose is working hard. This is evident from the tall plume of smoke, the brakeman on the top of the tender is shoveling coal to the front of the tender. (Newitt.)

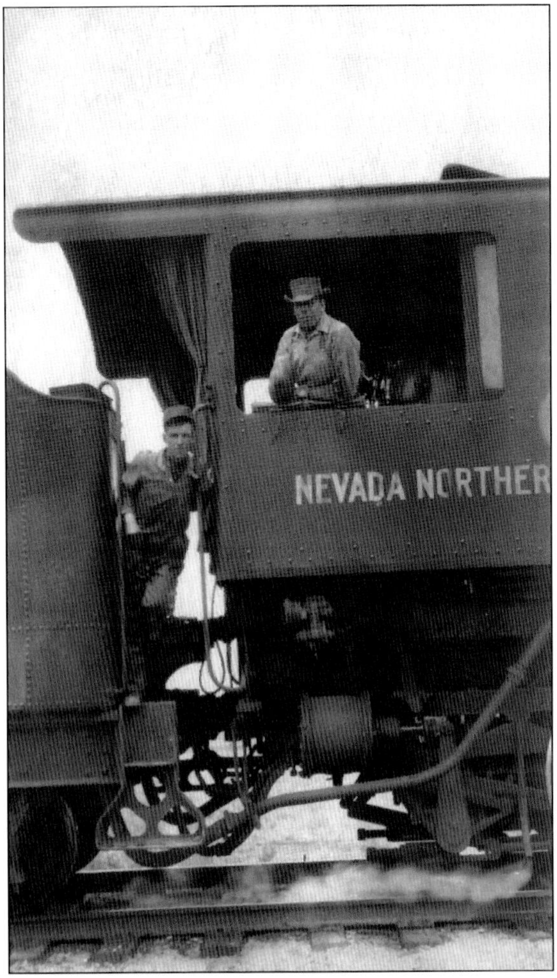

Posing in the window is the engineer; in the gangway is the fireman. The two work as a team to get a train over the road. The fireman will shovel coal, put water in the boiler, ring the bell, and watch the left side of the locomotive. The engineer will operate the locomotive and blow the whistle. (Newitt.)

Heading home to East Ely, locomotive 401 leads a southbound freight at McGill Junction. In the background the water tower is still visible even though the newfangled internal combustion machine did not need to stop for water. It would fill its fuel tanks at East Ely and run to Cobre with no stops. (Gardner.)

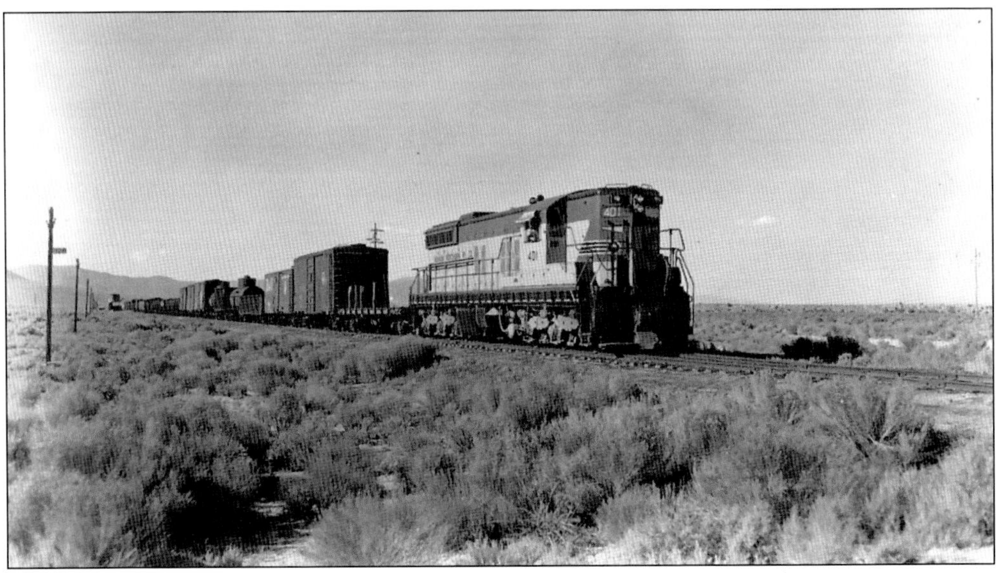

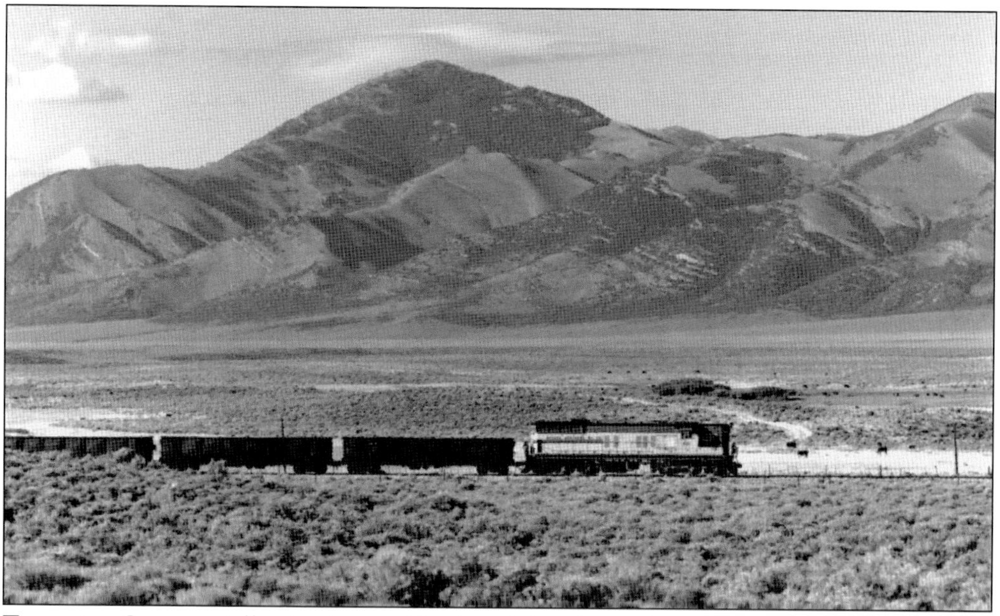

Traversing Steptoe Valley is Nevada Northern's handsome locomotive 401, nicknamed the "desert warbonnet." Here, it is leading a northbound freight train between Goshute and Currie on September 17, 1976. The scene is just as desolate today as it was when Mark Requa built the railroad in 1906. The only changes were diesel locomotives and longer cars. (Benson.)

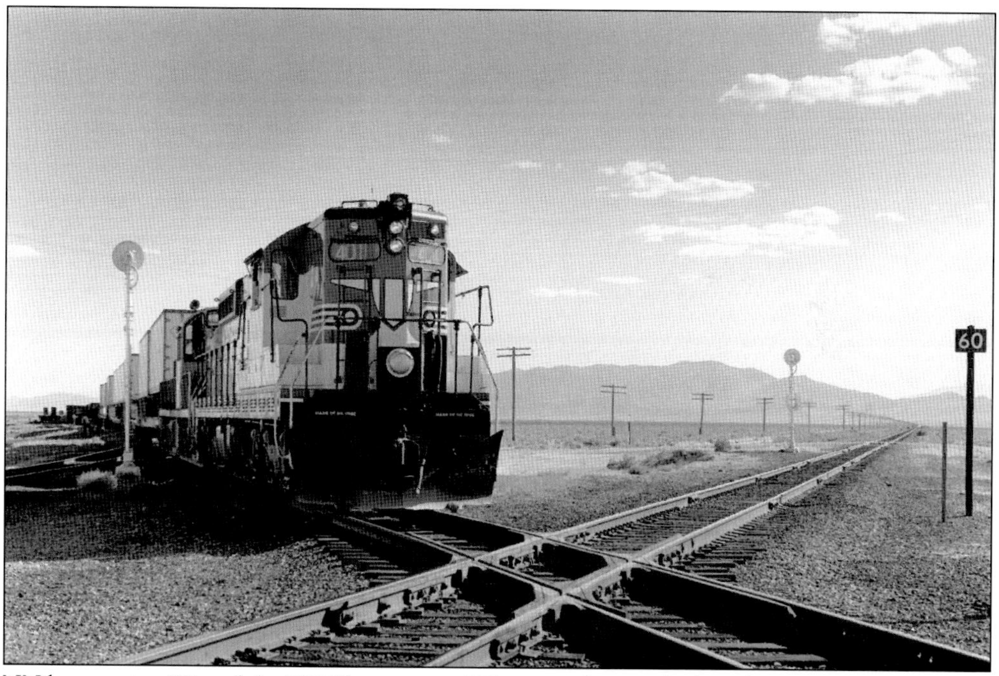

NN locomotive 401 and the KCC locomotive 105 occupy the interlocking limits of the WP crossing at Shafter on August 4, 1982. Yes, those are indeed piggyback loads behind the locomotives, which were bound for the SP connection at Cobre. Following a short layover, the southbound train for Ely would slip through Shafter hours before sunrise. (Benson.)

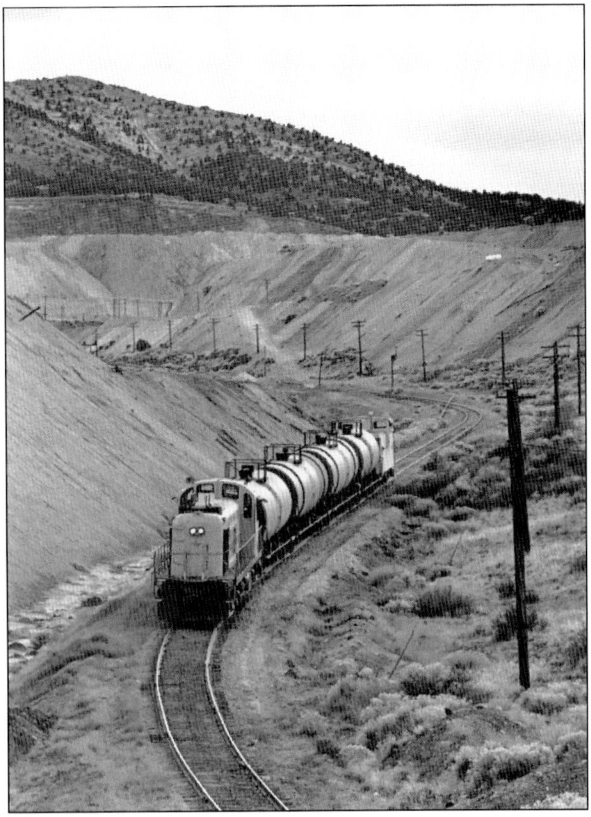

Back in the business of mining after reaching a truce with the Environmental Protection Agency (EPA), locomotive 101 leads four empty, acid-tank cars below Copper Flat approaching milepost 147 on November 17, 1977. The orange locomotive pictured was filling in for the railroad's normal freight locomotive 401 during its overhaul at Morrison-Knudsen in Boise, Idaho. (Benson.)

NN's Cobre Local, behind locomotive 101, rolls a quartet of outbound acid-tank cars past milepost 147 on November 17, 1977. Caboose 6, an extended-vision cupola model built by the International Car Corporation in 1972, trails the train past New Ruth. It was the second crummy to carry the number six on the Nevada Northern roster. (Benson.)

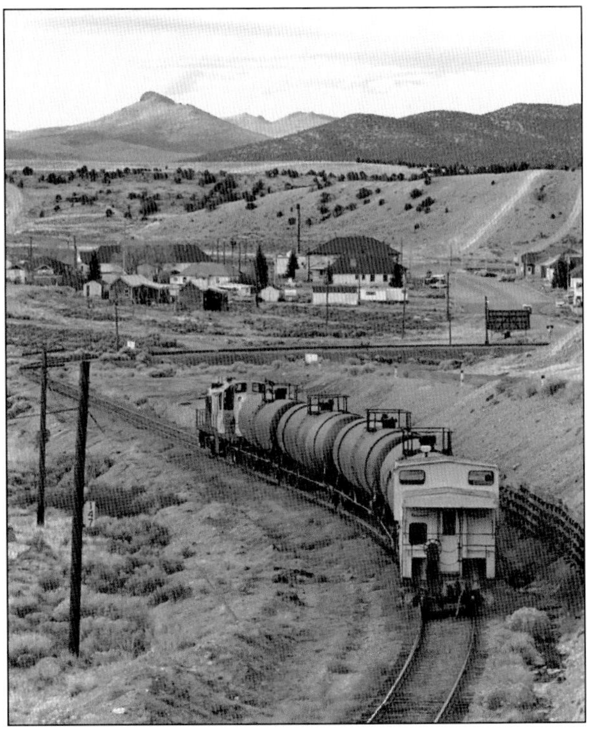

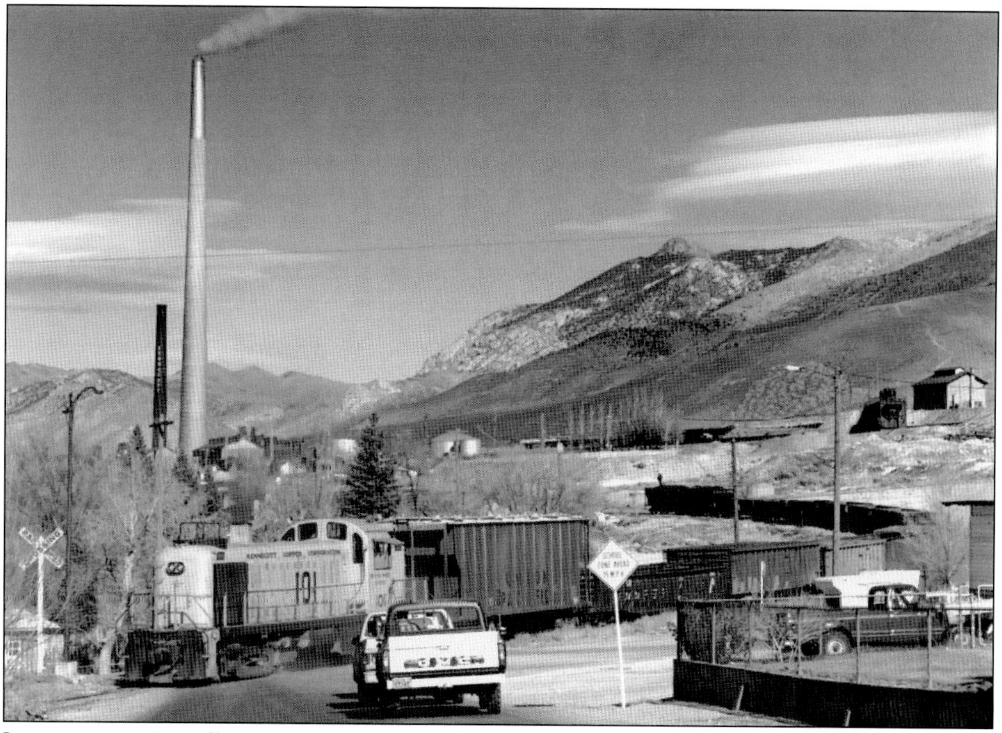

Locomotive 101 pulls a cut of cars across First Street in McGill on November 15, 1977. The brakeman can be seen on the last car protecting the move. The McGill branch provided common carrier service separate to McGill and served the depot. The Hiline branch, where ore trains operated on their own right-of-way, was farther up the hill. (Benson.)

The rails are the same, but the motive power is different. The exhaust plume from locomotive 101 recalls the days when Schenectady-built steam locomotives operated on the Nevada Northern. But it has been decades since the last external combustion locomotives stopped at the Cherry Creek water tank. The southbound NN Cobre Local is shown as it approaches on November 15, 1977. (Benson.)

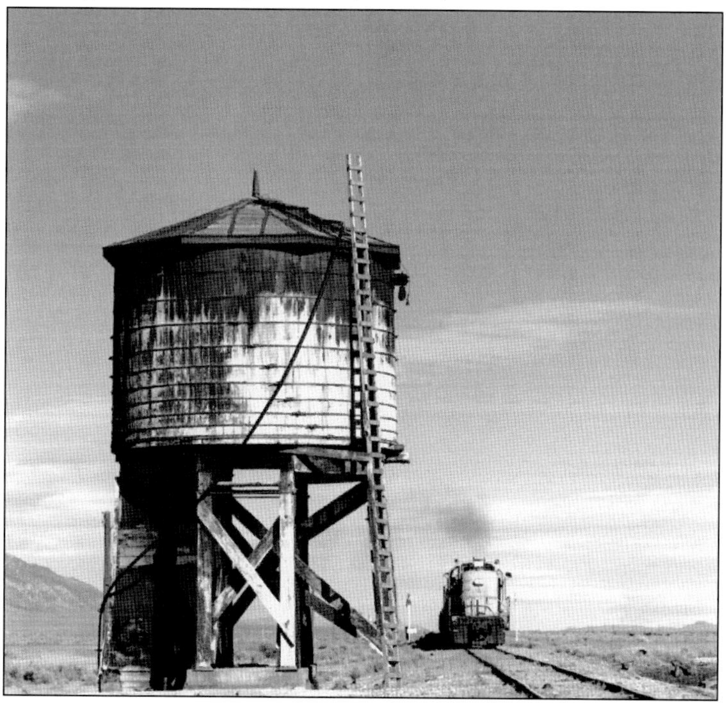

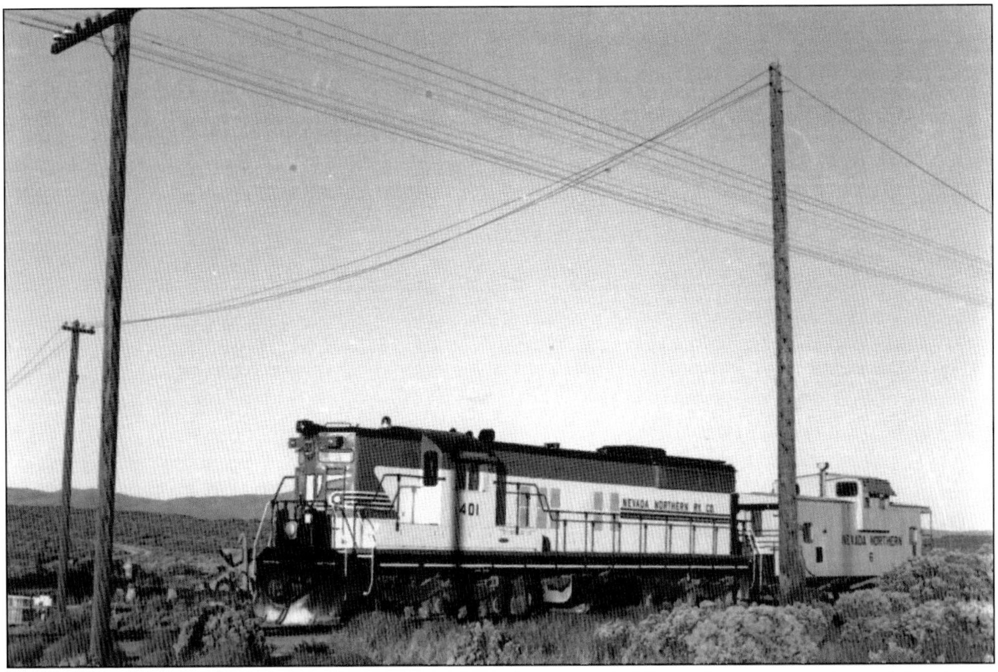

The last NN revenue freight train operated on June 20, 1983, with seven outbound loads for Shafter. After dropping the loads at Shafter, the locomotive and caboose tied up to overnight at Cobre. The next day, locomotive 401 and caboose 6 returned to East Ely, thereby ending 78 years of freight service.

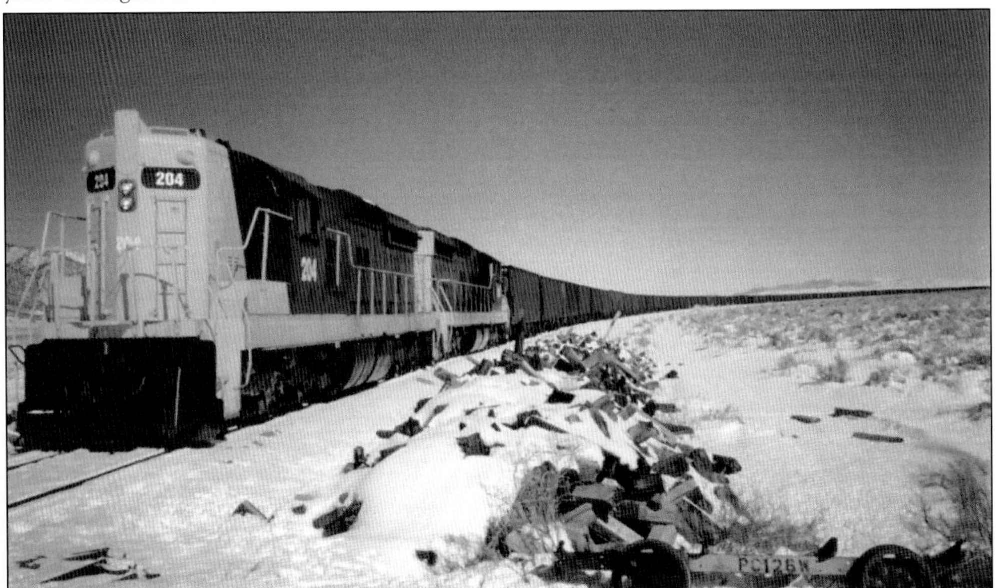

The Northern Nevada Railroad Corporation (NNRC) started a copper-hauling renaissance in White Pine County. It reopened the dormant railroad on February 6, 1996, with the first ore train to Shafter, but the NNRC was short-lived. BHP Nevada Railroad Company took over operations on June 7, 1996, and ended them three years later. In January 1999, the ex–Southern Pacific SD-9 locomotive 204 lead a train of 129 empties at milepost 87. (Timko.)

Five

A Century of Passenger Service

Since 1906, the railroad has provided passenger service to White Pine County. July 31, 1941, appeared to be the end of passenger service. No longer would it carry miners, emigrants, shoppers, school children, churchgoers, partiers, business people, or the US mail.

After the last run, the equipment was put back into the buildings. Some was scrapped, but most was kept waiting. In every decade since then, (except the 1970s) locomotive 40 has coupled up to her passenger cars and hauled people again.

The Nevada Northern Railway's principal purpose was to serve the copper mines. In addition to hauling ore from Ruth to McGill, it also brought in all of the supplies the community and the mines needed. Along with carrying ore and freight, it also provided passenger service. To truly understand the importance of the passenger service, a trip back to 1913 is necessary. Cars were a rarity and flying was only for the foolhardy or brave. For practical purposes, the only ways to travel were by walking, on horseback, or by train.

Today, we do not understand the impact that passenger trains had on society—it truly liberated them. With the coming of passenger service, they could travel in comfort across the country or across town. This is what the Nevada Northern Railway provided; a connection with the transcontinental railroads and to the towns along the lines. The passenger trains were completely intertwined with life. People rode shift trains, school trains, ping-pong trains, party trains, church trains, and even rabbit-hunting trains.

For the workers, the railroad provided shift trains. Since the county high school was a block away from the Ely Depot, school trains carried students from both Ruth and McGill. In the age before the automobile, the railroad offered ping-pong trains between East Ely and Ely. Because Ely was the established town with most of the amenities in the county, people needing to go shopping would hop the ping-pong train. On Saturday nights, a special train was run from McGill so the workers and their family could party. And on Sunday morning, a special church train was available to bring people to worship.

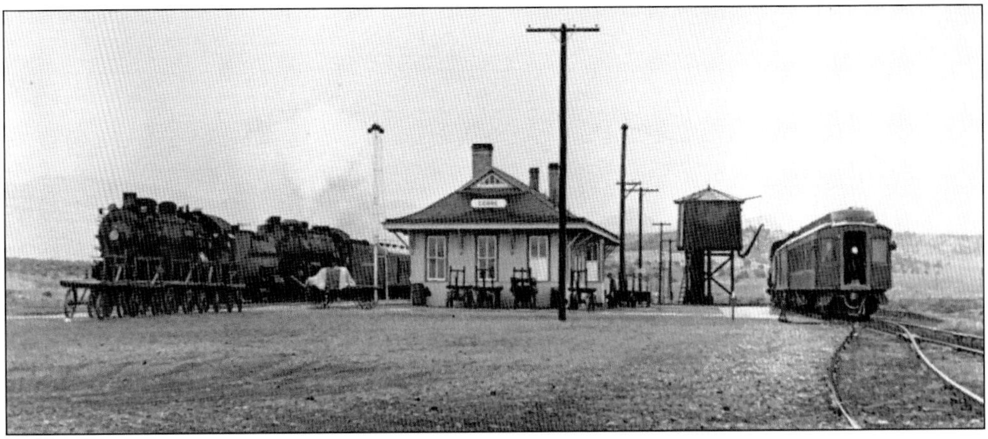

Since 1906, passenger trips on the Nevada Northern began at milepost 0 in Cobre, which is Spanish for copper. The name was considered appropriate for a copper-hauling railroad. The railroad interchanged with the Central Pacific (CP), the original transcontinental railroad. The CP morphed into the Southern Pacific Railroad. The 1913 timetable showed one train a day to Cobre and return. The train left Ely at 6:40 a.m. and arrived at Cobre at 10:50 a.m., traveling 140 miles in four hours and 10 minutes. At Cobre, 30 minutes were allotted to turn the train and water the locomotive. The trip back started at 11:20 a.m. and arrived in Ely at 6:25 p.m. Timetable speed was 33 miles per hour. (Below, Bechtold.)

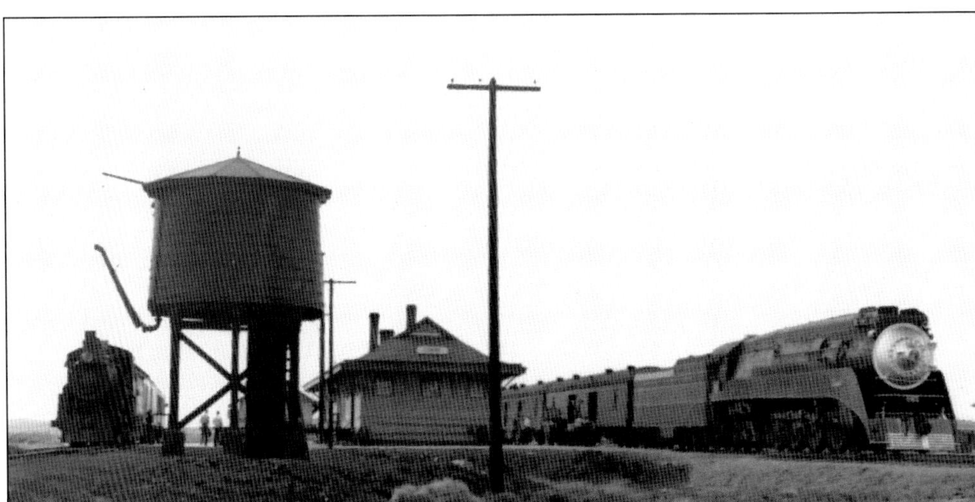

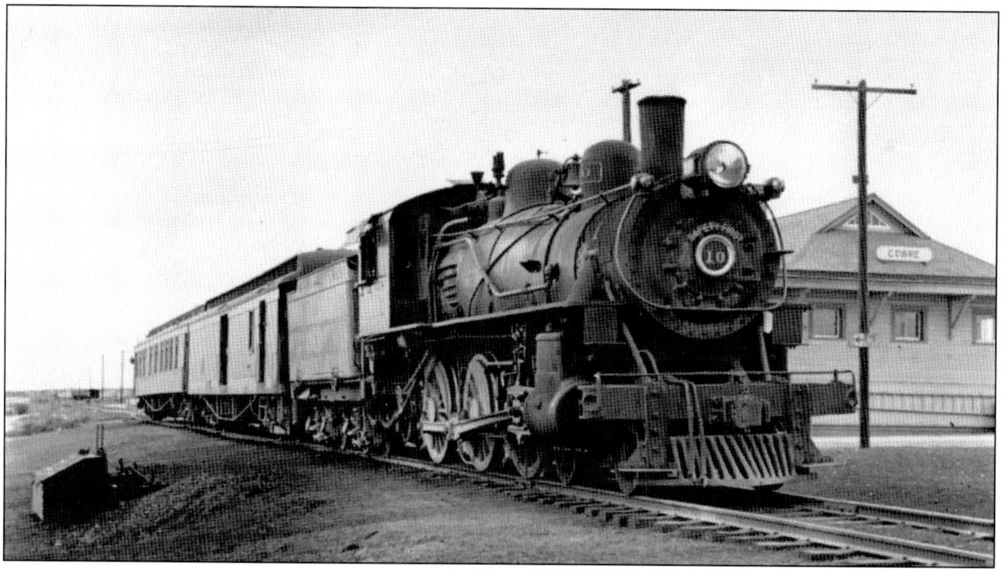

Cobre was a tiny collection of houses in the high desert. Nevada Northern buildings are located on the left side. To the right are the CP (later Southern Pacific) buildings and structures. Emigrants getting off at Cobre to continue their trip to White Pine County must have been shocked at the desolation. Today, Union Pacific Railroad trains still run through Cobre, but the Nevada Northern Railway left in 1983. Although its track is still there, all the buildings in the photograph, except for the cinderblock engine house and the old coal loading ramp and bins, are gone.

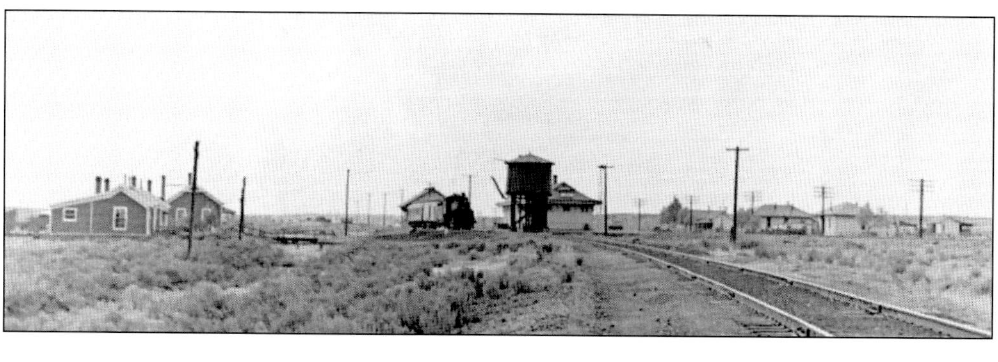

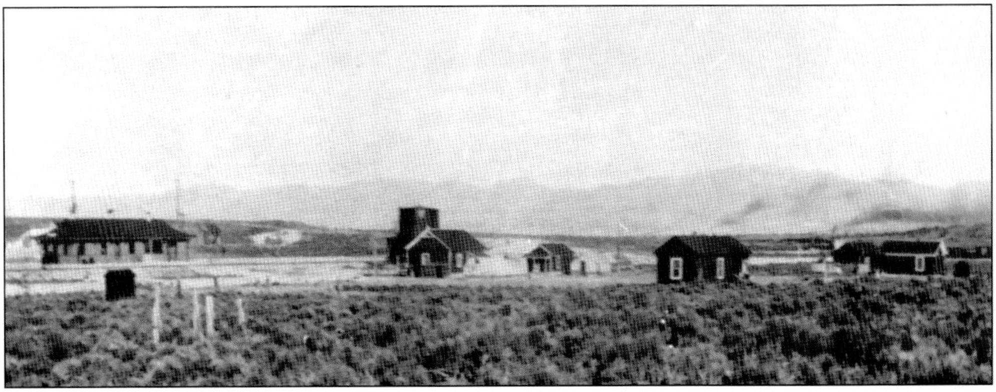

The first stop south of Cobre was Shafter. This was the WP interchange point. The Shafter Depot was on the left. The Western Pacific outfoxed the Nevada Northern. The same construction company had contracts for both railroads. WP crews got there first and built a railroad grade where the NN needed to build. This trick meant that the WP was the senior railroad, although their trains would not operate through Shafter for another year. After passenger service ended, the town disappeared. The photograph below shows locomotive 40 rolling through Shafter in the 1960s. Only a track shed is left. (Below, Gardner.)

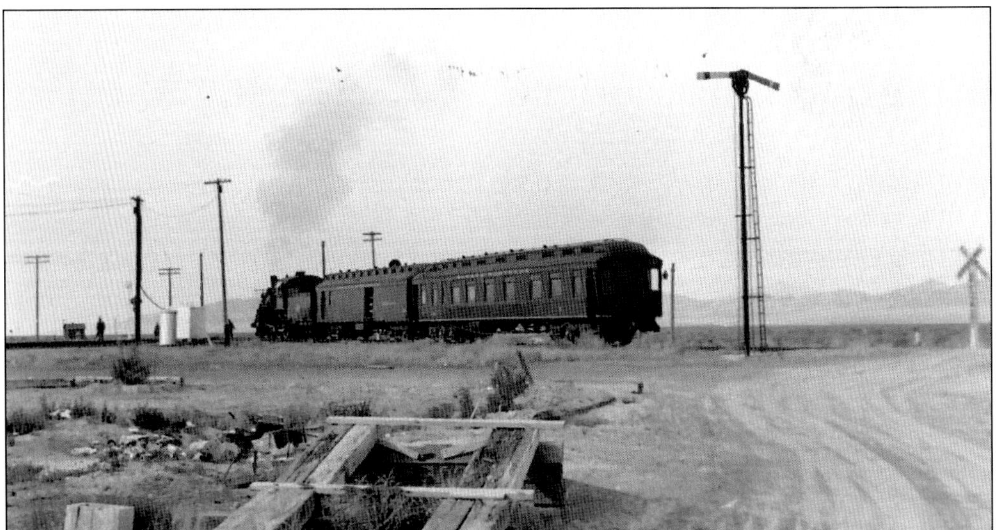

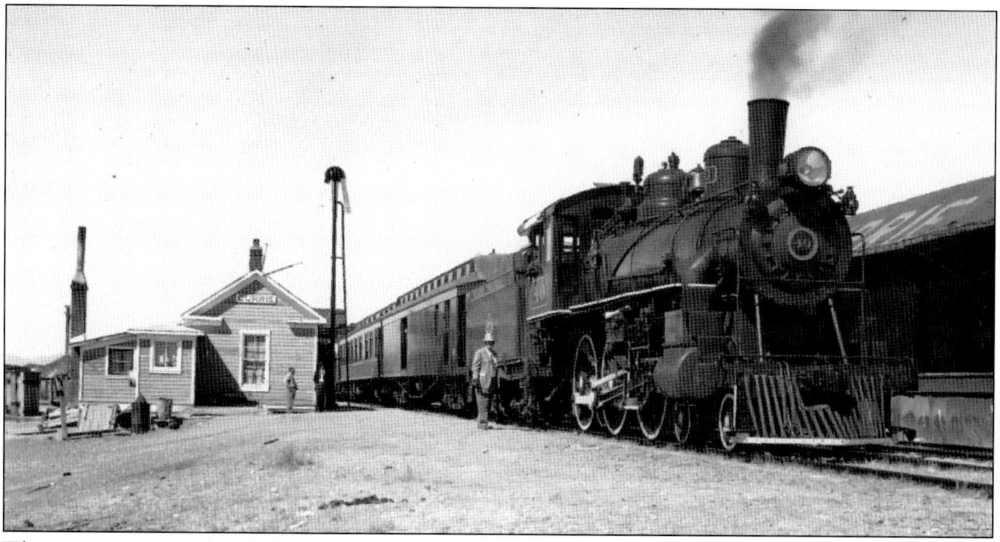

The next stop south of Shafter is Currie. Named after a local rancher, it is the approximate midpoint on the Nevada Northern between Cobre and Ely. In the background is the Currie Depot and train order board, which still exists. To the left is the Currie freight house, which now is gone. (Bechtold.)

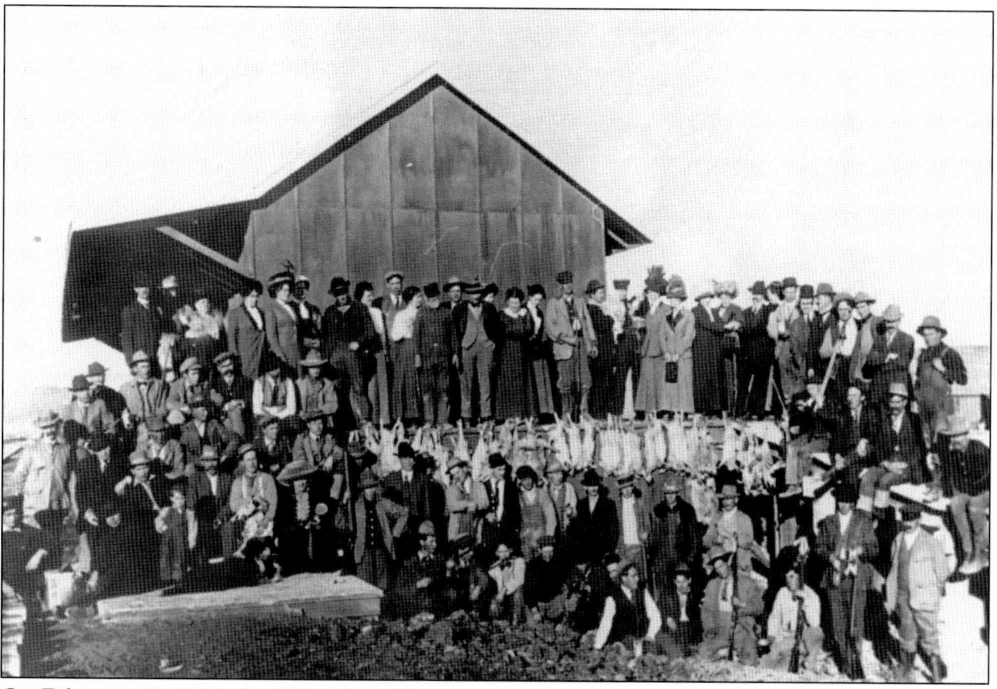

On February 13, 1910, the *White Pine News* reported, "Engine 1, the regular mainline passenger engine . . . [is assigned to] . . . the rabbit train and if she doesn't breakdown by straining herself pulling too many rabbits, she will resume the run on the mainline passenger tomorrow." The story appeared far-fetched until a note was found that before the rabbit train began, the Northern Nevada Railway Company storekeeper had ordered 5,000 rounds of ammunition for the train.

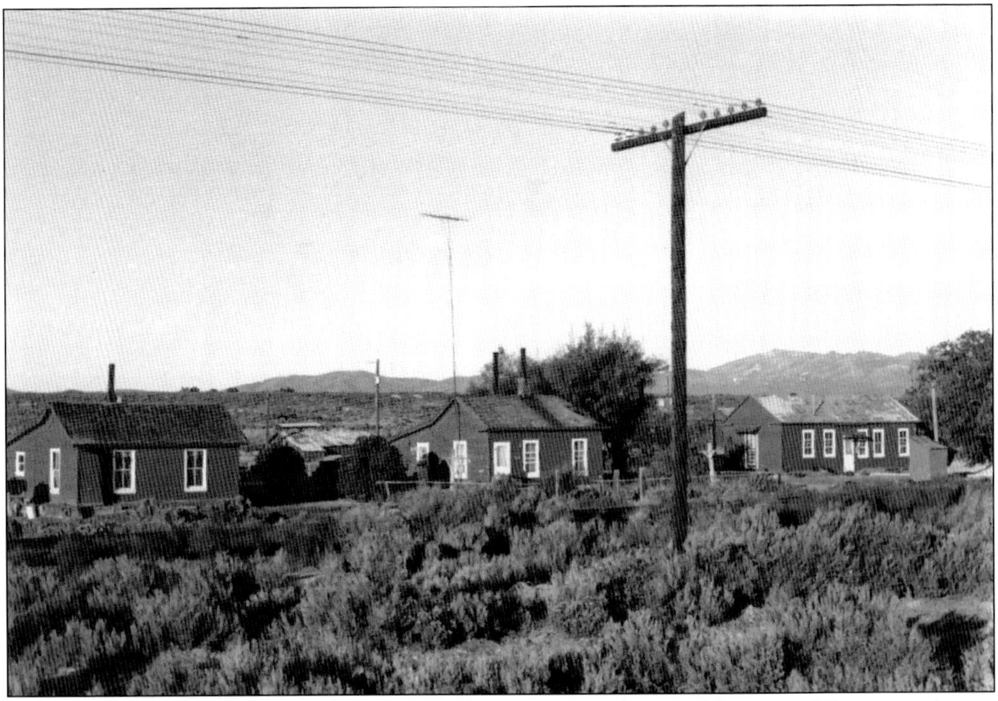

At Currie, the railroad maintained housing for the section boss and his crew. The center house was for the section boss, the house to left of it was for his helper, and to the right was a barracks for the section crew. The section gang was responsible for track maintenance in their section, including snow removal in the winter.

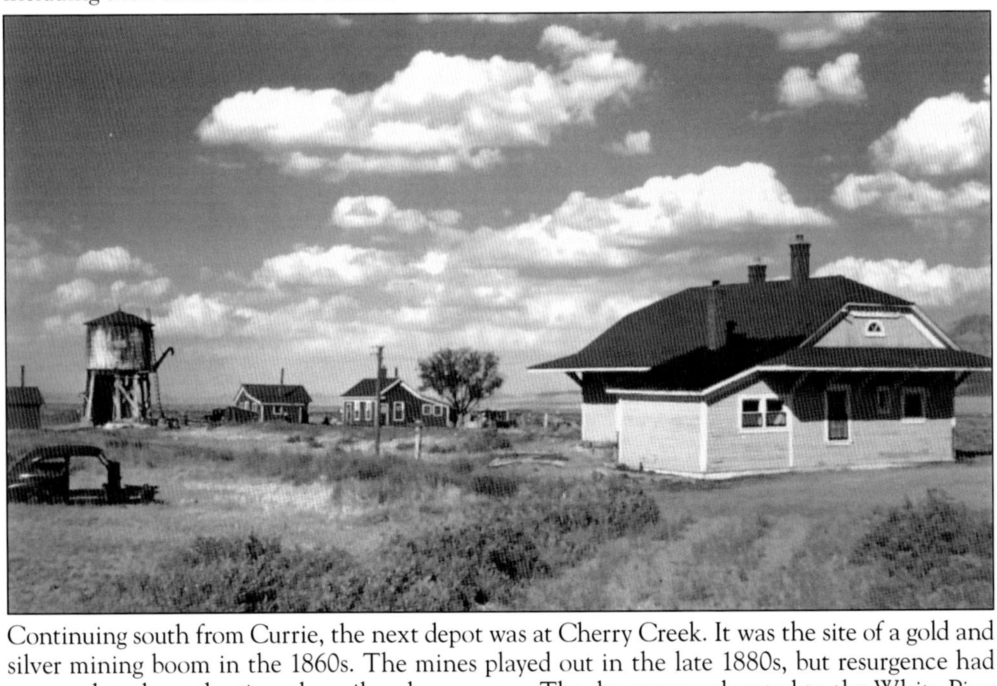

Continuing south from Currie, the next depot was at Cherry Creek. It was the site of a gold and silver mining boom in the 1860s. The mines played out in the late 1880s, but resurgence had occurred at about the time the railroad came near. The depot was relocated to the White Pine Public Museum in Ely. (Novich.)

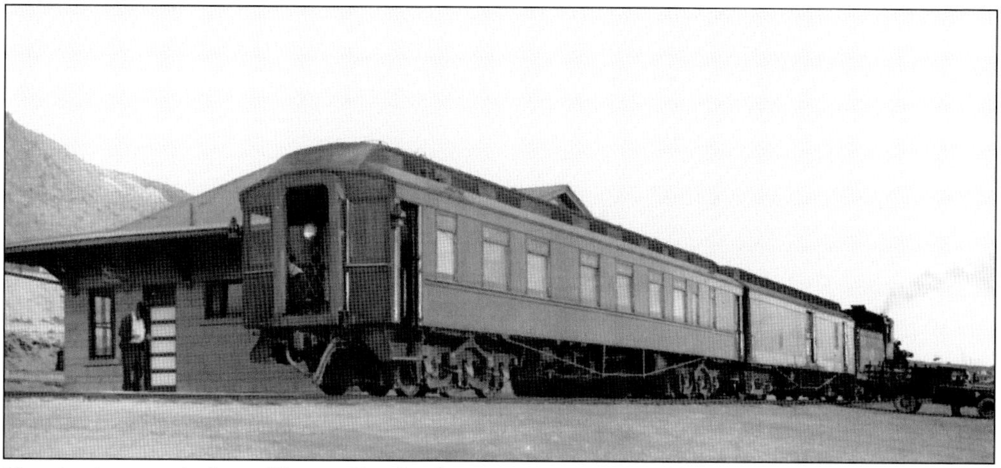

Continuing south from Cherry Creek, the next stop is McGill Junction. A wye that allows the trains to turn around ties into the McGill branch. NN passenger trains would travel the 2.6 miles to the depot in reverse. Once at the depot, passengers, mail, and express would be exchanged. (Bechtold.)

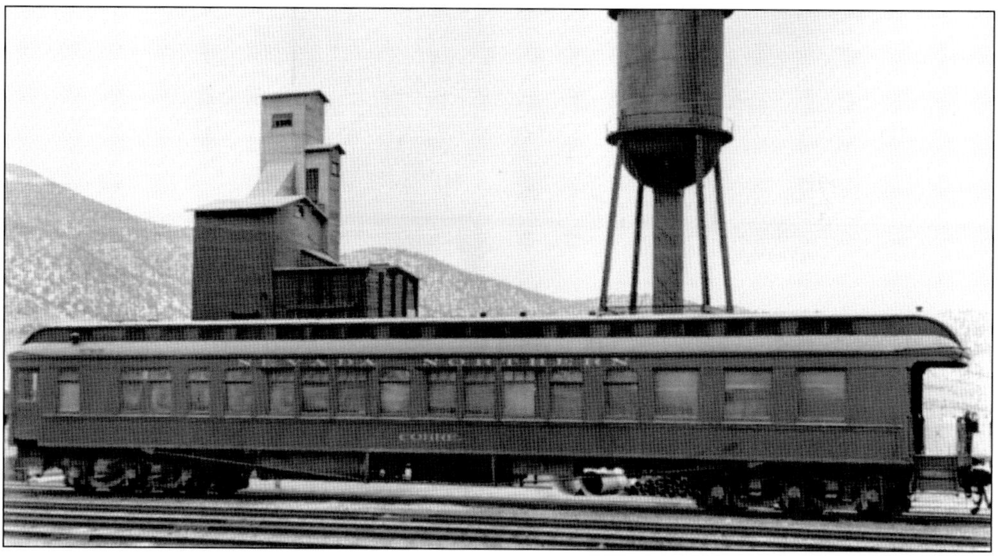

The *Cobre* was part coach and part observation car. In the rear of the car were big, high-backed chairs that swiveled all the way around. With the end of passenger service, it was retired in April 1942. The car was subsequently burned, but the precise circumstances (whether deliberate or accidental) remain unclear.

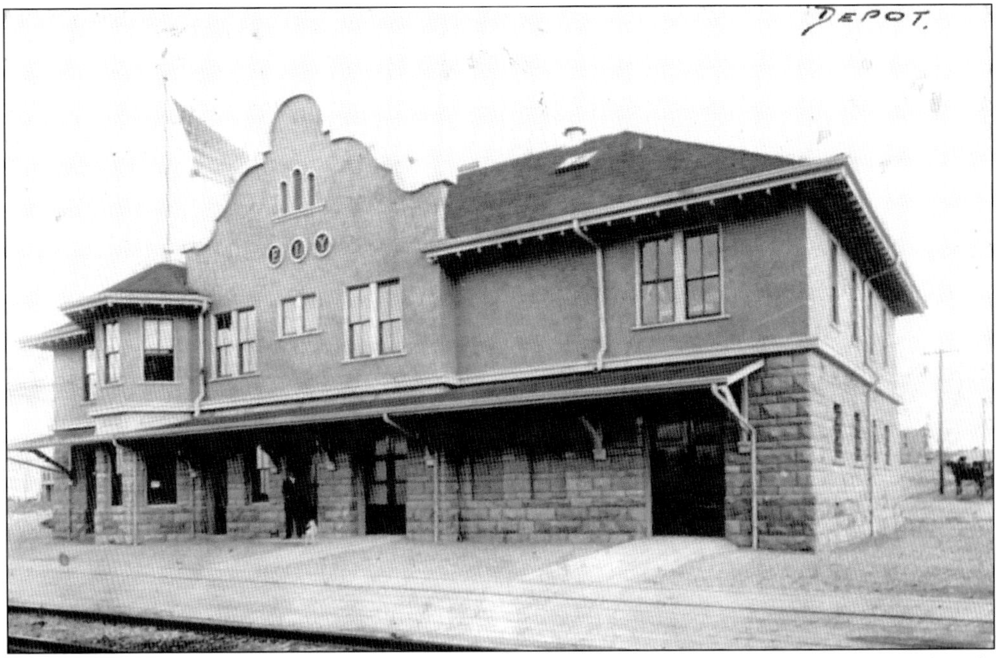

Upon its arrival in Ely, the railroad built its offices and yard east of the community. The Ely Townsite Company, a subsidiary of the railroad, purchased the land and laid out a new town. Once the depot was completed, the railroad put the word *Ely* on it. The residents of Ely objected. The railroad tried to placate the community by changing the name on the depot to Ely City, but this didn't work either. By 1908, after lawsuits and counter-lawsuits, the depot was renamed East Ely, and the railroad planned a new community. The *White Pine News* from December 25, 1906, contained the headline, "ELY CITY TO HAVE 50,000 POPULATION FIVE YEARS HENCE." The city was to be built of brick and stone with a water and sewage system, paved streets, parks, theaters, and handsome business blocks. Ely and East Ely combined when the mine closed. (Both, Novich.)

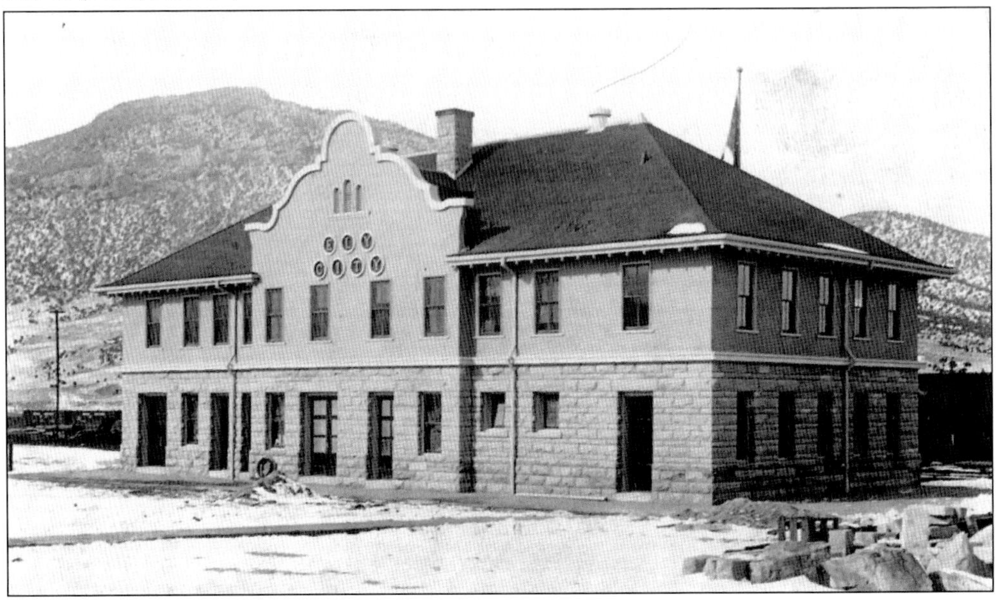

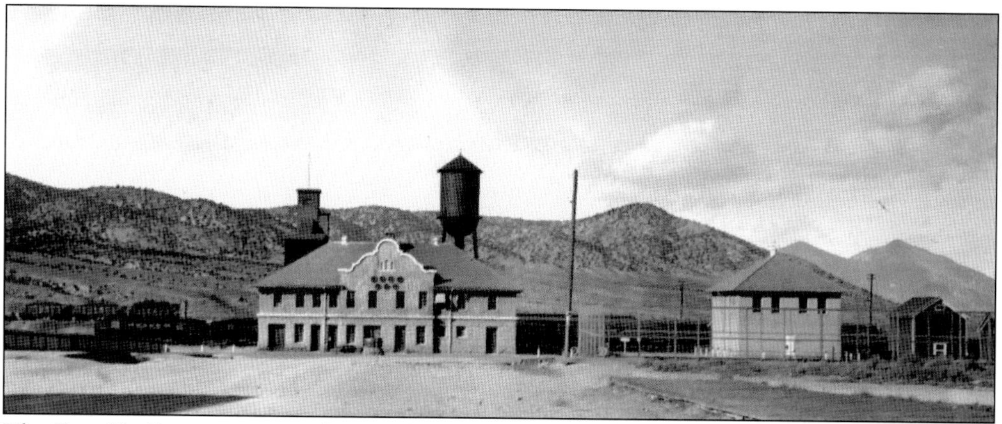

The East Ely Depot is pictured around 1920. It was located at the bottom of 11th Street East. Behind the depot is the coaling tower on the left and the water tower to the right. The building to the right of the depot is the transportation building, and to its right is the icehouse.

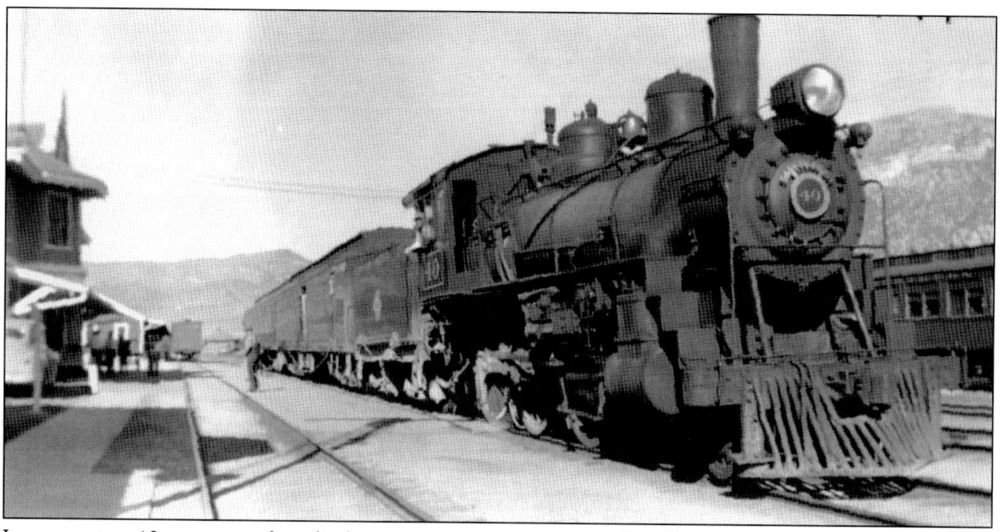

Locomotive 40 is pictured with the morning train at East Ely. Above the number plate are the words *safety first*, which is the slogan of the railroad, and even incorporated into its logo. Notice the shadow pointing to the locomotive's cab. This is a train order board controlled by the dispatcher in the transportation building. (WPCHS.)

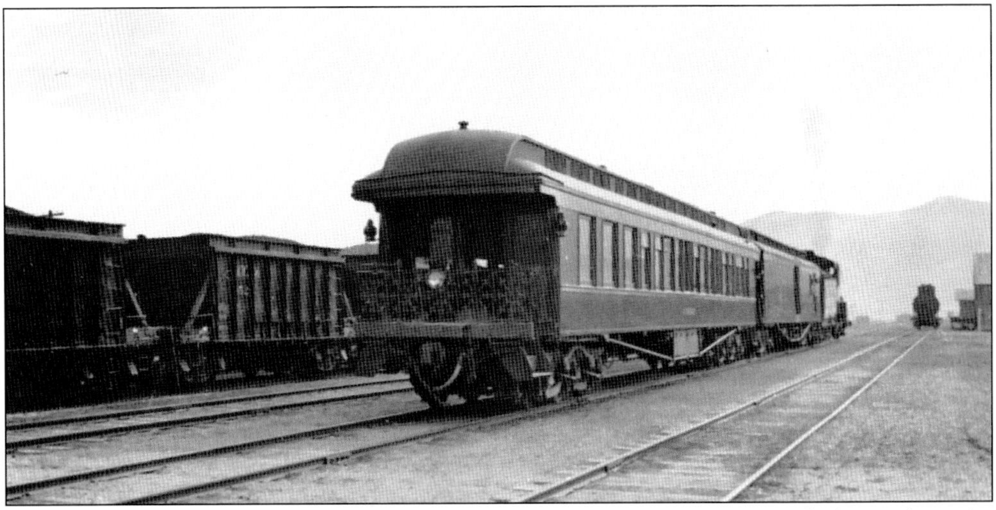

Played out countless times from 1906 to 1941, the passenger train has just pulled away from the East Ely Depot to begin its journey to Cobre. The train is powered by a 4-6-0 passenger locomotive and consists of a baggage/mail car—either 20 or 21. Bringing up the markers is the observation car *Cobre*. In 35 years, the railroad carried 4.5 million passengers.

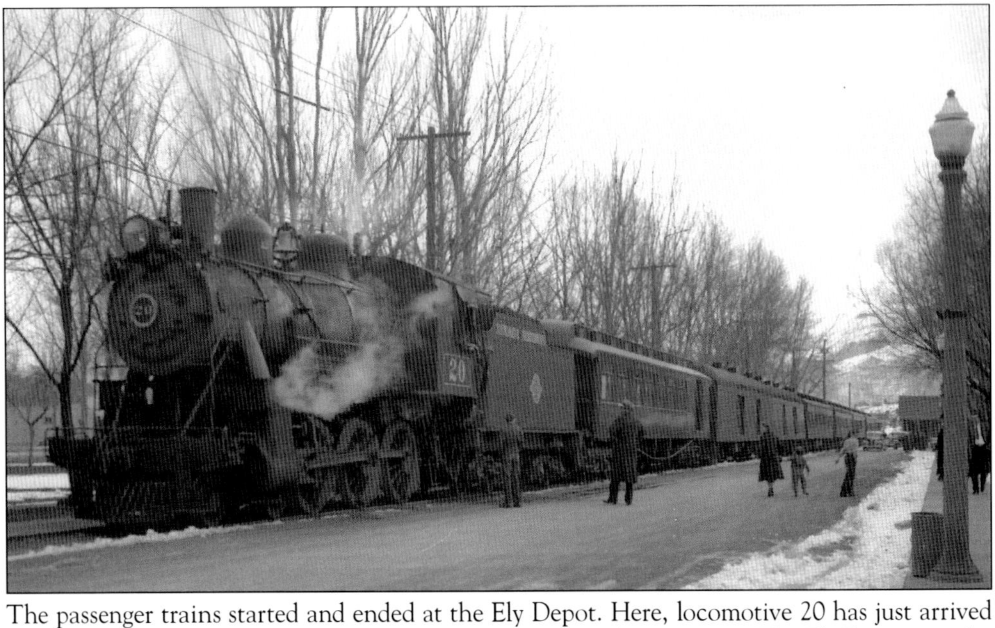

The passenger trains started and ended at the Ely Depot. Here, locomotive 20 has just arrived with a special charter consisting of eight cars, including two baggage cars. The Ely Depot is to the right of the train near the rear car. The mainline track was on Clark Street and would continue for another mile before joining the ore bypass track at Ely Junction.

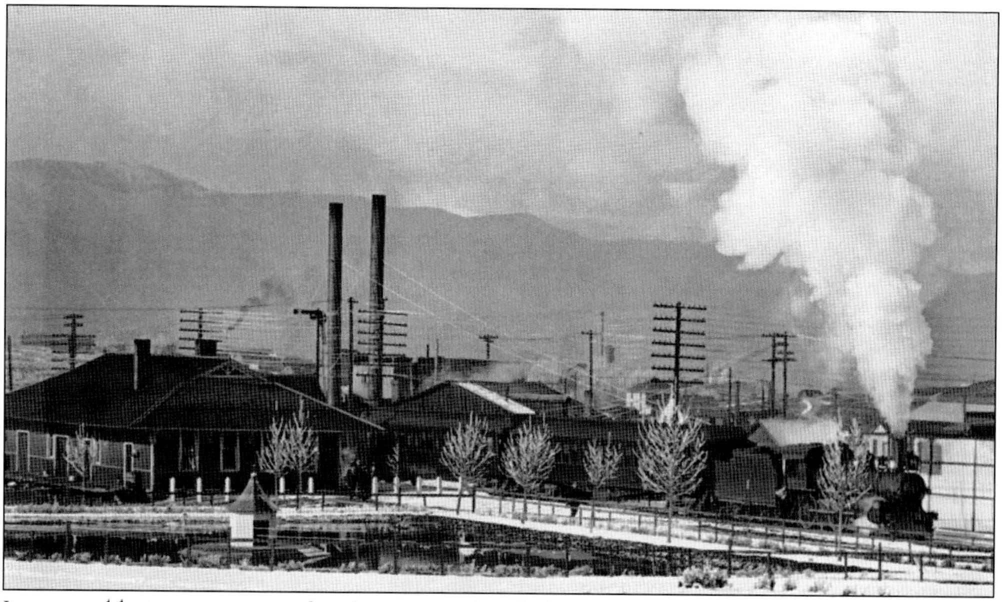

It was a cold winter morning when locomotive 1 pulled away from the Ely Depot in this photograph from around 1908. The duck pond was (and still is) located next to the depot. Notice the telephone poles and how many wires are strung from pole to pole. This is the reason for the railroad's existence—copper. The copper wire provided electric and telephone service. (NHS.)

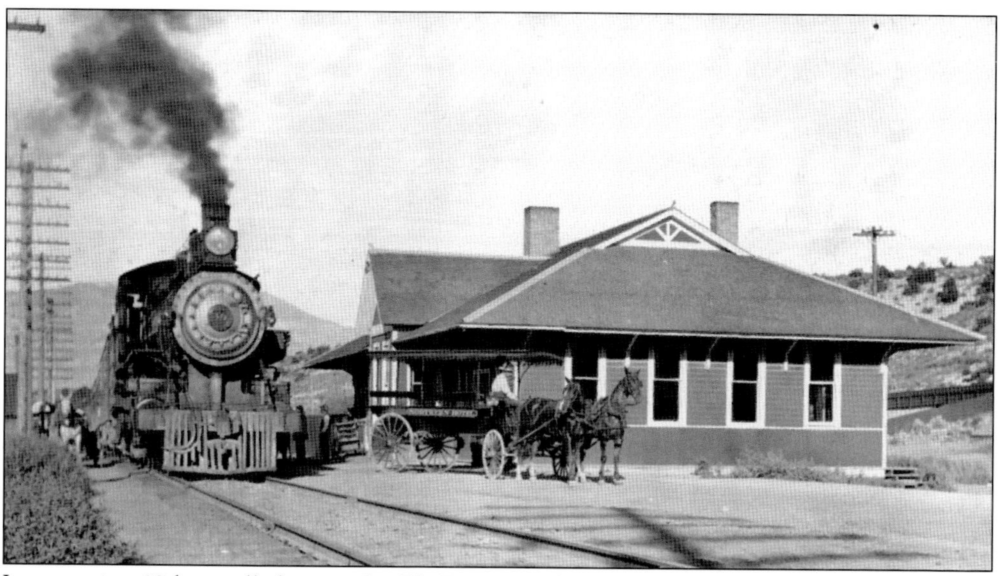

Locomotive 40 has pulled up to the Ely Depot to discharge passengers. Waiting is the two-horsepower station wagon from the Northern Hotel. When the railroad built the two-story depot at East Ely, the residents of Ely thought that they would not get a depot. After lawsuits, a depot was built in Ely. It still exists as the Mark Requa Senior Center. (WPCHS.)

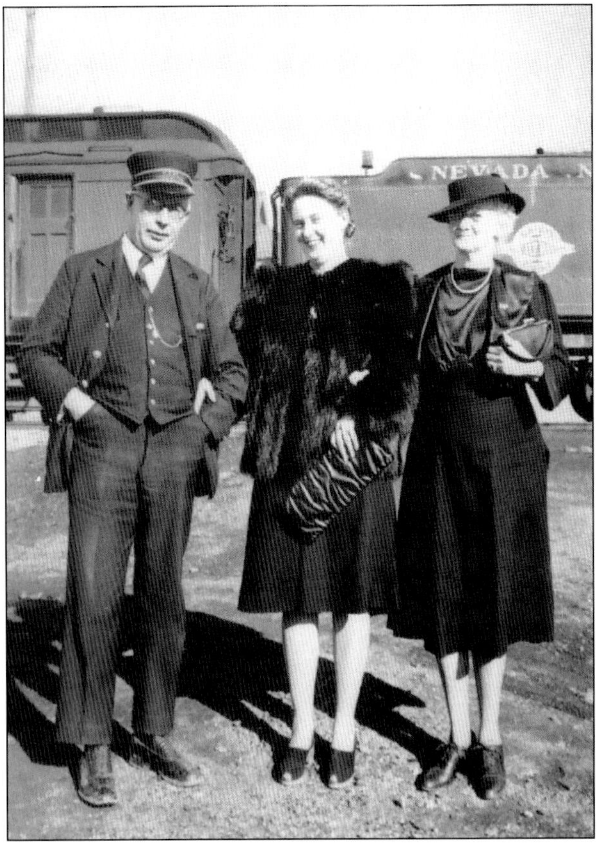

Philip Newitt started as a brakeman on the Nevada Northern Railway on November 7, 1910. He was promoted to Conductor on October 11, 1913. After 33 years, he retired from the railroad. Scattered through the book are photographs that Newitt took during his long career with the railroad. In this photograph, conductor Newitt, sister Kittie (center), and mother Georgiana are shown. The date is January 1941. (Newitt.)

Locomotive 94 has a special duty in this photograph from around 1915. Tied to a five-car passenger train, the engineer is reviewing his train orders prior to departure. The location appears to be Clark Street with the Northern Hotel in the background. Locomotive 94 was purchased in 1910 for $15,908. A 2-8-0 locomotive, it was normally used in ore service. It was scrapped at McGill in 1951. (Newitt.)

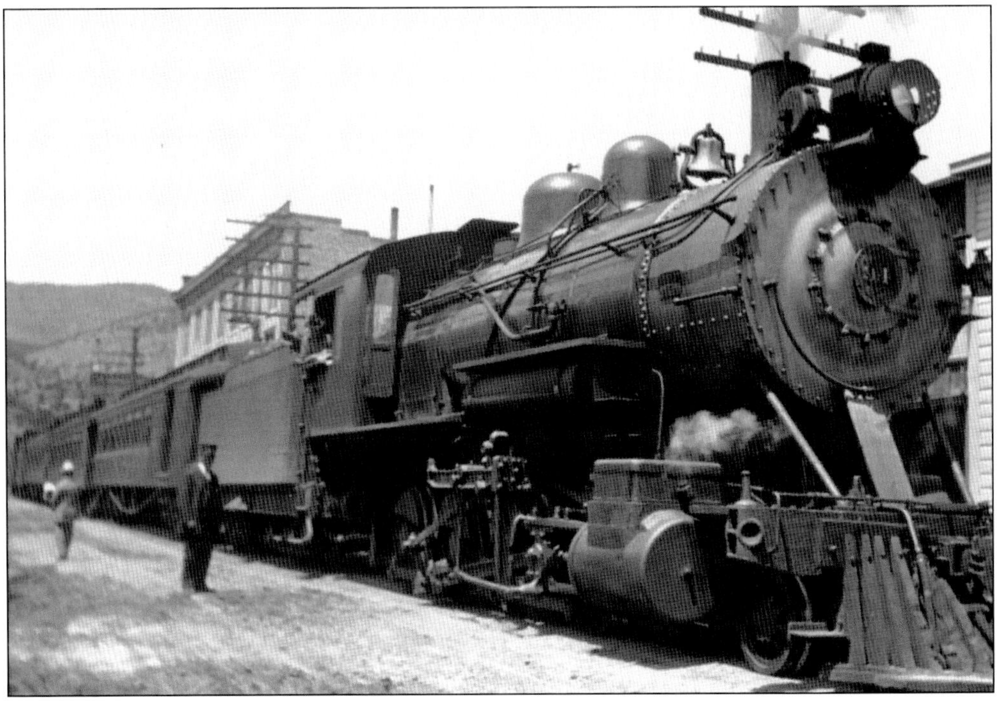

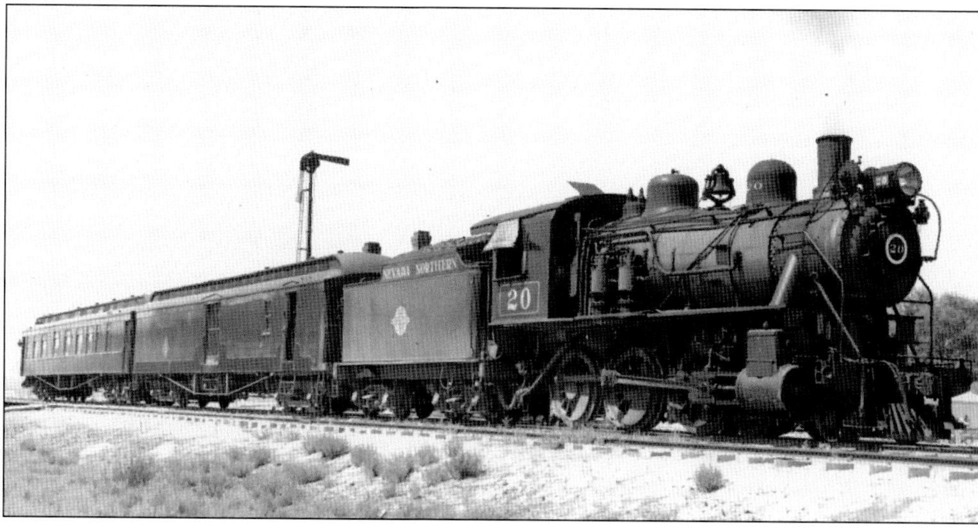

On July 8, 1941, photographer A.C. Phelps chased the Cobre-to-Ely passenger train. Shown above, the train is stopped at Cherry Creek. Rising above the train is the train order board set in the stop position. The station agent set the board manually. Below, it is late afternoon by the time locomotive 20 arrives in Ely with the passenger train. Standing in front of the pilot is the conductor and the engineer. It appears that two passengers have gotten off the train. Just 23 days after this photograph was taken, passenger service on the Nevada Northern Railway would end. (Bechtold.)

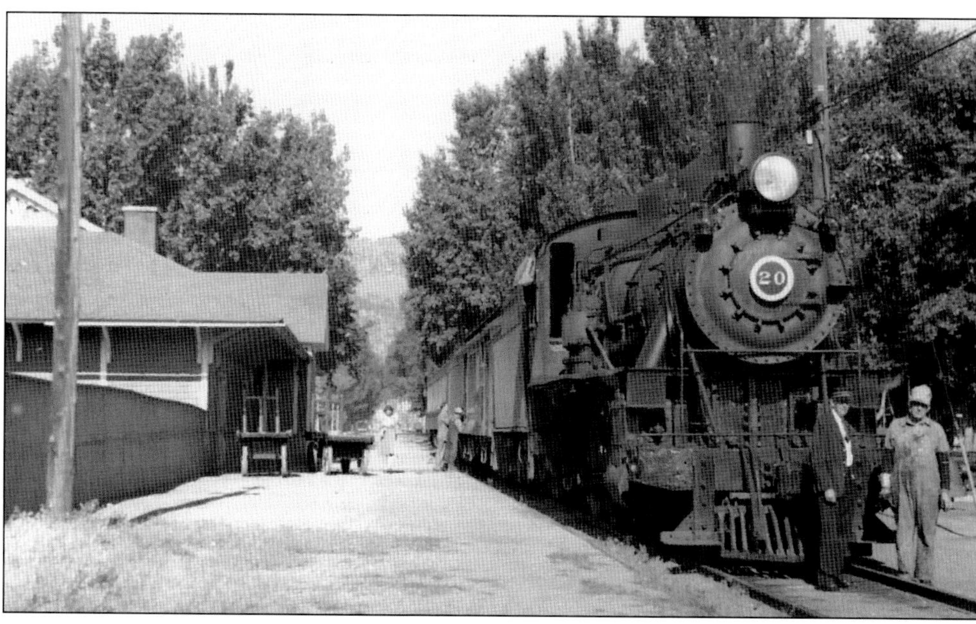

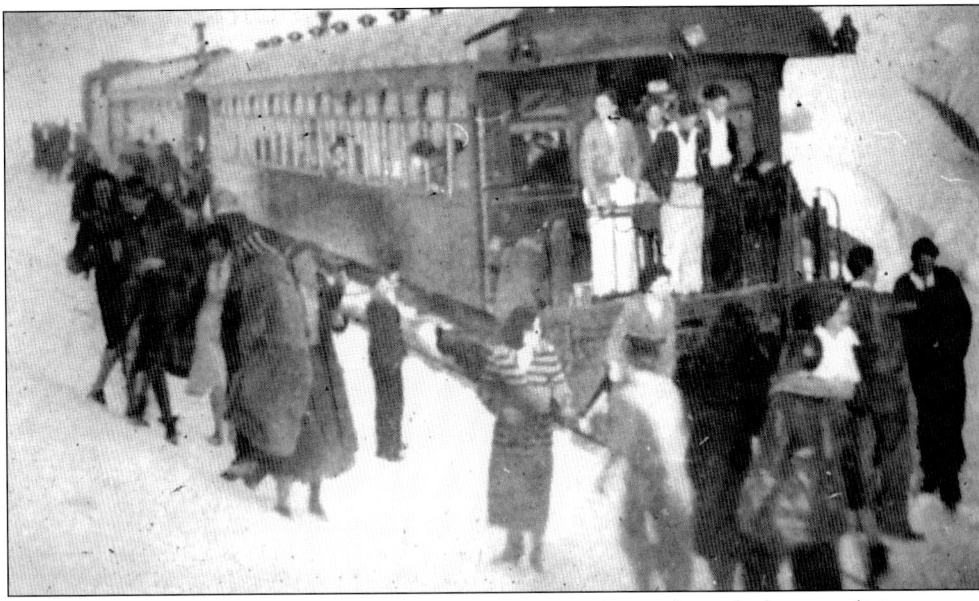

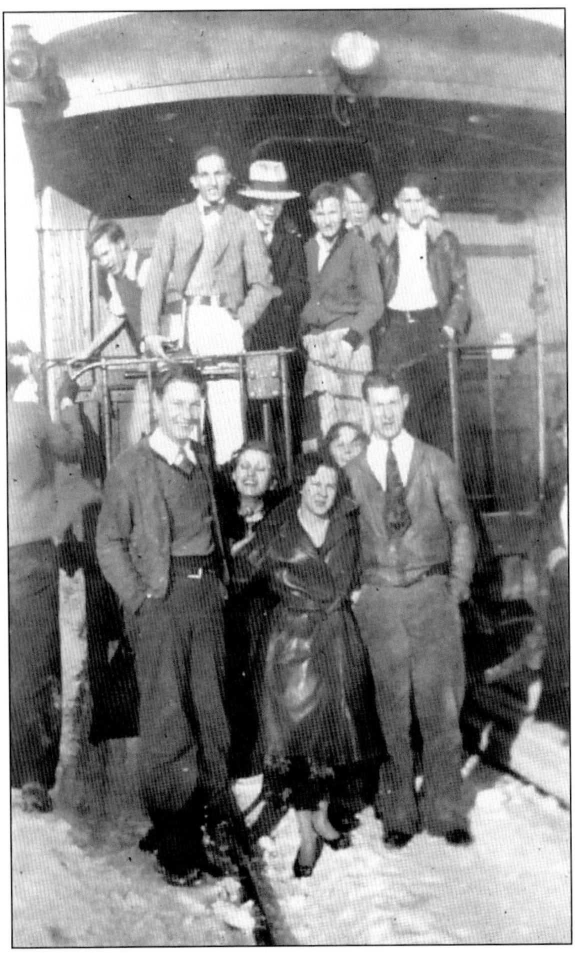

It was through the serendipitous combination of having the Ely Depot located within two blocks of the White Pine County High School and having track to both McGill and Ruth, that caused the Nevada Northern Railway to provide school train service to the community. In an era before paved roads and dependable school buses, the railroad would carry high school students from both McGill and Ruth to Ely. In Ely, they could attend high school. This saved the school district considerable money, because additional high schools were not needed in either Ruth or McGill. It was a rite of passage for high school students to take the school train to Ely. It appears that the train has made an unscheduled stop, possibly because of the snow. Today, there is still only one high school in White Pine County, but instead of trains, the students ride busses.

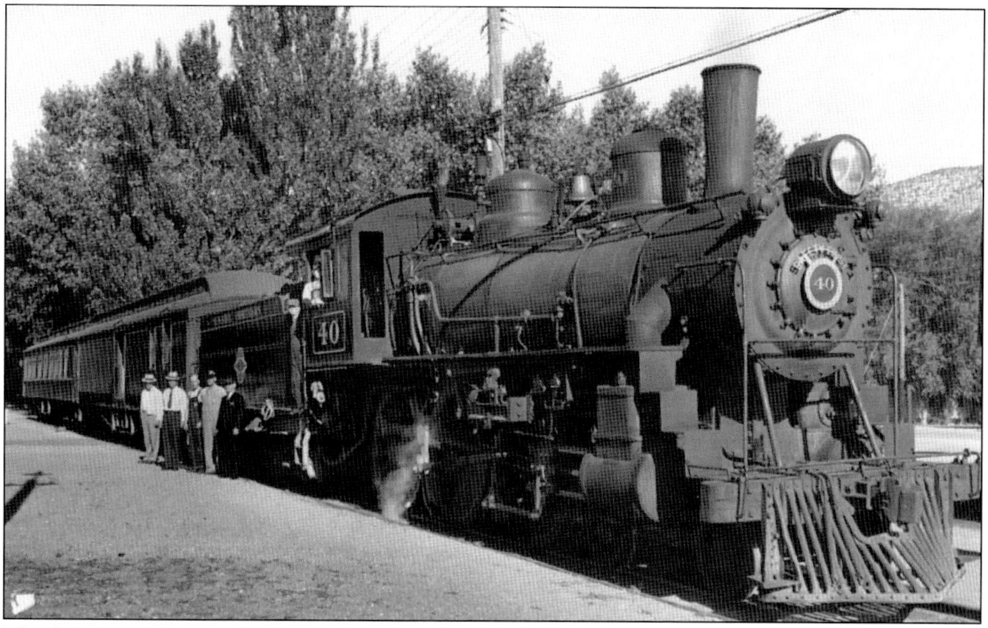

The last passenger train was July 31, 1941, with locomotive 40, baggage/mail 20, and coach 5. To witness the last trip were, from left to right, Harry Beem (superintendent), Harry Fravel (trainmaster), Val Walker (mail clerk), Paul Bennett (brakeman), William Padden (conductor), Loretto Labate (fireman), and William Young (engineer). According to the *Ely Daily Times*, "Without celebration and yet with a feeling of sadness . . . the passenger train . . . [made] . . . its last run to Cobre and return." (EERDM.)

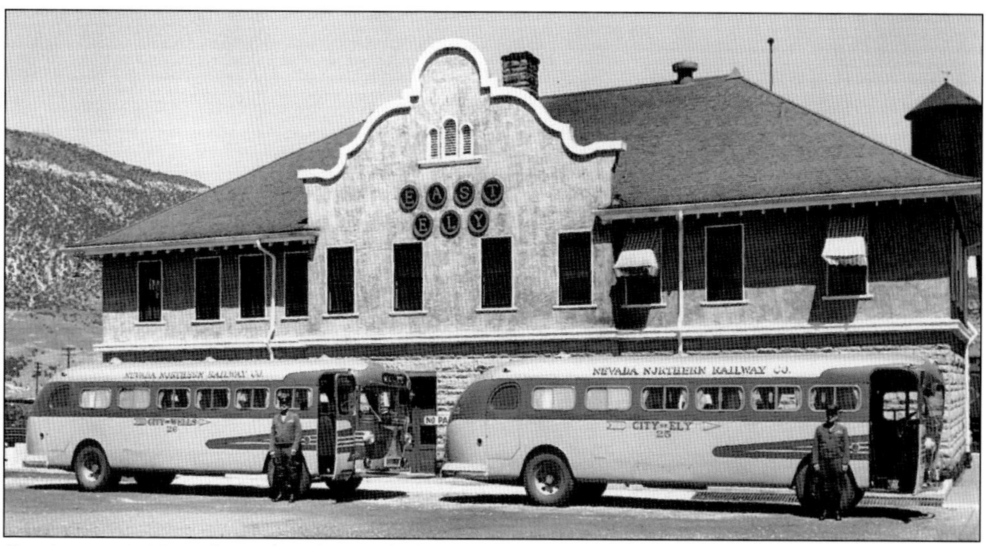

On August 1, 1941, the railroad provided two choices for passengers: take the new bus, or ride in a caboose. The Public Service Commission ordered the railroad to carry passengers on its freight trains. But Mr. Hickey, the general manager of the railroad, would make it difficult, noting that the freight trains "do not . . . show in Official Guide . . . as mixed trains. . . . These are strictly freight trains and will continue to be so, with arrangement as promised . . . that passengers would be carried." (EERDM.)

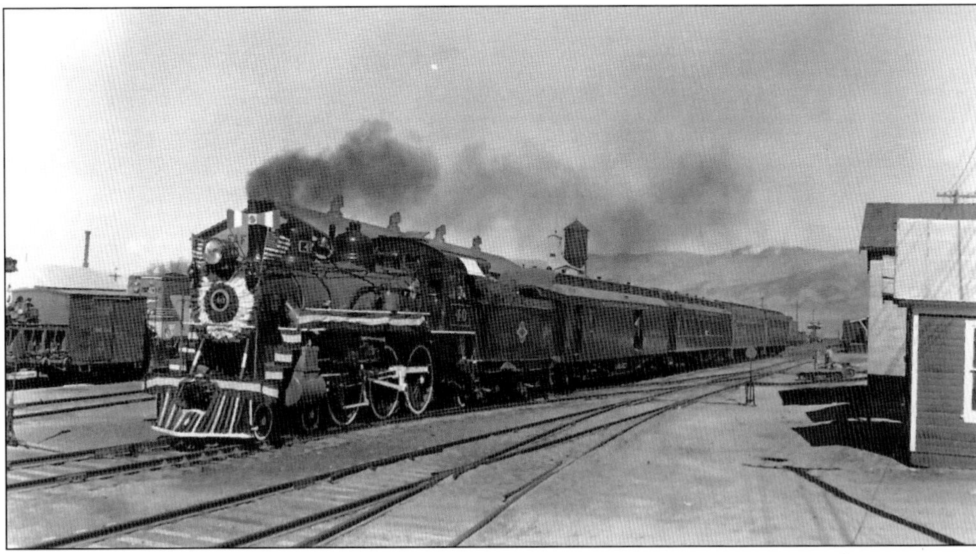

The Public Service Commission also ordered the railroad to preserve some of its passenger equipment in case the buses could not handle the passenger business. Because of this requirement, the railroad kept locomotive 40 and some of its passenger cars. On September 29, 1956, in celebration of the 50th anniversary of the railroad, locomotive 40 once again hauled passengers. The trip was rather short—just between the East Ely Depot and the Ely Depot—but it was well attended. In the photograph above, locomotive 40 is decorated and heading toward Ely. At the depot, crowds await their turn to ride the rails once again. (Both, Gardner.)

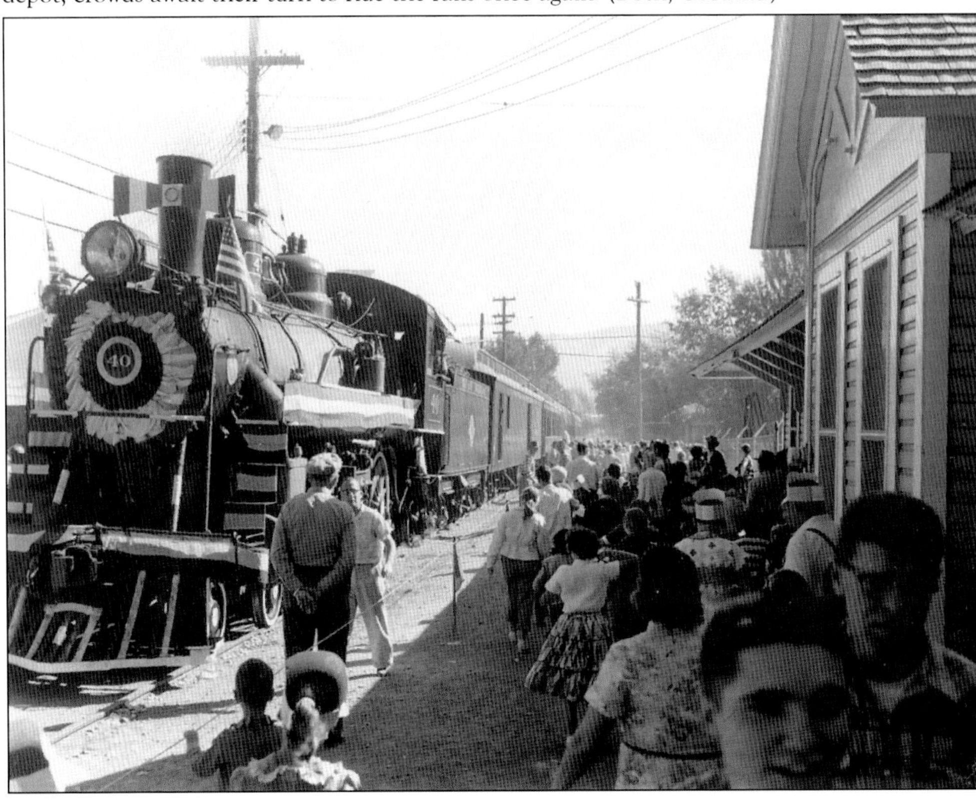

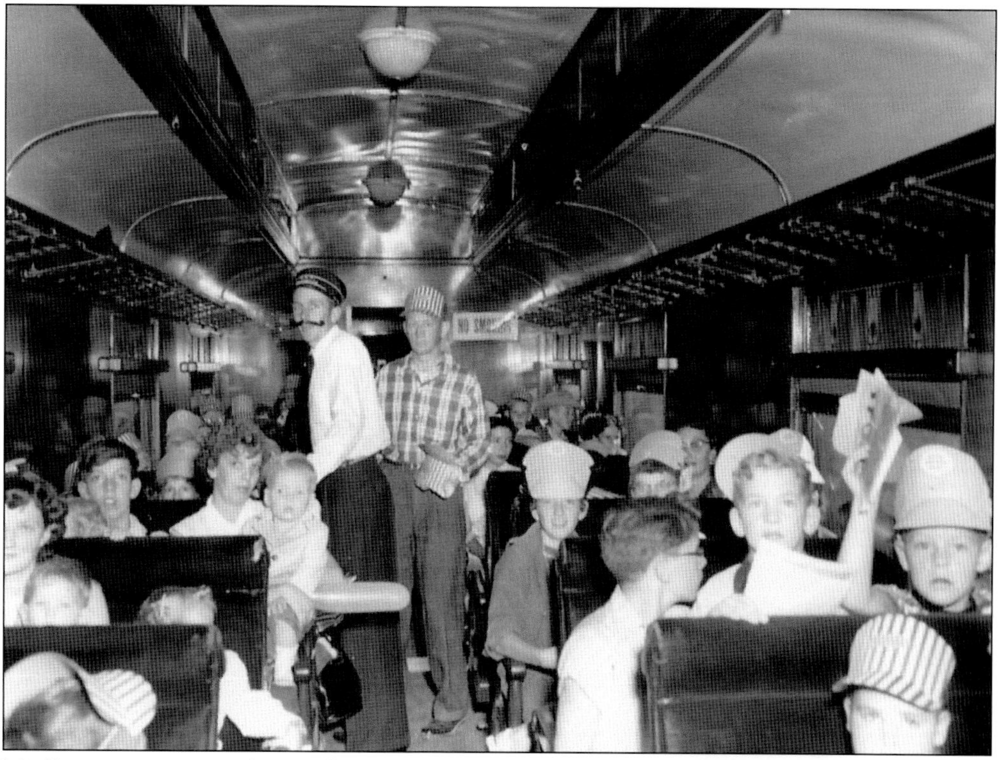

Mr. Peterson, vice president and general manager of the railroad, organized the 50th anniversary program. From his autobiography is this explanation: "I worried for a month about what to do [about the anniversary] and finally wrote to our President and asked for authority to spend several thousand dollars on the celebration. He agreed. We rented . . . coaches from Southern Pacific, and added Nevada Northern's old coach with the plush seats. Then we used our old #40 passenger engine to pull the train. We advertised free rides for children on the train, and counted a total of 6,000 rides that day." The crew got into the spirit of the day and wore fake mustaches. At right are Frank Agan (left), Walt Armstrong (center), and Harold M. Peterson. (Both, Gardner.)

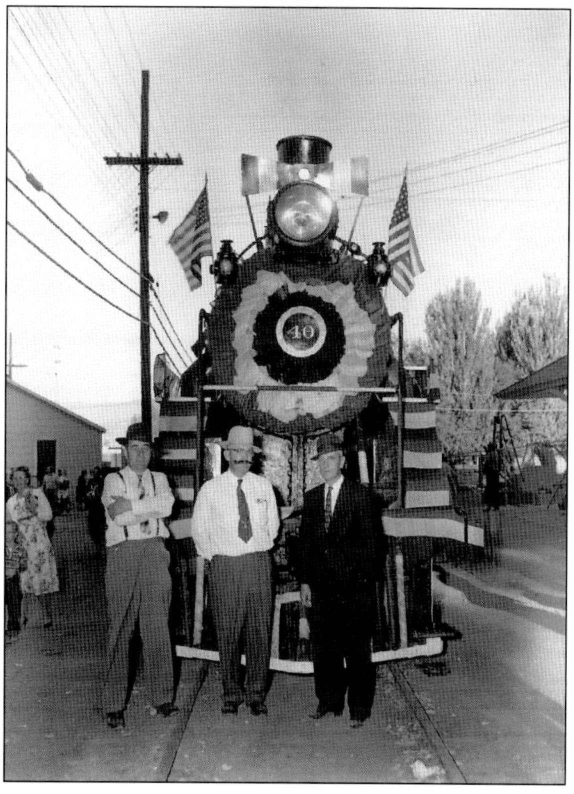

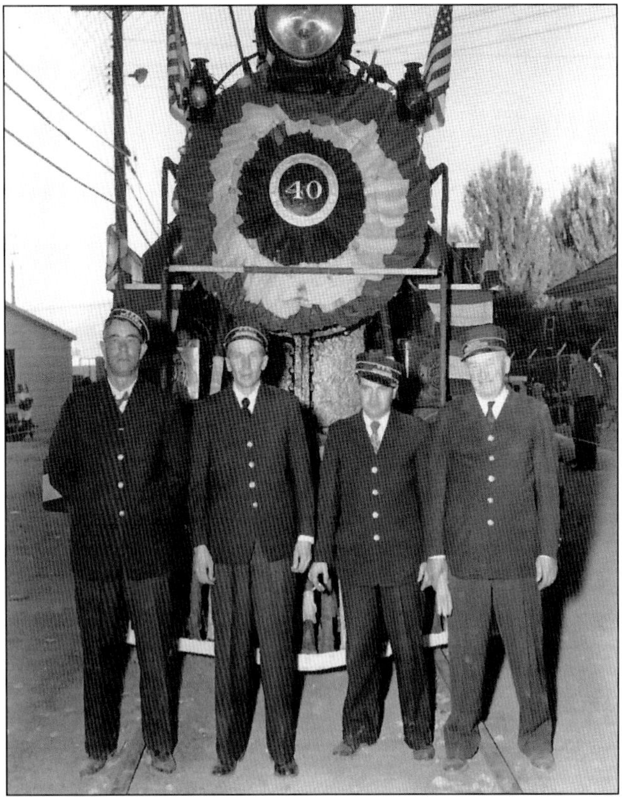

The conductors that handled 6,000 passengers in a day for the 50th anniversary trains were, from left to right, Dick Smith, Paul Tilby, Harold Jensen, and Jack Perry. The band around their conductor hats read in two lines, "N. N. Ry.," and underneath, "Conductor." Both were embroidered in heavy gold bullion thread. (Gardner.)

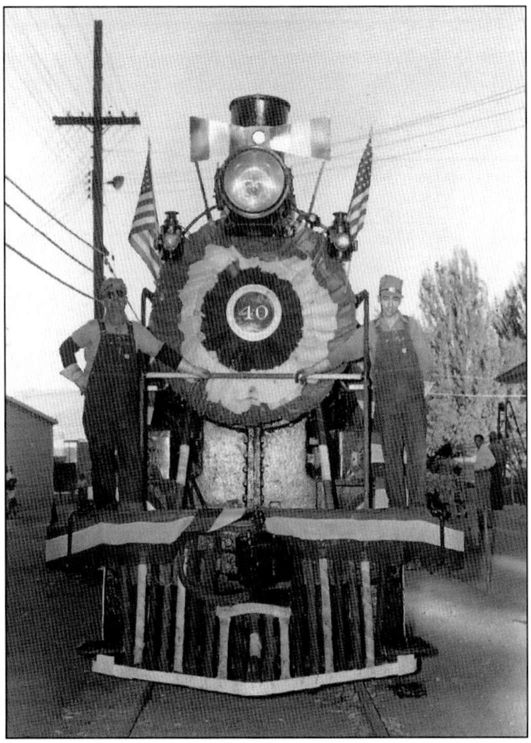

The engine crew that day included engineer Jumbo Labate (left) and fireman Ralph Morrow. The trains were reminiscent of the old ping-pong trains that operated between the Ely Depot and the East Ely Depot. The anniversary trains ran from the Ely Depot, to the East Ely overpass, and back to the depot. (Gardner.)

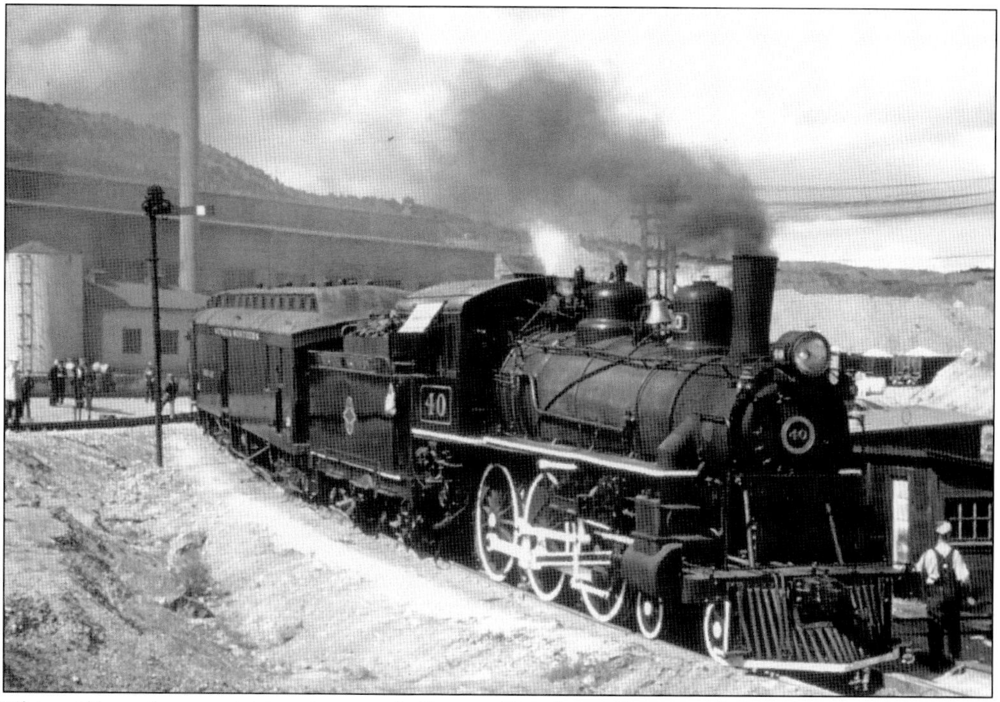

This railfan trip was visiting the mine's Copper Flat shop. The Nevada Northern Railway had a deserved reputation for friendliness toward railfans. It allowed the public to explore its facilities—a rare occurrence, especially on a workday. The Nevada Northern Railway Museum continues this policy for its visitors. (Duke.)

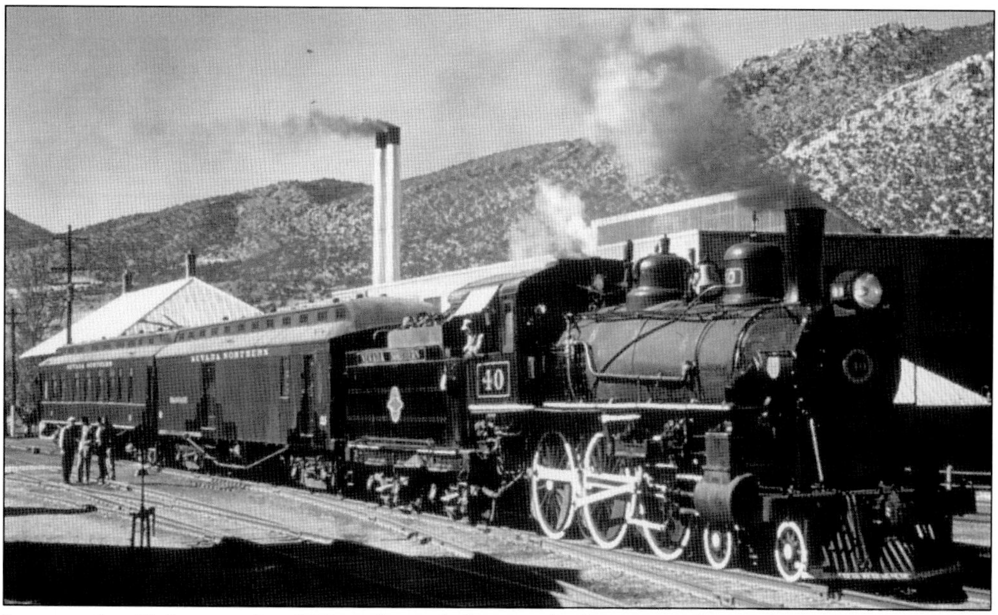

Locomotive 40, baggage/mail 20, and coach 5 are parked opposite the machine shop and engine house complex as railfans explore the shops. Even though passenger service ended 20 years earlier, standards had to be maintained. Locomotive 40 and the cars were freshly painted and polished. Not apparent in this photograph, but locomotive 40's boiler jacket is painted green. (Duke.)

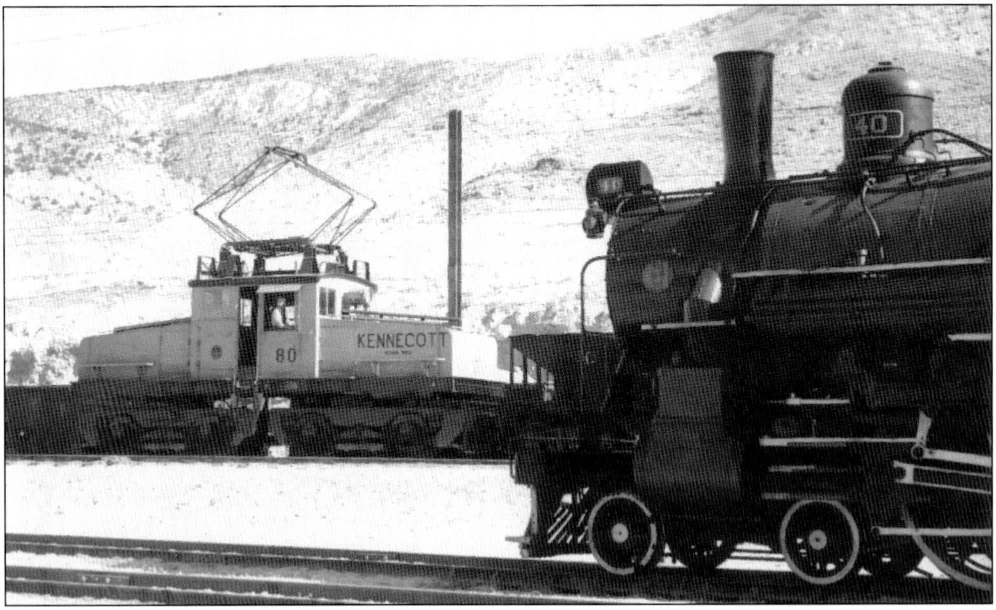

The railroad would pull out all stops to make sure visiting rail enthusiasts had an unbelievable experience. They would take them to the mine, to the railroad shops, and to the mill. Here, locomotive 40 is at McGill. In the background is electric locomotive 80. Both locomotives are preserved at the Nevada Northern Railway Museum. (Duke.)

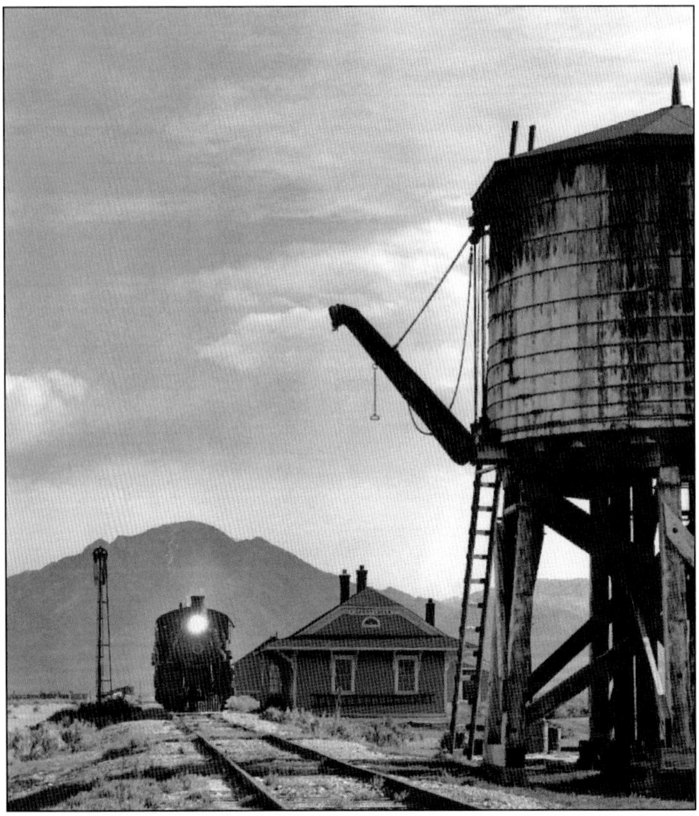

Locomotive 40 is heading northbound as it approaches the depot at Cherry Creek. The depot is closed and the train order boards are in the proceed position. Locomotive 40 and the Cherry Creek Depot will both experience a fleeting moment of fame when they appeared in the Willie Nelson movie *Once Upon a Texas Train*. (Duke.)

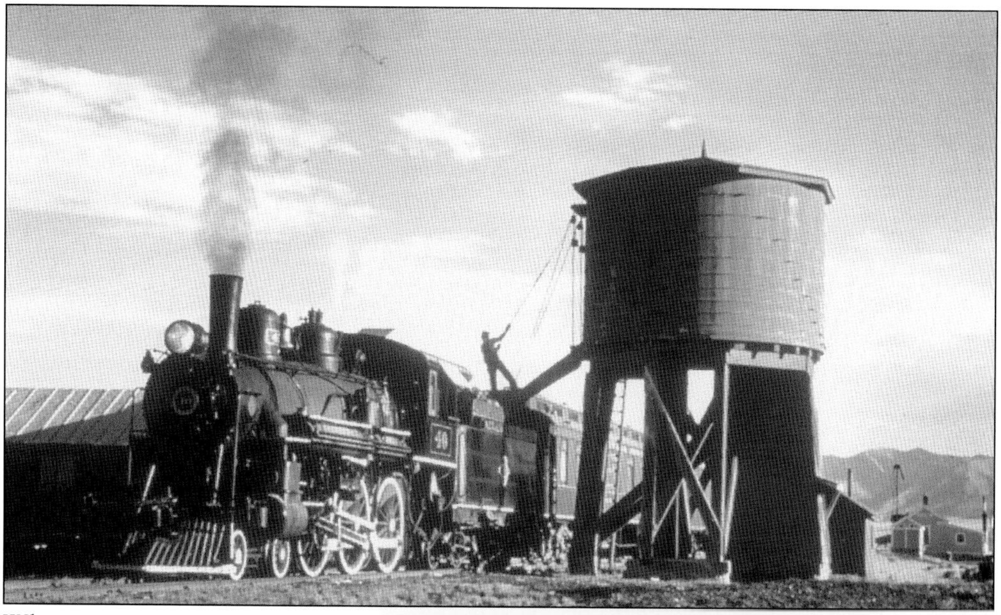

What was once a common occurrence is now a rare event, as locomotive 40 stops at Currie for water on a northbound charter trip. The fireman climbs on the tender and pulls down the spout so that water from the tank fills the tender. Keeping water available in the desert was a costly proposition. The wooden tanks and pumps needed to be maintained and protected from freezing in the winter. (Duke.)

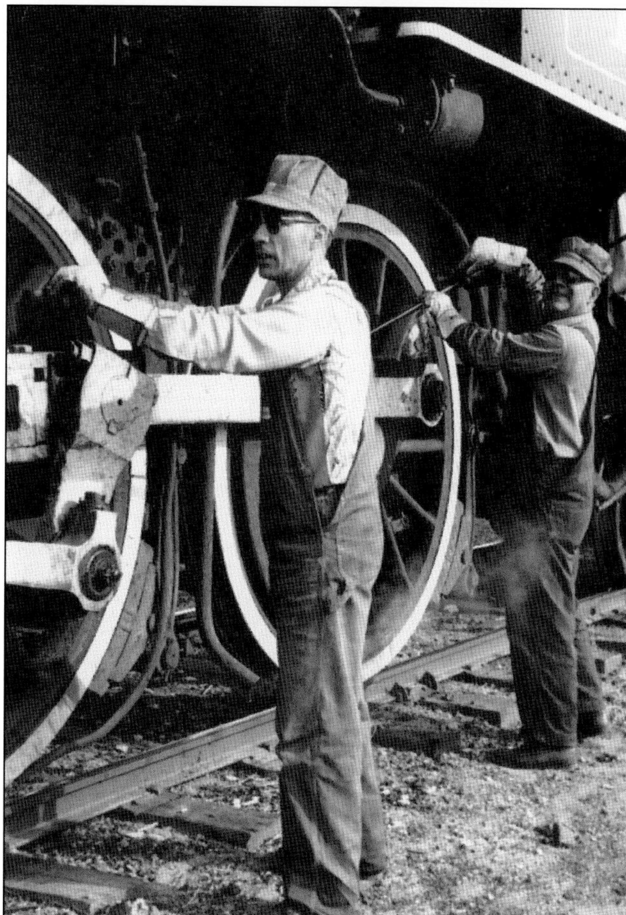

Water stops meant it was time to oil and check the running gear. Here, the fireman and the engineer are using their trusty oilcan to spread oil on wear parts in the running gear. Hidden behind the wheels in the locomotive frame is the drive box that the locomotive axles ride in. It slides up and down depending on track conditions and needs lubrication. (Gardner.)

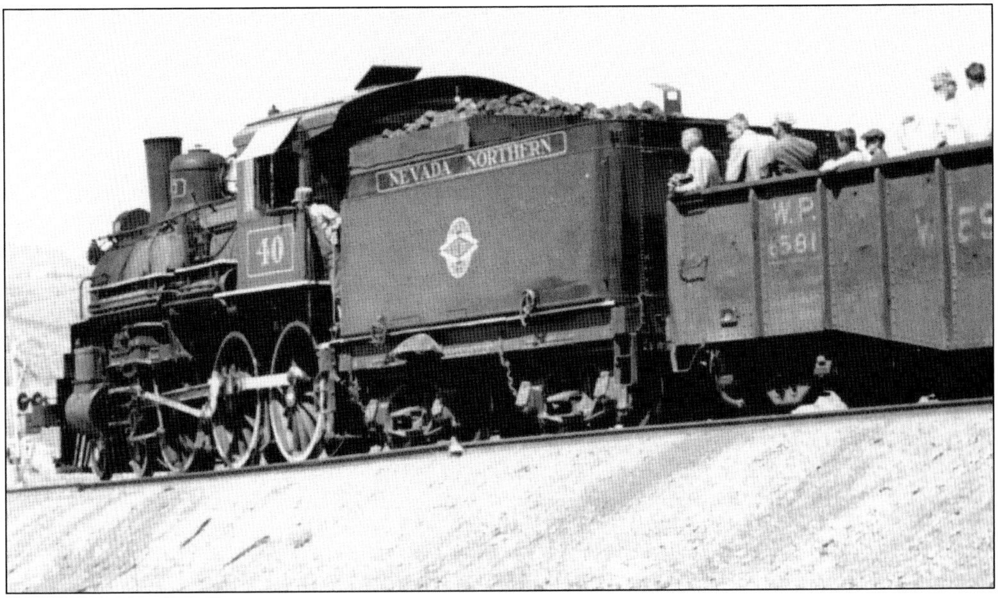

For the rail enthusiast, the Nevada Northern added rather primitive open-air cars to the train. The one shown is a WP gondola car. When the fireman shovels in the coal as locomotive 40 heads uphill, these riders will be covered with soot and cinders. For most of them, this is the highlight of the trip. (Gardner.)

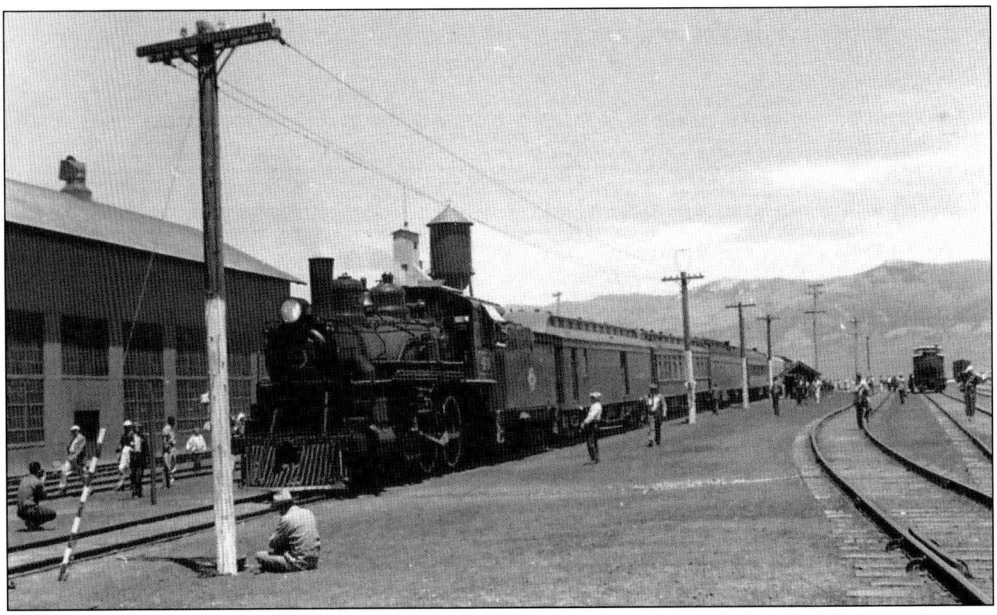

It is a summer day, and locomotive 40 has just arrived at East Ely with a rail enthusiast charter. The train consists of two NN passenger cars and four heavy-weight passenger cars from another railroad. As evident by the number of passengers, these excursions were popular. (Novich.)

Six

National Historic Landmark and Railroad Museum

From the 1850s until the early 1900s, gold and silver discoveries occurred all around Nevada. Legendary towns boomed. Unbelievably rich mines were developed. And storied railroads were built to serve these towns and mines. Ely, the county seat of White Pine County, was the site of one of the last major booms in Nevada.

The boom was different here. It was not gold and silver, but the new miracle metal, copper. Copper was needed to provide the wires for two paradigm-shifting inventions: the electric light and the telephone. The White Pine County boom followed the pattern of the other booms in some ways; cities sprang up where none existed. Mines, mills, and smelters were built where, before, there had only been sagebrush. The railroad made all of this possible.

The significant exception to the White Pine County boom versus the rest of the booms in Nevada is that here, the towns still exist, the mine is still producing copper ore, and the Nevada Northern Railway still functions.

Today, the railway demonstrates what it took to move a mountain of copper ore. It brings people from around the world to White Pine County. The reason? It is not a re-creation. Rather, it is an authentic working railroad, which exists today the same as it has for most of a century.

The original locomotives couple up to the original cars. Passengers purchase their tickets at the original depot ticket office and board their trains. Repairs are made in the original buildings using the original tools. It is a time capsule that is now recognized as a National Historic Landmark—the highest honor the federal government can bestow on a historic site.

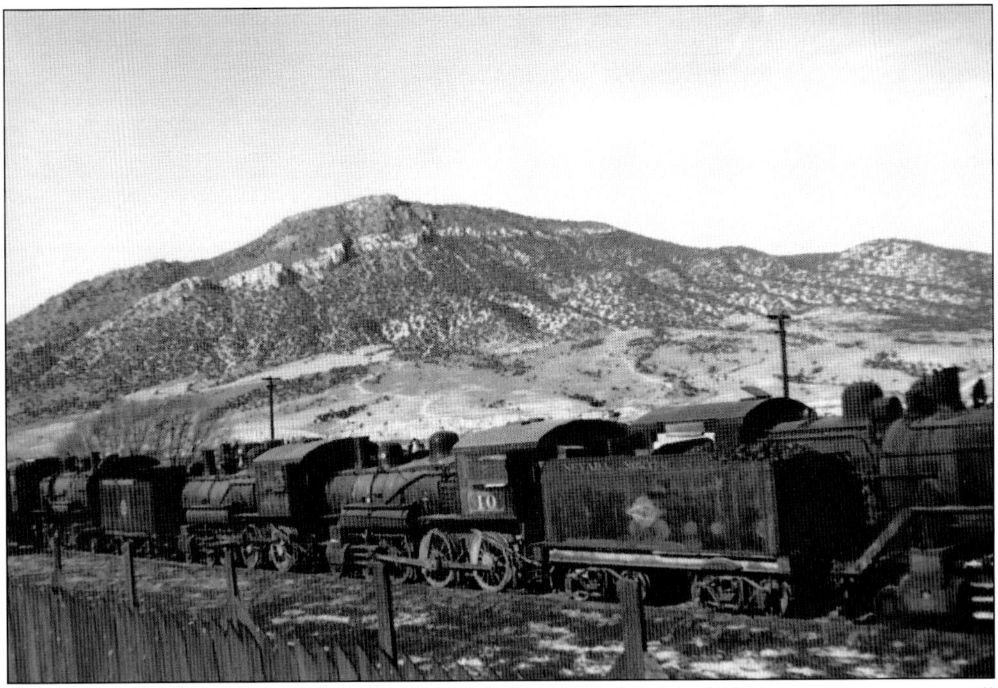

There was an insatiable scrap-metal-gobbling beast located in McGill. The concentrating mill used steel balls to breakup the copper ore, and the demand was voracious. Any available scrap metal was sent to McGill to be melted and tuned into mill balls. At the end of their service life, locomotives and ore cars went to the foundry. Ironically sitting in the old coal yard, the locomotives (above) and ore cars (below) await their turns. The surviving locomotives and ore, freight, and passenger cars all share one trait—serendipitous luck. There is no reason why they should have survived, but they did. (Below, Sundance.)

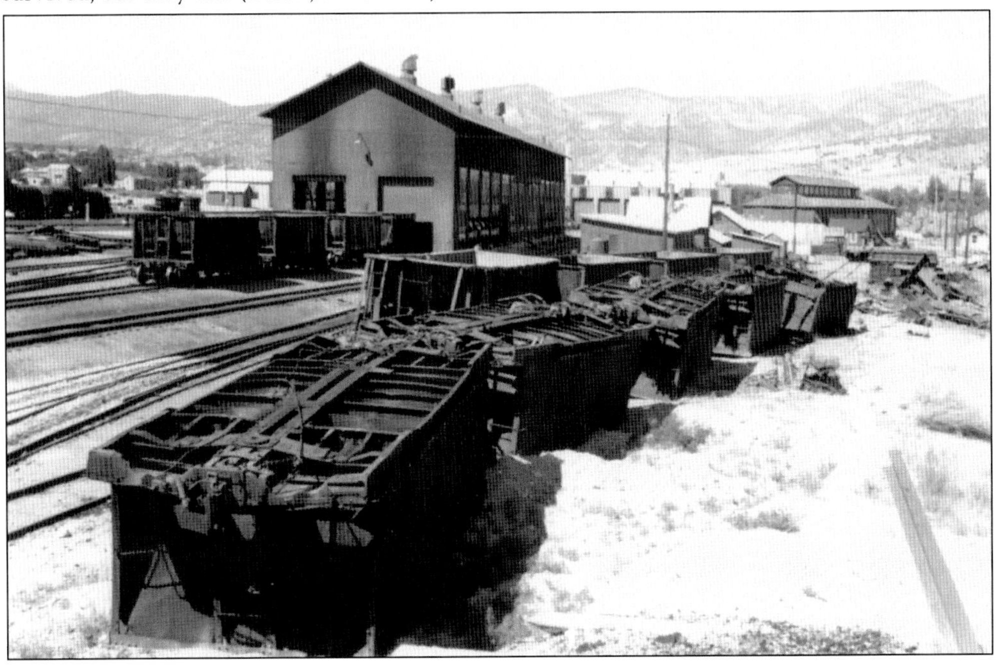

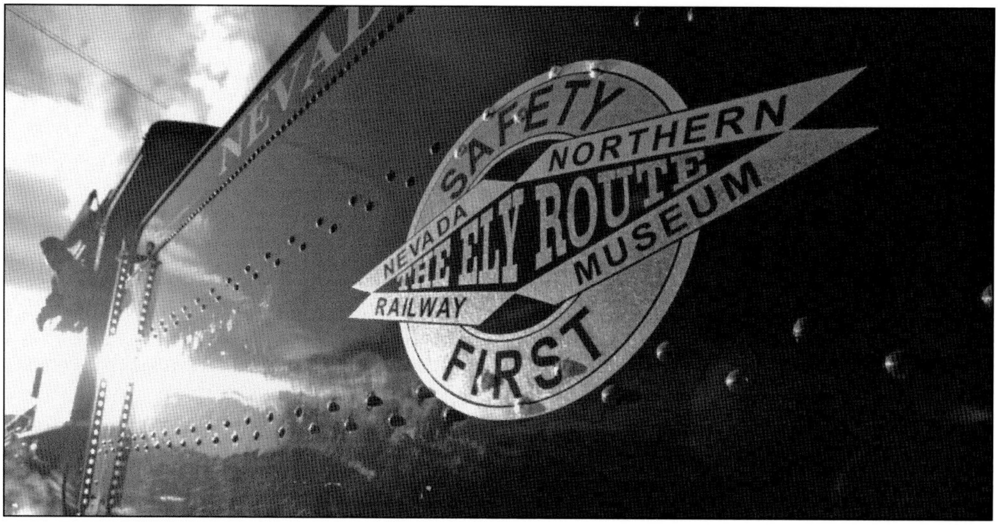

The logo on the tender of locomotive 40 says it all: "Nevada Northern Railway Museum." The closure of the copper mine and then the McGill complex ended the copper dream. Nevada's history is full of railroads and mining communities that are no more. This railroad could have followed the other short-line railroads in Nevada, disappearing into the desert as a faded memory. All of its contemporaries are gone now; track has been torn out, buildings demolished, and equipment cut up and scrapped. That didn't happen here. Instead, the museum was created. Here, history is touchable—there is no need to wonder what it is like to operate a steam locomotive. Perhaps the crown jewel in the collection is the copper spike that Mark Requa drove a century ago. (Both, Crise.)

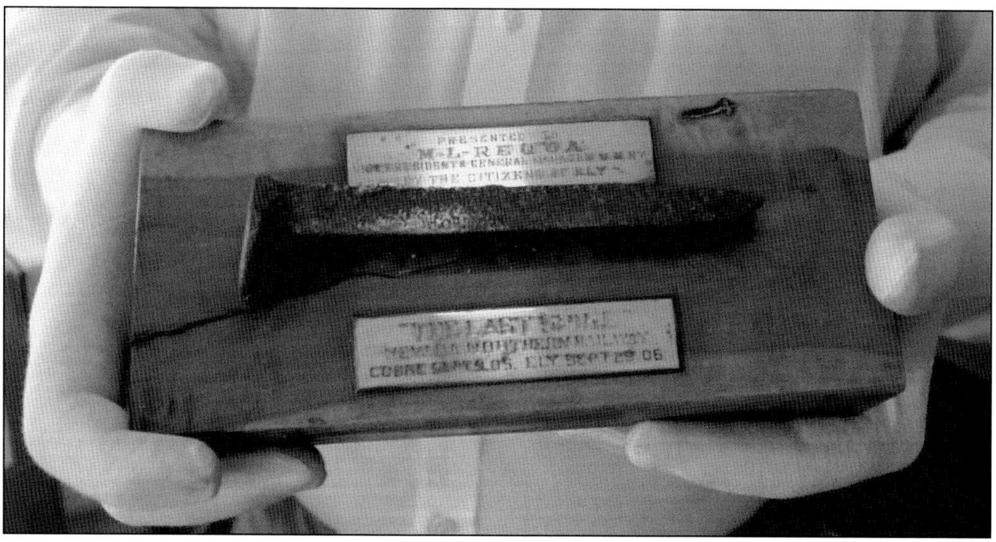

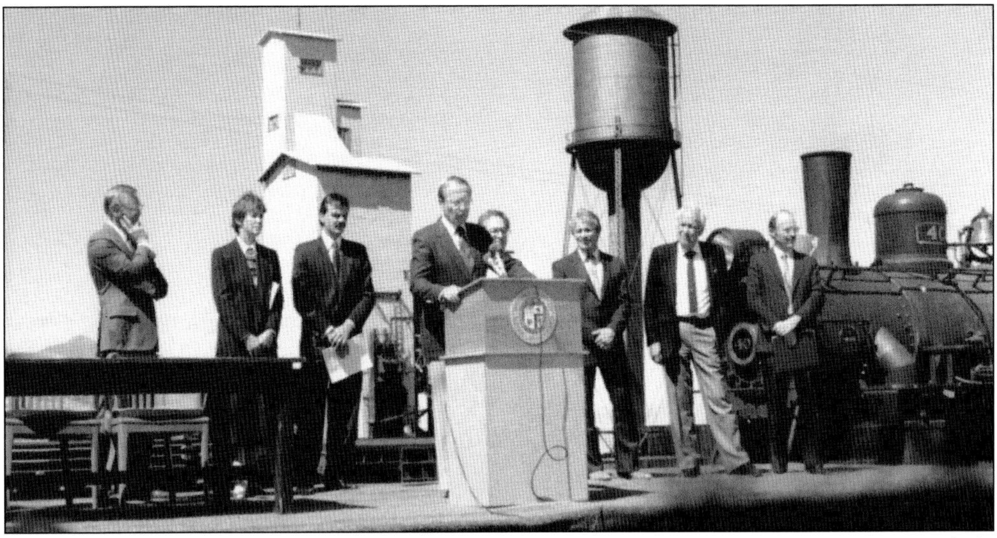

Community leaders approached Kennecott requesting that they operate excursion trains to help the economic health of the community after Kennecott shut down. Kennecott replied that they were a mining company, not a tourist railroad. Undaunted, the community then ask Kennecott if they could have the railroad, considering Kennecott was not planning to use it. After negotiations, Kennecott gifted the railroad to the community. Governor Bryan is shown addressing a crowd after the good news.

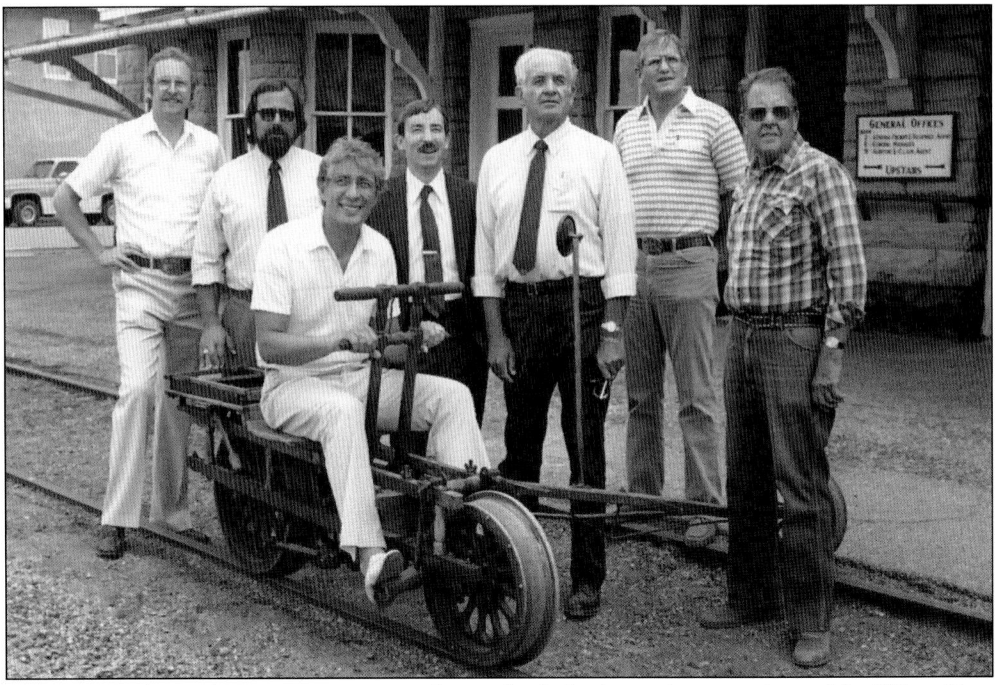

Ely mayor Barlow White prepares to test a three-wheeled velocipede as members of the White Pine Historical Railroad Foundation watch. They include, from left to right, Marshall Coppersmith, Robert Spellbery, Barlow White, Jerry Martin, Ralph Orgill, Dave Tilford, and Joy M. Bybee. The railroad was given jointly to the White Pine Historical Railroad Foundation and the City of Ely and is managed as a living history museum.

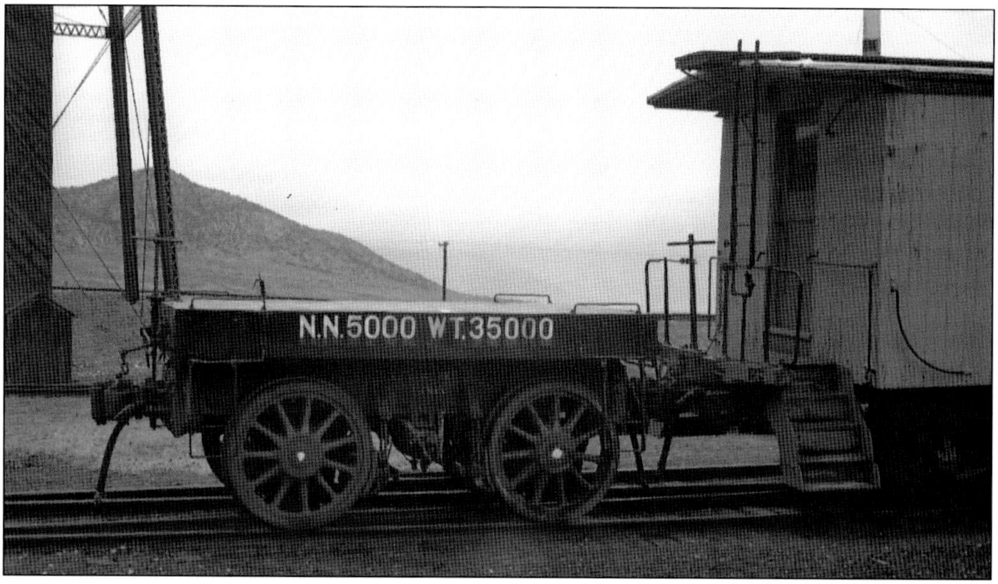

Scale-test car NN 5000 (above) has an interesting history and a direct tie to the ouster of Mark Requa. Below is a builder's photograph of NN locomotive 5, which was purchased by Mark Requa to service the mill and smelter at East Ely. The tank locomotive carried its own coal and water. When Requa was forced out, and the mill and smelter moved to McGill, locomotive 5 was out of a job. The railroad tried to find a use for locomotive 5. In 1913, it was converted to a 2-8-0 locomotive and renumbered to locomotive 80. The conversion was not a success; the vehicle rocked and foamed easily. During the conversion, the original pilot and trailing trucks were removed, and the two extra wheel sets were the basis for the scale car. (Below, Chappell.)

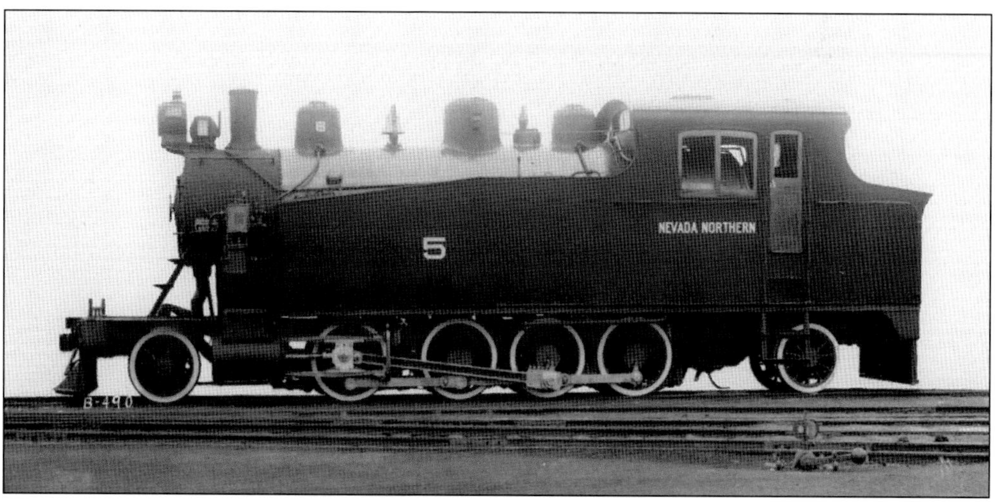

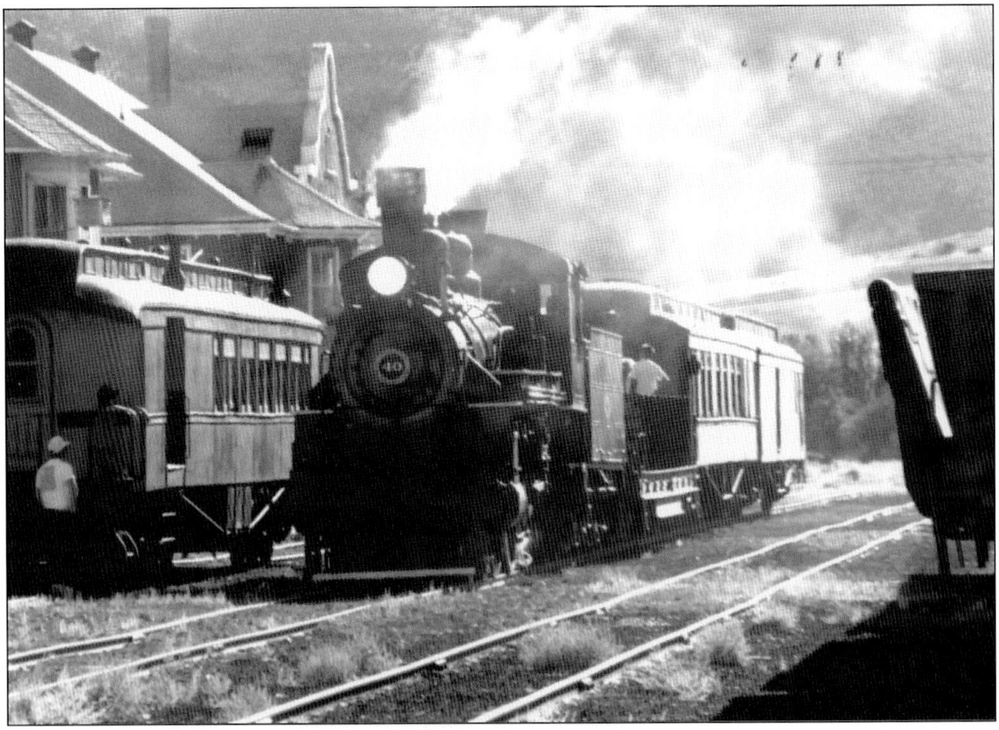

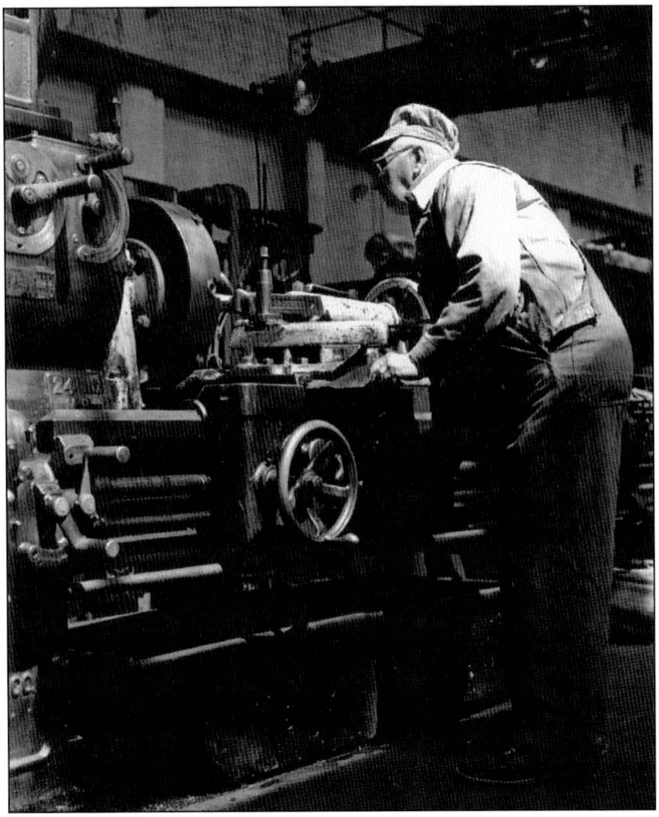

The community asked for the railroad because they wanted to build a tourist train business to help offset the loss of mining revenue; they received an entire railroad. In 1987, excursion trains were started using locomotive 40, flatcar 23, coaches 2 and 5, and baggage/mail 20, seen here departing the East Ely Depot.

Steam locomotives are incredibly high-maintenance machines; operating them would require some work. Included in the gift from Kennecott was the complete machine shop. Here, volunteer Tom Lake, a former Kennecott employee, is fabricating a part on one of the original lathes, which qualifies as a museum piece in its own right.

All operating steam locomotives will eventually need to have the boiler rebuilt. Locomotive 40 is in the machine shop; the smokebox cover is off, and the old boiler tubes are being pulled out. The work is difficult, heavy, and dirty. The project was successfully completed in 2005, and locomotive 40's new boiler should last until 2020.

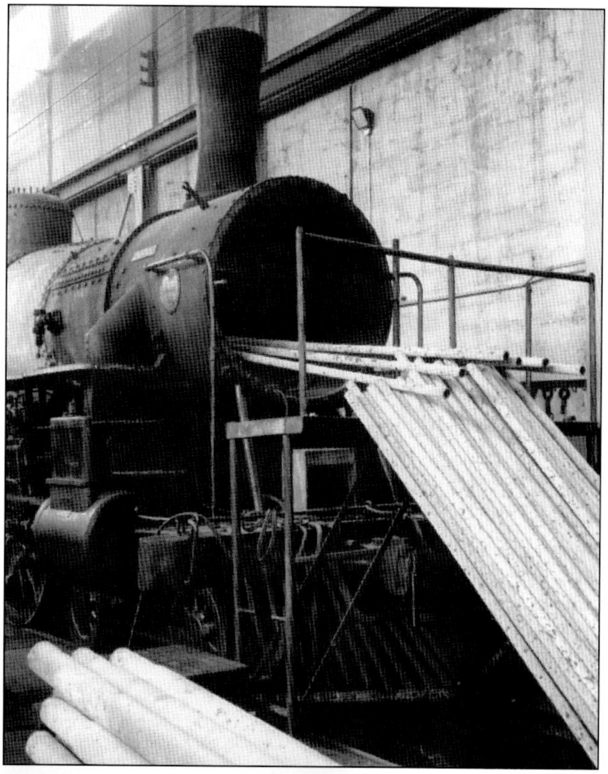

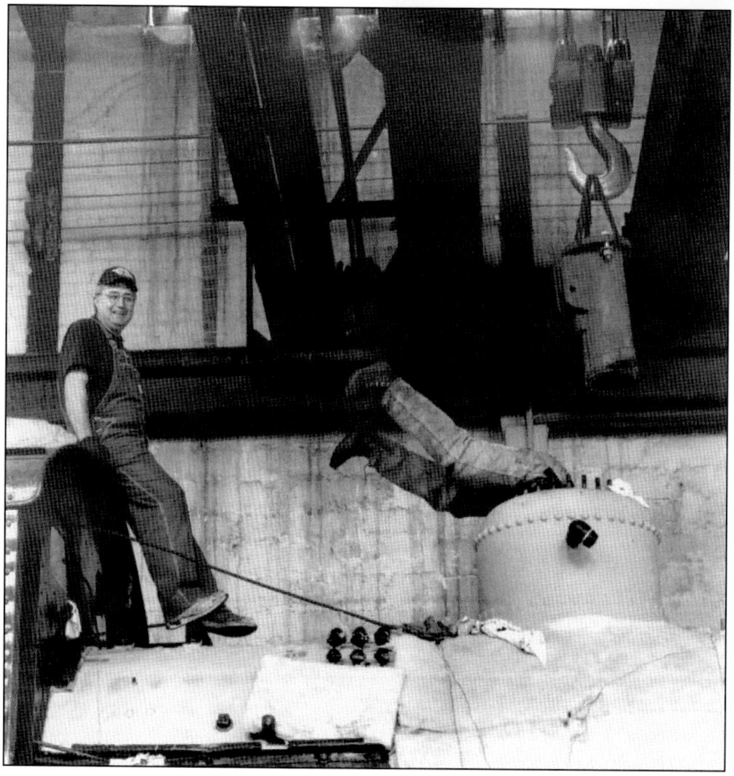

The only way into a steam locomotive's boiler is through the steam dome, a tight fit. Suspended over the lucky individual heading into the boiler is the throttle valve that was removed to provide access. Kelvin Martinez, a longtime museum volunteer, is waiting for his turn to go in.

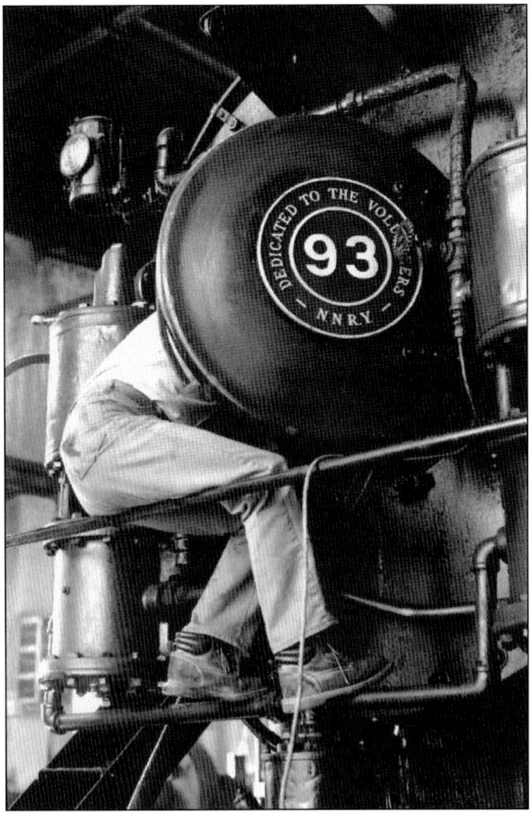

The core of the success of the Nevada Northern Railway Museum is directly linked to its volunteers. Without the volunteers' unstinting dedication and unbelievable hard work, the railroad would not have survived into its second century. The number plate on locomotive 93 recognizes the contributions of the volunteers. (Jensen.)

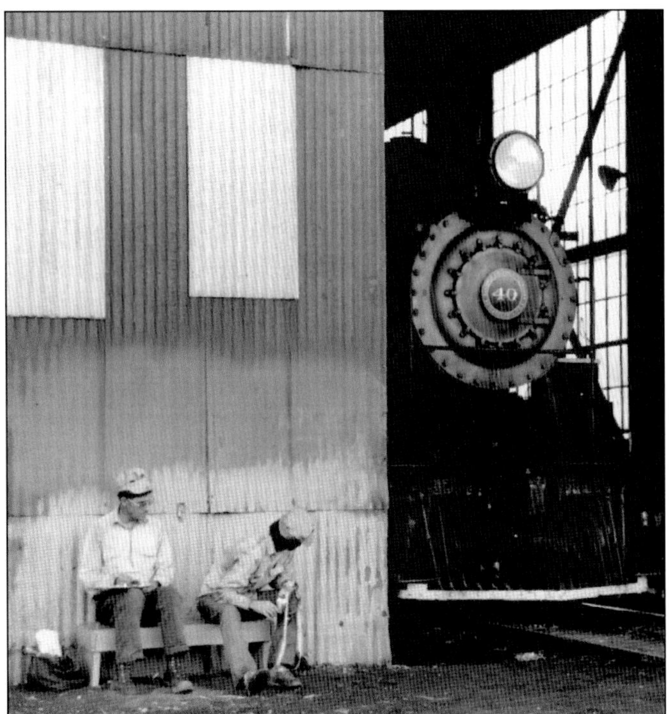

Longtime volunteers Ron Taylor (left) and Tony Bond sit outside the RIP building after spending hours in Locomotive 40's cab. To the public, being in the cab of a steam locomotive seems glamorous. But it is hot, dirty, backbreaking work. For just one trip up the hill, 2,000 pounds of coal must be shoveled by hand into the locomotive's firebox. (Jensen.)

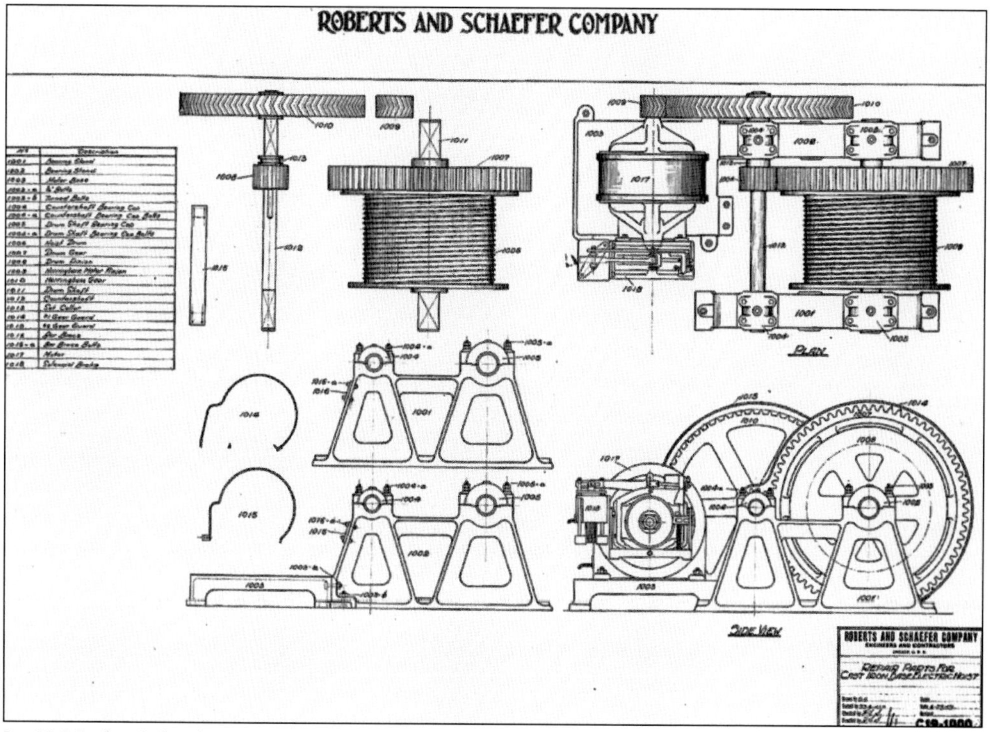

In 2006, the federal government recognized the railroad as a National Historic Landmark because of its exceptional value and quality in interpreting the heritage of the United States. This is the highest form recognition that the government can bestow upon a historic site. The Nevada Northern Railroad is unique. Not only did the buildings and structures survive; the steam, diesel, and electric locomotives and the passenger and freight cars survived, too. But perhaps more importantly, is that the paper record was saved too. Above is one tiny example, a drawing of the parts in the coaling tower.

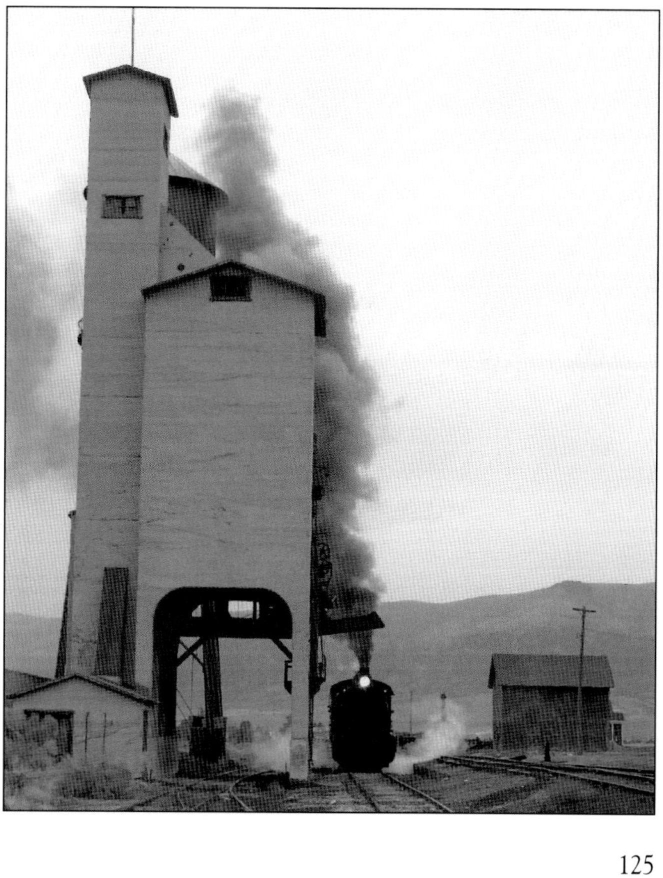

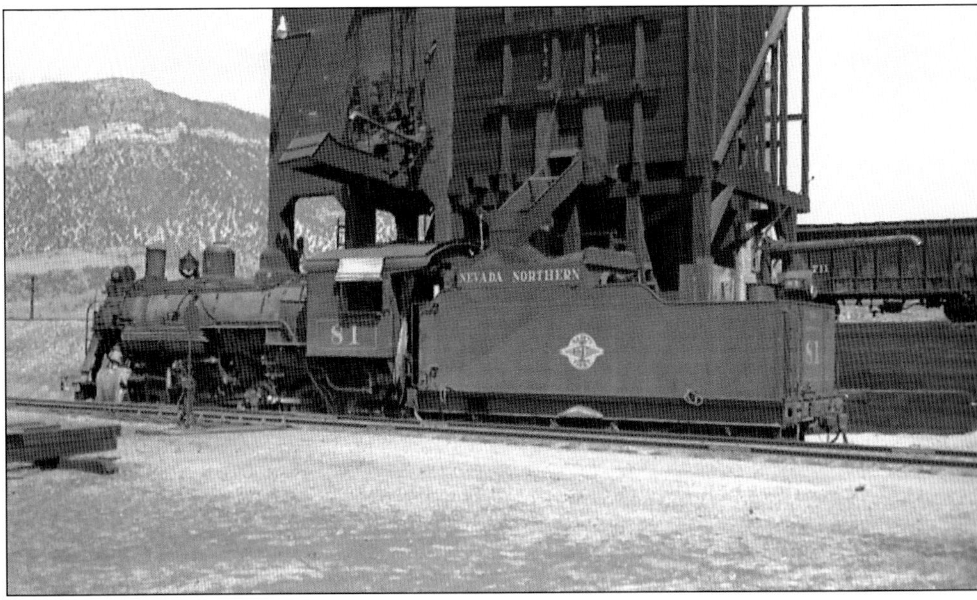

The Nevada Northern Railway Museum is unique. It is stuck in the 20th century. The staff and volunteers work diligently to maintain the feel and atmosphere of the railroad as it was during its heyday. Above, locomotive 81 is being coaled. Both the coaling tower and locomotive 81 still exist, but they need restoration. Someday, this scene may be duplicated. Below, NN rotary snowplow B and locomotive 93 are getting ready to plow more snow—or are they? This photograph was staged in 2010, but it could have just as easily been 1910. Regardless of the century, the challenges, hard work, and bitter cold remain the same. Here, time travel is possible. (Above, MacGregor.)

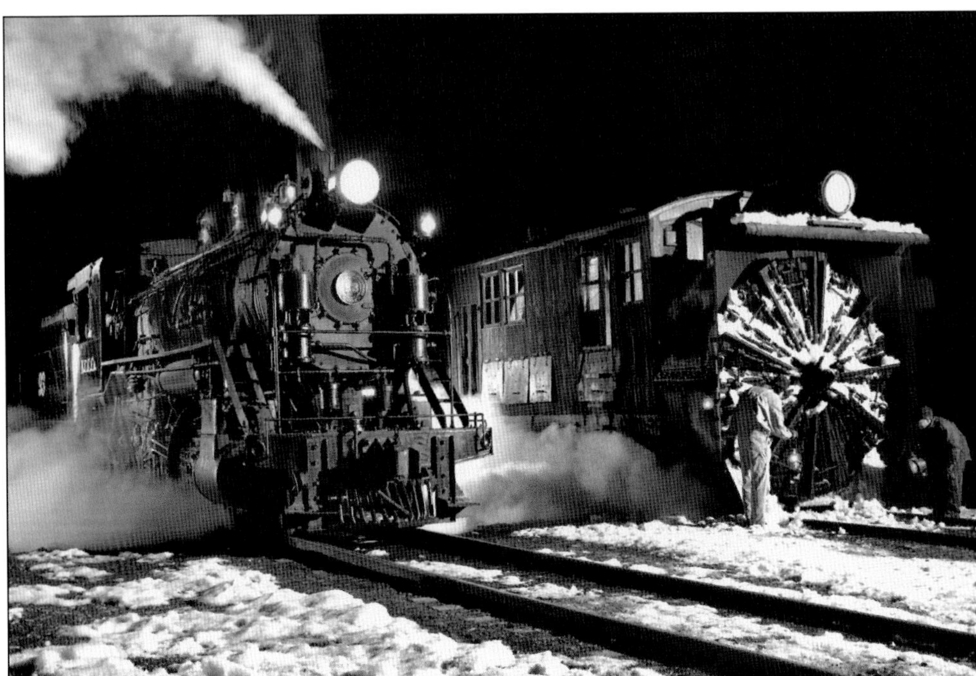

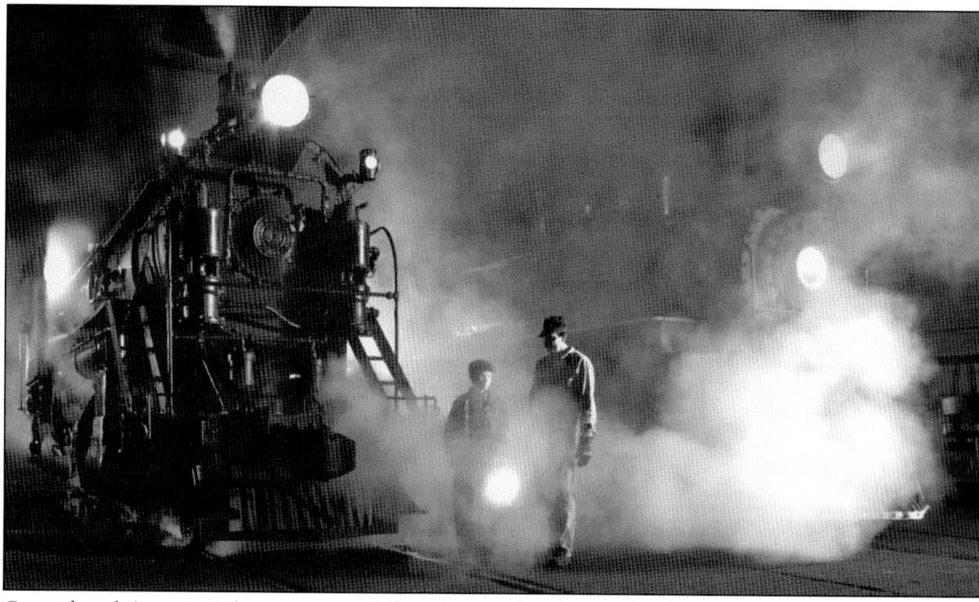

Considered America's best-preserved short-line railroad, it is the last of its kind. Now a National Historic Landmark, the Nevada Northern Railway Museum takes visitors back in time. Instead of relics in glass cases and old equipment repainted for static display, visitors experience a real, working steam railroad. It is gritty and dirty. It smells of coal smoke, creosote, and sweat. Here, visitors can peek behind the curtain of history. The 56-acre museum with 70 buildings and structures shows visitors firsthand what it took to move a mountain of copper ore. Guests can go into the shops and watch as century-old techniques are still used today to maintain antique locomotives and cars, and they can climb aboard a steam-powered passenger train to experience travel from the last century.

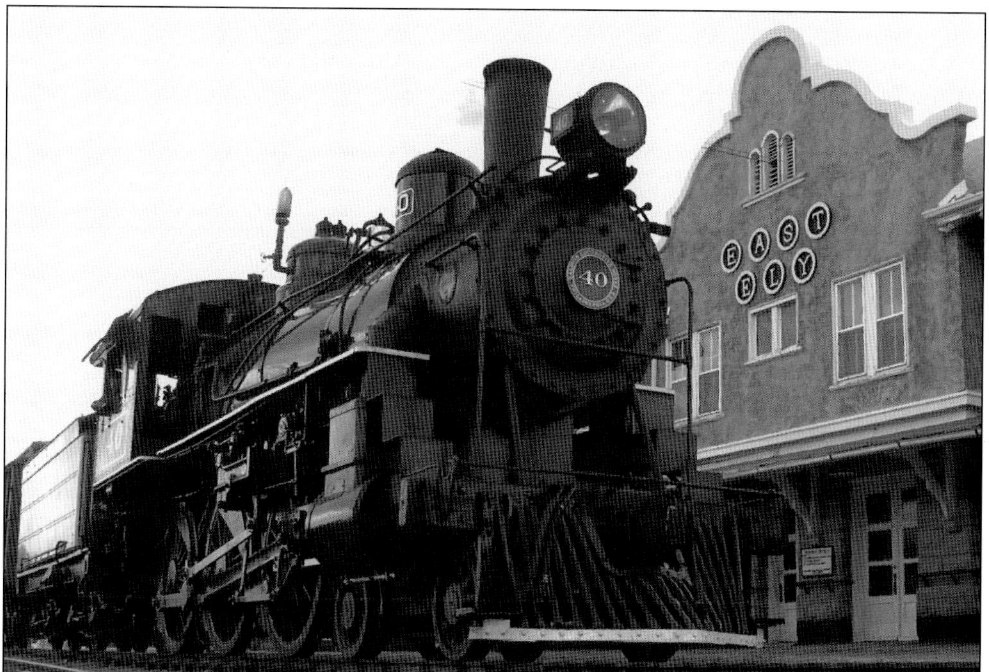